Yesterday, Today, and Tomorrow

The Harvard Class of 1950
Reflects on the Past and Looks to the Future

Yesterday, Today, and Tomorrow

Edited by George S. Mumford

*Privately Published by the Harvard Class of 1950
at the Time of Their Fiftieth Reunion*

FIRST EDITION

ISBN 0-9671833-1-6

Library of Congress Cataloging-in-Publication information is available.

Privately published by the Harvard Class of 1950
at the time of their fiftieth reunion.

PRINTED IN THE UNITED STATES OF AMERICA

Contents

PREFACE

Those of us who graduated in 1950 and are still present on this planet have lived through an extraordinary three-quarters of a century marked by astonishing changes in society, science, technology, and more is still to come. Who, at the time of our graduation, would have predicted the arrival of the information age, to the point where, from the comforts of our living rooms, we could follow bombs into Baghdad targets; or that American astronauts and Soviet cosmonauts would be peacefully at work beyond the earth's shielding atmosphere on a joint space-age venture; or that the Soviet Union would collapse and that Russia would become an impoverished country controlled by mobsters; or that new diseases could cover the globe in a day? In his essay, "The Big Change: Fifty Years of the Press, Television, and Politics," Charles W. Bailey, a free-lance writer and editor who spent a major portion of his career with the *Minneapolis Tribune,* rising from reporter to chief of its Washington Bureau to editor, continues: "who would have thought that . . . we would have fought two major wars (Won 0, Lost 1, Tied 1)? watched men walk on the moon and float in space? seen five Presidents and would-be Presidents of the United States killed, wounded, or shot at? elected, by a landslide vote, a movie actor as President of the

United States? re-elected him — by an even larger majority? heard one President say (with a straight face) that he was not a crook? heard another President say (with a straight face) that fellatio is not a sex act?"

There were probably few among those of our class who met one day in June 1997 to discuss projects for our 50th Reunion who really appreciated the wealth of creativity, experience, and talent available among our classmates — artists, composers, poets, philosophers, scientists, theologians, engineers, teachers, lawyers, judges, physicians, and on and on. We were indeed fortunate that some of these exceptional classmates would respond and bring to fruition the rather nebulous idea generated at that meeting — a consensus that the primary thrust at our reunion should be on creative and intellectual achievement; that our symposia should be the major attractions; and that a reunion on a millennium was something special and warranted extra effort, a different sort of publication.

An *ad hoc* committee began meeting later that year to discuss and make recommendations regarding possible subjects for essays that might become the basis for symposia. We started to identify potential authors among members of our class. We were a diverse group including a former superintendent of schools, a banker, a realtor, a college professor/dean, an environmentalist/author, and a businessman, augmented at various times by other members of the class.

From an initial brain-stormed list of some fifty ideas, covering just about everything from advertising to X-rated movies, about a dozen were selected for further, in-depth exploration. Categories were quite general: business and finance, science and technology, religion, and so forth. Based on information available, notably class reports and personal knowledge, lists of likely authors were generated.

Considerable discussion ensued on a unifying theme. Who was our audience? What was our objective? Did we want reviews of the past fifty years, or something more? How personal should the stories be? Should they be scholarly works or something else? We concluded that we wanted snapshots, not histories and, if possible, some insights into the future — hence the buzzwords: yesterday, today, and tomorrow. Within these parameters, authors were given essentially free rein being told a total of twenty pages plus references was what we were after. Our goal was to combine these essays into a single volume and distribute them to classmates well ahead of our reunion.

The completed volume is not a compilation of self-improvement essays with titles such as "How I made My First Billion," or "Living Healthfully into Your Nineties." Rather it is a collection of expert insights and, in a number of cases, suggestions for future action. The contributions range from the quite personal to the truly scholarly. An example of the latter is John Woolverton's "From Word to Therapeusis — and Back Again?: An Overview of Religion in America since 1950." An Episcopal minister, and practicing American church historian, John serves as editor for the *Anglican and Episcopal History,* an international, historical journal published by the Historical Society of the Episcopal Church. He has written in an area in which he is truly an expert.

John Train, investment counsel, author of eighteen books and about 400 columns in the *Financial Times* (London), *Forbes, The Wall Street Journal, Harvard Magazine,* in "The New Prudent Investor Rule" provides some pertinent ideas that those engaged in passing along wealth to the following generations should consider.

Among the more personal contributions is that of Pulitzer Prize-winning author, and Harvard-faculty member Robert Coles. His discussion in "A Witness to Public Education" of the trials and tribulations faced by those involved in school integration, from the time that six-year-old Ruby Bridges walked to classes at a previously all-white school in New Orleans to the present day in Boston, is full of insights.

Frank Jones also writes about minority students. His essay "A Half Century of Change: Race, Admissions, and the Harvard Community" is based primarily on his own experiences. Frank has retired from the Massachusetts Institute of Technology, where he was the Ford Professor of Urban Affairs. His father was for thirty years the president of Bennett College in Greensboro, North

Carolina, one of two colleges oriented primarily to the higher education of Afro-American women. Thus, with this heritage, it is not surprising that from 1943 to 1992 Frank dealt with the education and development of himself and others in, successively, Phillips Academy, Andover, MA; Harvard College; Harvard Business School; and MIT.

The legal grounds for affirmative action are described by John Ingram, Professor of Law at the John Marshall Law School, in "100 Years of Evolution from 'Separate but Equal': 1950 – 2050." He concludes: "I am still an idealist, and hope that we can some day have a society that is truly colorblind in the best sense — where we can recognize our different skin colors as a physical characteristic like hair color, but where none of our governmental, economic, or social decisions are based on race . . . we've made some real progress toward that goal, but we still have a long way to go."

Several contributions are autobiographical in nature. Gordon MacDonald's "Environment: The Evolution of a Concept," serves as one example. Currently Gordon is director of IIASA (originally the International Institute for Applied Systems Analysis), an international organization that conducts policy-oriented, multidisciplinary research in areas of energy and technologies, population and society, environment and natural resources. After graduating with our class, he earned a master's and a doctorate in geophysics at Harvard. In 1992, he served as the first chairman of the Environmental Task Force, sponsored by the Office of Vice President Al Gore, and then chaired its successor organization until 1996. Much of his involvement with the federal government is discussed in his essay which he concludes with: "Harvard, like other colleges and universities throughout the world, clearly understands the central role environment will play in the years to come. The university has responded to student needs by developing an interdisciplinary curriculum focused on environment. . . . If 'the best and the brightest' have identified environment as central to their lives, can we doubt that it will play a central role in the twenty-first century?"

In a similar vein, George Lodge, Jaime and Josefina Professor of Business Administration, Emeritus, at the Harvard Business School, describes his involvement on the international scene, especially in Central America. In "The World Economy: Convergence and Conflict," he calls for the creation of a World Development Corporation (WDC) to augment the International Monetary Fund and the World Bank. It's his view that the WDC would be chartered by the Bank and composed of managers from a number of multinational corporations. These persons would provide the range of competencies: ". . . agriculture and related industries, and also access to world product and credit markets and the latest technology," required to develop such sites as rural Brazil.

"At first," George writes, "the WDC would need to be subsidized, but eventually it should return a profit; and virtually any amount of subsidy would be more worthwhile than current practices that frequently put money down a rat hole. I proposed a WDC to the World Bank's president, James Wolfensohn, without success."

Robert Ashenhurst, Professor of Applied Mathematics in the Graduate School of Business at the University of Chicago, is a specialist in computer and information systems. After graduating in 1950, he worked at the Harvard Computation Laboratory for seven years while earning a master's and a doctorate in Applied Mathematics, thereby becoming involved with the computer age at an early stage. His essay "Information Systems in the Year(s) 2000 ± 50: The Two Cultures of the Information Age," describes some of his career in academe. Having started in Cambridge, he soon followed in his grandfather's footsteps to the University of Chicago. There, besides his appointment to the Graduate School of Business, he has also served as Director of the Institute for Computer Research and Chairman of the Committee on Information Sciences. Throughout his career, Bob has been deeply involved with the Association for Computing Machinery, a leading professional organization in his field. His essay develops the thesis that the gap between "the applications-oriented [who] do not understand the depths of the technology, and feel (rightly) that they should not have to;" and "the systems-oriented [who] think they understand the issues facing the organization, but fail to appreciate the finer points that are only felt through direct user experience" has to be bridged.

Our contributor on the "Family," is Nicholas Cunningham, Professor of Clinical Pediatrics and Clinical Public Health at the College of Physicians and Surgeons of Columbia University. He also serves as Attending Pediatrician and Director of Outpatient Pediatrics at the Babies Hospital Division of the Presbyterian Hospital in New York City. Following graduation Nick went on to receive his M.D. at Johns Hopkins University, his Doctor in Tropical Health from the University of London, and his Doctor of Public Health from Johns Hopkins. The Peace Corps took him to Togo, West Africa, early in his career. In November 1998, he returned from a mission to Baghdad to assess the effect that various sanctions were having on women and children in Iraq. His essay is entitled "Investing in Today's Families for Our Common Future." He concludes that parenting dysfunction "due to ignorance and inadequate support from community and society," is at the root of many of today's social problems. His prescription for the family and for all of us includes "For both parents, love and nurturance . . . for every family professional outside support . . . for every community, quality, universal childcare . . . for every citizen, political action . . . to move national priorities until families and children have found their rightful place — #1 — in social policy."

Charles Bailey devotes a large part of his contribution to the role of television and the decline of the daily newspaper. "There are any number of ways to bring public scrutiny to bear on media performance. Maybe it's time for another Hutchins Commission, to bring that seminal 1947 study of the press into the Internet Age. Maybe it's time for the resurrection of the National News Council, that noble experiment that was suffocated by the bitter opposition of the *New York Times* and other major news organizations. Certainly it's time for many local and state news organizations to propose and support local news councils. And it's past time for many newspapers and television stations to create an ombudsman's position on their staffs.

"We can choose from any number of remedies. But one thing

is certain: if the media don't figure out how to clean up their act, someone else will do it for them — and it won't be a pretty sight."

Four essays have been selected to be discussed at prereunion symposia. Miles Shore's "A Cottage Industry is Getting Organized" was the topic at the Harvard Club of Boston in May; Jack Ingram's (see above) was discussed in Chicago by a panel including former Harvard College admissions director, Fred Glimp, contributor Frank Jones and moderated by John Simon, Augustus Lines Professor of Law at Yale Law School; Arden Albee, author of "Electrons, Genes, Society, and Nature: Science and Technology in the 20th (and One-Half) Century" presented his paper in Los Angeles, classmate-panelists included Plant Biologist Winslow Briggs and Historian Jonathan Goldstein. Early in the coming Spring, Bill Harrop will discuss "The Conduct of American Foreign Policy" at a Washington, D.C. locale.

Miles Shore is Bullard Professor of Psychiatry at Harvard Medical School and Visiting Scholar at the Kennedy School of Government, where he is studying the dramatic changes affecting the health care system in this and other countries. Discussants of his paper were Dr. Robert Carey of the Lahey Clinic and George C. Lodge. Harvard Medical School Dean, Daniel Federman (H '49) served as moderator. "Much has happened," writes Miles, "in medical practice since 1950. The cascade of scientific advances, and the implications of those advances for the economics of health care, mean that the practice of medicine of the highest quality probably exceeds the capacity of the human brain to function adequately without assistance. To move into the future, health care needs the medical equivalent of power steering, of fly-by-wire aircraft, or of the combination of global positioning system and automatic pilot that guides ships through the Norwegian fjords. Many of these aids to medical practice are already developed and are being applied, albeit piecemeal; others are in the developmental stage almost ready for implementation; while still others lie in the future. For such aids to be adopted across all of health care will require a change in the health care marketplace so that value is placed ahead of profit, and a change in the medical culture to accept a host of technological innovations as a valuable step toward the results that patients and health professional alike desire — health care that is broadly accessible, affordable, safe, and of the highest quality."

Arden Albee is currently Dean of Graduate Studies and Professor of Geology and Planetary Science at the California Institute of Technology. Since 1959, his entire career has been spent at Caltech, where he was a member of the Lunatic Asylum, a group who analyzed the lunar rock samples as they were returned from the moon. He has served as Chief Scientist at the Jet Propulsion Laboratory and as the Project Scientist for the Mars Observer Mission. He is the Project Scientist for the Mars Global Surveyor Mission, currently in orbit about that planet. "There are," Arden concludes, "moral, societal, and economic consequences to change. It is not clear whether society can accommodate itself to rapid change or will react by smothering the change as it has done with the promises of nuclear power. International, national, and personal diplomacy will have to rise to this challenge of a rapidly changing world. Only if society can address the problem of the distribution of technology can it ever hope to bring about the worldwide cooperation required to adapt to the fundamental limitations of the global atmosphere, the ocean, and the land before it is too late. The benefits of evolving technology must be distributed to the developing nations in return for the conservation and rational use of dwindling resources.

"The greatest challenge to the technologists — scientists and engineers — in the new century will be the need to make their voices heard and to step up to new responsibilities of leadership. Technological evolution must be for society's sake, not for technology's sake."

Bill Harrop, a retired career diplomat who was ambassador at various times to Guinea, Kenya, Seychelles, Zaire, and Israel, and who was also Inspector General of the State Department and Foreign Service, writes "As we approach the year 2000, American leadership in international matters is less certain. The United States is not fully exerting the role it could and should exert — in its own self-interest and in the world's interest. If, in the two decades before us, the American political system can produce another generation of competent, decisive leaders, capable of convincing the American public and Congress that the United States must be fully engaged internationally and must allocate substantial resources to support the political and economic development of the poor countries, then world conditions at mid-twenty-first century need not look so bleak as has been outlined above. But that is a large 'IF'."

One of the issues that the committee spent considerable time addressing concerned the lack of material related to the arts. We could think of no way to include in this publication samples of paintings or photographs or musical compositions. For what we had in mind, creative writing seemed out of place. There are, however, in today's world other venues to choose, CD-ROMs for example, that contain far more capabilities than the printed page. These are being explored.

Thanks to the great generosity of one classmate, and contributions from members of the Class Committee, the collection has been published privately and distributed free of charge to all classmates. Considerable effort was spent by many, including several of the authors, to get either university or commercial presses interested. Classmates in the publishing world were contacted and virtually no stone was left unturned. But in the interests of timeliness the private route seemed the preferable way to go.

Through the hard work of many we have reached this present stage — the final product. We are particularly grateful to our authors for their outstanding contributions and cooperation. The symposia committee, chaired by Nat Ober and including Fred Glimp, Bill Allen, Dave Stone, and John Chase, has been closely involved. Thank you, Bruce Harriman, for your reviews and comments; thank you, Phil Winsor, Ted Reynolds, and Rollie Algrant, for your reactions and ideas on possible publishers. Special thanks are due to Robin Higham for his suggestion that we take on Bill Siddall's wife Abby (Radcliffe '52) as copy editor; she has done a super job. And of course the final production would not have transpired without the input of Susan Hayes. The contributions and suggestions from Pem Hart and John Temple Swing deserve special mention too. And, finally, thank you essay committee members: Gordon Abbott, Shep Brown, Mark Gordon, Peter Hewitt, and Nat Ober, without your input and support this would never have happened.

George S. Mumford
Dover, Mass
August, 1999

Yesterday, Today, and Tomorrow

ELECTRONS, GENES, SOCIETY, AND NATURE

Science and Technology in the 20th (and One-Half) Century

Arden L. Albee

As members of the Class of 1950 we can each assess our own fifty years of experience and attempt to use this experience as a base from which to look fifty years into the future — Yesterday, Today, and Tomorrow. We can use our own perspectives based on those things that fall within our own direct experience, or we can utilize a collection of all those things that the various pundits have said. History has clearly shown that both approaches fall short. Almost all predictions describe a future that is shiny or gloomy, glorious or doomed, smooth or perilous.

Each of us has experienced firsthand the failure of simple extrapolation into the future. In 1946 I arrived in Cambridge on a coal-burning train, with one trunk, a manual typewriter, and a 40–watt desk lamp. By graduation my roommates and I had added a radio, a record player, an electric coffeepot, and a shared phone. In 1996, new members of the Class of 2000 probably arrived on a jet plane or in their own cars. As seniors, their room has fluorescent lights, wide-screen color TV, video-tape-player, microwave oven, CD and tape player with stereo speakers, computer, printer, scanner, fax, a phone and internet connection, cell phone, electric razor, and half a dozen battery operated ames.

Can we use these observations to predict the appearance of the room of the Class of 2050? We might extrapolate another ten-fold increase in the number of gadgets, a ten-fold decrease in their size, and a ten-fold decrease in time spent attending lectures. On the other hand, it may be more likely that Harvard 2050 will be a virtual class, one linked by distance learning over a wireless network. Its members might never appear in Cambridge until June 2050 when, having paid their $100,000 tuition bill by electronic funds transfer, they would don their crimson robes and march forward to receive diplomas written in Latin with a goosequill pen on synthetic sheepskin. But Neil Rudenstine said, in kicking off the 1994 University Campaign,[1] ". . . It matters that we are a residential college and university. The energy we feel in the air; the excitement and intensity that are the essence of our life here; the visible history present in these buildings; the friendships that have grown from the days and years spent together in this singular place: these depend deeply on the fact that we are rooted here, that we are a residential community whose values still echo the independent and questing spirit of our founders."

So much for making a simple extrapolation into the future!

YESTERDAY

A commencement speaker addressing the Class of 1900 about the 20th Century would probably not have even mentioned airplanes, radio or television, antibiotics, nuclear energy, electronics, computers, or space exploration. He might have talked about an era of great civil engineering projects — dams, roads, bridges — and of advances in manufacturing; but he might well have missed the explosive growth of the automobile and its effects on society. Would he have predicted two worldwide wars and the societal changes of the 1930s? We can assume that the speaker of 1900 would have been a "he," and he was unlikely to have predicted that the commencement speaker of 2000 would very likely be a "she."

In 1946 our class was swollen by returning veterans and became the largest class in Harvard's history. The GI Bill of Rights brought an entire generation of Americans back to college, transforming the United States from a system of elite higher education (less than 10% of its citizens) to a system of mass higher education (more than 50%). We were beginning to understand some details about nuclear weapons — beyond the stark facts of Hiroshima and Nagasaki — and to understand that they had been developed by the largest and most expensive organization of science ever brought together by a nation. Smaller concentrations of scientific and engineering efforts had brought about the development of radar, computation and computers, cryptography, jet aircraft, analytical instruments, drugs, and other technologies. Vannevar Bush's report entitled "Science: The Endless Frontier" appeared, expressing the confidence in science that helped to lead to the founding of The National Science Foundation and to the "Golden Age of Science." The enthusiasts for nuclear power and those concerned over the threat of nuclear annihilation were beginning to voice sharply opposite views, opening a debate that still continues.

In 1950 we probably looked to the future with optimism — even with the feeling that science and technology would make life effortless and joyful. A World's Fair or a Disney movie might have envisioned the "average family" (two adults — one wage-earner — two children, and one dog) living in a solar-heated plastic home with robotic vacuum cleaners and lawn mowers. The family would enjoy their extended leisure with mind-fulfilling television on large, flat screens set in the wall. We did not accomplish these things (except for big-screen TV), but we went far beyond the most outrageous predictions that might have been conceived at that time. We walked on the moon and watched from our living rooms as the robot Sojourner Truth explored Mars; we brought back pictures from the farthest reaches of the solar system and from an orbiting telescope that looks at light that originated at a time near the beginning of the universe; we crisscrossed the earth with fiber-optic links and networked the entire planet with high-speed digital communications; we created microchips containing millions of transistors and costing so little that anyone can have a computer more powerful than could have been conceptualized with the use of vacuum tubes; we unraveled DNA and probed the fundamental building blocks of life.

But did these awesome scientific and technological advances change the basic conditions of our lives? Life's everyday problems and the deeper problems of our civilization seem highly resistant to quick fixes by technology. In retrospect we cannot avoid the conclusion that we must frame all our scientific and technological advances in the context of society. We would have had to predict the Cold War and the disintegration of the Soviet Union. We would have had to predict the expansion of the nuclear race into a nuclear missile race, and then predict that this would be replaced in our fears by "small" wars and racial and ethnic strife. Would we have predicted that the economic consequences of continued technological advances would lead to the decay of both inner cities and vast rural areas? We would not have predicted that environmental concerns would become a major driver of governmental policies or that malnutrition, illiteracy, illegal drugs, terrorism, and religious and ethnic fundamentalism would become forces of worldwide concern. Most families do not have two parents and a single income. They have large-screen television, but not a flat screen on the wall, and the programming content will hardly satisfy the mind.

Yet still we are optimistic about the future.

Technology can change our lives in very commonplace ways. Some changes are the result of major scientific discoveries, and others are simply the result of technological evolution. I like to consider the mundane example of the small, internal combustion engine. In 1959, as I crossed the United States in my move to California, I noticed for the first time that all the farms along the way had mown lawns (including my grandfather's, which had previously been "mowed" by a horse tied to a stake with a rope). And anyone who visited Europe in that period remembers the special sound made by motor scooters rushing down narrow streets in the middle of the night. Today, one can scarcely imagine the economies of Minnesota, Wisconsin, and Michigan without outboard motorboats, snowmobiles, jet-skis, and ATVs. Small outboard motors and snowmobiles now dominate travel in Greenland, northern Canada, and Alaska, replacing the kayak, umiak, and dog team, and surely the ready availability and low cost of chain saws has contributed to the clear-cut harvesting of forests throughout the world. *Garden Design* notes that there are about ninety million gasoline-powered garden tools in the U.S., and their small engines spew some seven million tons of pollutants into the air each year, about 5% of our total air pollution.

Even in this simple example of small-engine development we can observe a variety of interactions with society and culture. Here was a commercial technology that succeeded beyond anyone's dreams. Yet there was no new basic invention or design change involved and this development could have been predicted early in the twentieth century. It was sparked by manufacturers paying careful attention to basic engineering practices and evolving an engine that was cheaper, lighter, more reliable — and useful. This engine led to major societal changes in several geographic areas and it now presents a major pollution problem.

As I thought about the theme of "Yesterday, Today, and Tomorrow" I used "electrons, genes, society, and nature" to characterize the three fifty-year periods and as a way to organize my thoughts. The internal combustion engine dominated the first third of the twentieth century with the explosive growth in the number of cars, trucks, buses, and airplanes. It spawned a manufacturing industry that dominated the growth of cities, and led to the societal unrest and changes of the 1930s. But the use and understanding of the electron, discovered by J. J. Thomson in 1897, has had more impact on science, technology, and our daily lives in this century than any other single discovery. Although the electric light and power industry was well established before the actual discovery of the electron, by the 1930s the TVA and the REA were bringing electric lights and milking machines to every part of the United States. Subsequently, every element of the revolution in information flow can be traced back to this understanding of the electron. It has become a cliché to note the pivotal role that the fax machine played in the revolutionary changes in Russia and China by opening free communication. And television does not respect national boundaries.

By the end of the Second World War, communication equipment and the early computers had come to depend on a wide variety of vacuum tubes that seemed capable of meeting all future needs. Of course we now know that building a modern computer with vacuum tubes would be impossible. Its size would make it too slow, and the millions of vacuum tubes would fail so frequently that the machine would be permanently broken.

In 1945 Mervin Kelly established a research group at Bell Labs to focus on the use of a semiconductor device that might eventually replace the vacuum tube and the relay switch. Remarkably, in a period of only five years the invention of the transistor was essentially complete, understood, and well documented. By the late 1950s the scientific discovery of the transistor had a secure engineering foundation and the integrated circuit was born in the laboratories of Texas Instruments and Fairchild. The foundations had been laid for Nobel Prizes as well as for fortunes, but it was not until 1971 that the concept of the stored program design was brought together with the transistor into the Intel 4004 microprocessor. By now Moore's Law (named for Gordon Moore, the founder of Intel) is well known. It states that every two years the number of transistors doubles on chips of the same size. Today's Pentium 2 chip has 7.5 million transistors, more than 3,000 times as many as were on the 4004 chip in 1971. Yet current development should soon produce a microprocessor that contains more than 100 times the number in the current Pentium 2. In 1996 David Patterson predicted in a special issue of *Scientific American* improvements such that "... one desktop computer in 2020 will be as powerful as all the computers in Silicon Valley today,"[2] and that the high-end microprocessor of 2020 would combine processors and memory on a single chip, increasing the speed and reducing external connectors and size. The fall 1998 alumni magazine of the UC Irvine Engineering School describes such a chip, and predicts it will be in common use within the decade. This chip is an evolutionary development, but beyond this evolutionary potential many laboratories are working on novel new technologies.

The science and engineering successes of the war years led both government and industry to massively increase their investments in research and education. The bulk of federal support for research and development, including basic research, came from the Atomic Energy Commission and the Department of Defense. Vannevar Bush's report in 1945 demonstrated the high prestige in which science was held. The direct influence of the report has been debated, but this prestige led to the "Golden Age" of Science, or of Physics, or of Space, or of Graduate Education, or of Education, etc., depending upon which group is speaking. The National Science Foundation (NSF) was established in 1950 and became a major force in research and education in science. I received an NSF Graduate Fellowship early in the 1950s and almost fifty years later about fifty of our graduate students at Caltech are receiving NSF Fellowships to support their study and research. These Fellowships have been exceedingly important, not just for their financial support of graduate education, but also for their role of bringing students from smaller schools and minority backgrounds into graduate study.

The founding of the NSF reflected a crucial Washington decision to rely primarily on our already existing major universities and national laboratories for America's basic research effort and not to build a separate system of government research institutes. The strength of the research universities, as we know them now, can be traced to this decision. Research support comes from almost every agency of the federal government. Tremendous numbers of significant breakthroughs have had their origin in research universities, where the research was largely funded by our federal government.

After the war the federal government increased its R&D expenditures to about $50 billion in 1970 (in 1992 dollars). This figure then lost ground to inflation but rose to a peak of about $60 billion in 1988 before dropping back to $50 billion in 1997.[3] However, industrial R&D expenditures rose steadily well above inflation in this same period, from about $35 billion in 1970 to $110 billion in 1997 (in 1992 dollars). The federal government throughout this period provided the majority of the funds for academic R&D and, as a result, has been a major supporter of graduate student thesis research.

The number of Ph.D.s increased dramatically throughout this period to a total of about 37,000 science and engineering degrees awarded in North America in 1995. But the "Golden Age of Physics" was declared over in the mid-90s when professional groups sounded an alarm about the "oversupply of physicists" and recommended remedies. David Goodstein pointed out that the growth in the number of scientific journals from 1870 to about 1970 was matched over the same period by an exponential growth in the number of U.S. Ph.Ds in physics.[4] But things changed about 1970 — such growth could no longer be sustained by society. And with more than half of the nation's high school graduates already going beyond high school, it is clear that any further academic expansion is also constrained. In 1998 the National Research Council issued a similar alarm about life sciences: an "oversupply" of life scientists was announced and "restraint of the rate of growth of the number of graduate students in the life sciences" was recommended.[5] How do we equate this with the widespread feeling that the revolution in molecular biology will transform our lives in the next century? Won't this require that the very best minds continue to work in molecular biology?

A major feature of graduate education during this period has been the large number of highly qualified international students studying in the U.S. Around 1970 the number of our most-qualified students going into graduate school, excluding professional schools, began to decline. International students replaced those students. American science had become the best in the world, and students everywhere who wanted to be serious scientists felt that they had to come here for part of their education. Various studies have shown that large proportions of these students remain in the U.S. and that they have started many of the increasing number of "startups" in information technology and biotechnology. However, the international student enrollment in U.S. engineering programs has begun to decline. Although this is partly attributable to global economy, the increase in the international capacity to provide science and engineering education means that students from foreign countries need no longer come here to obtain good graduate education. Moreover, the number of first university degrees in science and engineering is increasing much more rapidly in Asia and Europe than in the U.S. We must remind ourselves that science and engineering are now global enterprises fostered by the rise of science, higher education, and research in other countries; by the migration of scientists and engineers across national boundaries; and by the development of new communication technologies. Maintenance of our technological development has become dependent upon the importation of foreign talent.

Global politics brought about the "Golden Age of Space." It was initiated by the launch of Sputnik in 1957, which led to the founding of NASA in October 1958, and was further fueled by the failure of the Cuban invasion in 1961, which led to President Kennedy's decision to put men on the moon in that decade. These events also convinced Washington that we weren't educating enough scientists and engineers. Space expenditure increased to be a major part of our R&D expenditures and the manned (human) space program continues to claim what may be a disproportionate share. The immense efforts that led to the success of the Apollo missions, similar to those of the Manhattan Project, provided a bond for another generation of engineers and scientists.

The true "Golden Age," however, was provided by those robotic missions that explored the planets and observed the cosmos — Explorers, Mariners, Pioneers, Vikings, Voyagers, Magellan, Galileo, Casinni, Pathfinder, Mars Global Surveyor, and all the "Great Observatories." For the first time we opened "the picture book of the planets" and saw the canyons and craters of Mars, the sulphurous colors of Io, the contorted ice floes of Europa, and the many, finely detailed rings of Saturn. Our children and grandchildren have "Golden Books" in their classrooms with actual photos of the planets and their surface features. They will never be able to look at the planets and their satellites with the same sense of awe and humility that we had when we first viewed our accomplishments.

On a personal note, I studied the lunar samples returned by each of the Apollo missions (except XIII); served on a seemingly infinite number of proposed mission studies; served as chief scientist of the Jet Propultion Laboratory (JPL); and am currently the project scientist for Mars Global Surveyor as it orbits Mars. Beyond the thrill of discoveries and the satisfaction of accomplishment, two events stand out in my mind —the Apollo XI Science Conference, January 1970, and the opening-up of the Russian space effort after the Reykjavik summit conference in 1986.

The Apollo XI lunar samples were distributed to scientific teams throughout the world with the proviso that all results would be embargoed until all the teams came together at a conference two months later. This conference brought together scientists from dozens of disciplines, scientists who had never talked to one another and who talked in different jargons; but, at this meeting each was trying to understand what insights the others offered. The competition among leading scientists for "firsts," for the most precise results, and for being "right" electrified the atmosphere and led to sleepless nights for many individuals. This conference marked the arrival of a whole new set of instrumental and analytical techniques and of a whole new integrative approach that has transformed the observational sciences.

At the Reykjavik Summit Conference in 1986 it was agreed to form a Joint U.S.-U.S.S.R. Treaty Working Group on Solar System Exploration with an emphasis on sharing information and data from our respective missions to Mars. As a member of this group I was privileged to make about fifteen visits to Russia during that period of immense political and cultural change. Initially, our meetings were very formal, with official translators, State Department oversight, formal communiqués, and restricted movements; but as time passed scientists and engineers engaged in open and informal communications. The whole atmosphere changed and we visited our homes in each other's country. I interviewed students and we brought them back for graduate study at Caltech.

If I were to choose a single significant event out of those visits, it would be the night of April 14, 1970, which was the Russian

Orthodox Easter. We had had dinner in downtown Moscow with the extended family of a Jewish space scientist. As we walked to the Metro we noticed a small crowd, mostly older people, observing traditional Easter-eve services at a small church in the center of the city. Later, in the southern suburbs of Moscow, as we came out of the Metro into below-freezing weather, we encountered an actual traffic jam, albeit a small one, of automobiles taking young, suburban Russians to Easter services at another church, one which had been closed for many years and was being rededicated for Easter and its "onion" top had been regilded for the occasion. From our hotel window we watched lines of candles extending across the outer ring road and into the countryside. The juxtaposition of these images — religious observances and traffic jams — stood in marked contrast to our understandings of cold-war, communist Russia, and we understood that future changes were inevitable.

YESTERDAY AND TODAY

The space program may have had its most lasting accomplishment in helping to initiate our environmental concerns while simultaneously providing tools to address these concerns. Looking back from space at Earth with its thin layer of blue water and its white patches of clouds did more than thousands of words to illustrate the fragility of our environment and the fact that mankind is embedded in nature and cannot escape it. Satellite systems do far more than provide us with phones and directional finders in cars. They are a vital part of our worldwide communication system. In October 1998 more than 120 satellites in low earth orbit provided mobile voice service, and more than 250 geostationary satellites provided a wide variety of communication and meteorological services.[6] Hundreds of additional launches are planned for communication needs. More than twenty satellites currently provide multispectral and radar images and other types of data for agriculture, fisheries, mineral exploration, land use, ocean productivity, meteorology, climate, and other applications. Hurricane tracking is one of the most visible products. Satellite mapping and global monitoring of our land, oceans, and atmosphere are major keys to the survival of mankind on this planet.

Advanced computational hardware and software have made it possible to effectively use the torrents of data being returned from satellites. More importantly, the data can be assimilated into complex physical models that permit forward extrapolation. So it is that we can begin to understand the ozone hole and the potential of global warming through numerical models. Models exist for Atmosphere General Circulation, Ocean General Circulation, Atmosphere Chemical Tracers, Ocean Chemical Tracers, and work is ongoing to combine these and others into an interconnected model of the entire climate system. We can begin to look seriously at the issue of climate change, on both Earth and Mars. Basic data sets from many nations are archived and used electronically by scientists and planners throughout the world.

Computational modeling and sampling have become two of the most important tools of science and engineering, and their use will undoubtedly continue to grow into the next century. Already this use is so pervasive that the distinction between observed data and computed "data" is becoming somewhat blurred, as is indicated by a recent exchange of letters in the *Journal of Geophysical Research*.

In some sense we are already taking the word of electronic circuits for vital information on increasingly vital issues. Most computer models are based on our concepts of physical laws and use a complex set of basically linear equations representing discrete interactions that can be represented sequentially. But increasingly we will be asking questions about patterns and the interactions within immense data sets. Seymour Cray has noted, "Adding two and two together is no longer the issue: it's pattern recognition, pattern generation, and interpretation." James Bailey suggests that "new evolutionary intermaths . . . like cellular automata, genetic algorithms, artificial life, classifier systems, and neural networks . . . will change the way we ourselves experience the world and our appropriate role within it.'[7] The patterns of entities such as environments, economics, and embryos can be computed by posing interactions of the entities and parallel evolution. But we tend to think sequentially, and these new maths are parallel; "... there is no direct way for the human mind to understand where the answer came from, because the formulation is constantly changing along the way." The pattern may be resolved by the computer and produce a useful and believable result, but we will be unable to understand the process within the computer that produced the result.

Deciphering the structure of DNA and the ensuing growth of molecular biology rendered our college biology textbooks obsolete. In a similar manner the discovery of reversed polarity magnetic stripes on the sea floor and the development of the understanding of plate tectonics made our geology textbooks totally obsolete. Earth science was further changed by the discoveries of planetary science, in particular the role that the impact of other objects on Earth must have played in its history. Astronomical understanding exploded under the impact of terrestrial and space observations over the entire range of the electromagnetic spectrum, thanks to an array of new sensors.

TODAY AND TOMORROW

Probably the most prominent of the miracles that are being promised for the new millennium fall into the explosively expanding realms of molecular biology and of information technology and computation. Both areas were introduced by discoveries in the latter half of the twentieth century and both affect broad aspects of our lives.

Molecular biology promises more miracles in both agriculture and medicine. Technology has pushed agriculture and protein production higher and higher during this century. About seventy million acres of gene-spliced corn and soybeans were planted in the U.S. in 1998. Richard McConnell of Pioneer Hi-Bred International, Inc., predicts that the use of gene alteration to help corn withstand bad weather and pests will double current yields, and that the price of corn over the next quarter-century will remain the same despite a 40% increase in the world's population.[8] The increased productivity of new varieties and the better control of disease and insect pests are well known. The advances in aqua-culture are much less known to the U.S. citizen, but we consume its products. More than one-quarter of the salmon and shrimp con-sumed already come from farms. Aquaculture was a $26 billion industry by 1993, involving several hundred species, and the World Bank estimates that aquaculture could meet 40% of the demand for fish by 2005 with appropriate investment.[9] Gene alteration is expected to double the growth rate of farm-raised salmon and trout.

In medicine, gene therapy promises a new revolution. W. F. Anderson writes that there have been three great leaps in the abil-ity of medicine to control disease: Control took its first step when society, utilizing new knowledge, began to take public health mea-sures, such as the introduction of sanitation and water systems. Next, surgery with anesthesia and, later, antibiotics enabled doctors to cure illnesses such as appendicitis and to aid the healing of wounds and injuries. Then the development and introduction of vaccines and antibiotics made it possible to prevent or treat many of the diseases that are spread by microbes.[10] (Anderson did not include the argument of Susan J. Blumenthal, assistant surgeon gen-eral, that low-cost individual behavior changes — those involving diet, exercise, seat belts, guns, substance abuse, and smoking — could decrease premature death in this country by half and could cut chronic disability by two-thirds and acute disability by one-third.)

Looking ahead, Anderson says, "Gene therapy will constitute a fourth revolution because delivery of selected genes into a patient's cells can potentially cure or ease the vast majority of dis-orders, including many that have so far resisted treatment. . . . Con-sider that almost every illness arises in part because one or more genes are not functioning properly. Genes give rise to proteins . . . and defective genes can yield disease when they cause cells to make the wrong amount of protein or an aberrant form of it." A wide variety of conditions ranging from cancer to viral infections appear to be due to damage or impairment of single genes. Although the precise genetic base for many diseases is still not well known, the Human Genome Project has already mapped all forty-six human chromosomes and expects to obtain the complete sequence of three billion base pairs in human DNA within the early years of the new millennium. Gene therapy is already being used to deliver corrective genes to damaged cells and its use is expanding rapidly. During the early part of the next century the use of gene therapy will probably be confined to the genetic alteration of non-reproductive cells, a treatment that affects only the patient. People have always resorted to the doctor when they are sick, but, if medicine could *prevent* everything from heart disease and cancer to TB and AIDS, the need for expensive surgery and drug treatment would drop. "Prevention leads to not only a longer, healthier life, but also much cheaper medicine," argues former Surgeon General C. Everett Koop. Eventually such treatment is predicted to be much less costly than current interventions for many conditions, and we should look forward to a longer life, one less burdened by disability, dysfunction, and impairment.

Genetic alteration of reproductive cells may alter the genetic makeup of all subsequent generations, thereby opening a Pandora's Box of ethical concerns. While it is tempting to try to eliminate inherited conditions, it is also true that misguided or even malevolent alteration of the genetic composition of humans could cause problems for subsequent generations. And do we really want to design our descendants?

Many other advances of medical technology are closely tied to the use of computers and electronic developments. These include advanced diagnostic tools such as magnetic resonance and ultrasound imaging; microchip implants for releasing drugs; smaller, longer-lived, and programmable heart implants; amplifiers to transmit brain waves from paralyzed patients to laptop computers; the development of designer drugs, etc. The Human Genome Project could not be carried out if the computer were not able to sort through the three billion base pairs, rejecting errors and putting the code into proper order. Computer comparisons can then be made between healthy and diseased tissue. A software program can describe the DNA code of a protein produced by a newly discovered gene and then search databases to find similar substances and make intelligent guesses about the properties of the new protein. Other programs visualize a protein in three dimensions and searches for small molecules that might bond to the surface or fit into crevices to modify the protein's action.

Beyond medical technology, scientists are learning to create a range of tiny devices that will have far-reaching effects on every-day life and across diverse disciplines. Micro-electromechanical systems (MEMS) are built with lithographic processes and combine computers, sensors, and tiny actuators. Currently their largest market is as a sensor for airbag systems, but their use is being extended to a host of other applications. "Smart matter" technology would link groups of hundreds to millions of MEMS into machines or structures. Nanotechnology seeks to create self-replicating machines that build mechanical parts such as gears, atom by atom or molecule by molecule.[11]

A special 1996 issue of the *Scientific American* entitled "Key Technologies for the 21st Century" had major sections on information technologies; transportation; medicine; machines, materials, and manufacturing; energy and environment; and finally "Living with New Technologies" — a total of twenty-four individual chapters and seven commentaries. Unlike similar articles of 100 years ago, these chapters express strong confidence in the future and in the ability of science and technology to move forward at an ever-increasing rate. However, in detail most of the essays only look ahead several decades and do not try to predict mid-century. John Rennie, in the introduction to the volume, does sound a cautionary note as he states, "New technologies also pose moral dilemmas, economic challenges, personal and social crises."

An even more cautionary note was sounded at a 1991 symposium entitled "Visions of a Sustainable World."[12] Murray Gell-Mann said, "The key concept is probably the achievement of sustainable quality . . . quality of human life and quality of the biosphere, including survival of many of the organisms with which we share the planet and the ecological systems that they form." The contributors to the symposium assumed that major advances in technology would occur, and they tried to address how to "manage human behavior in the global commons: space, atmosphere, oceans, Antarctica" and to examine the challenges to a sustainable world. Problems such as population growth, the oncoming energy crunch, the availability of potable water, the warming of the atmosphere, the shortsightedness of current decision-making — all these and others demand a more effective international coordination and a new pattern of international politics. But beyond international diplomacy it is also necessary to change individual human behavior. Each person must believe that using his can of aerosol may provide the last straw leading to a global catastrophe. Such belief can only be achieved through understanding, and such understanding can only be achieved through education; and we have not yet achieved such a level of education on technical issues even in the U.S.

When confronted with these questions a United States senator is quoted as saying: "All of history and most of human nature are against you; what have you got going for you?"

Al Gore is credited with coining the term "information superhighway" to describe the World Wide Web network. In some ways this is a most unfortunate term. The superhighway played a major role in the decline of rural communities and inner cities by facilitating a tremendous internal migration in most developed countries. Migration into cities is now a worldwide problem as the networks of highways, power lines, and phone lines begin to dominate the distribution of people and work in each country. Fortunately, wireless networks, towers and satellites, are already being established in China, Argentina, and other countries — bypassing the building of a wired network infrastructure. Just as the outboard motor and the ski-mobile sustain isolated communities in the North, so an individual's cell or satellite phone is already helping to sustain other isolated communities, and will help to stem the migration to cities. The wireless network offers the only possible hope of providing the kind of open communication that can build consensus among humans on how to address global environmental problems.

Advanced technology should be able to provide sufficient

answers to at least two important future concerns — the supply of energy and the supply of food. Every year the sun provides Earth with about ten times as much energy as is contained in all the known reserves of coal, oil, gas, and uranium combined: this energy will have to be tapped in sophisticated ways. The developed nations use at least ten times as much energy per person as do the developing countries, but the demand for energy continues to rise everywhere in the world. Solar technology will enable the developing areas to skip the construction of a generation of infrastructure and move directly to a distributed source of energy, one that does not contribute to global warming or otherwise degrade the environment. Wind power and solar cells convert solar energy into useful electricity but do not provide a means of energy storage. However, sunlight can also be used to produce hydrogen fuel.[13] Sunlight falling on an electrode can produce an electric current to split water into hydrogen and oxygen by photoelectrolysis. But many biological systems produce hydrogen directly, and current research is leading to photocatalysts that will allow sunlight to split water directly into its chemical components. Hydrogen can be stored, transported, burned as a fuel, and used to produce electricity in a fuel cell — the only by-product being water, which is environmentally benign.

These solutions will not happen overnight. It seems certain that in the near term we must use nuclear energy to generate electrical power and that therefore we must learn to use it intelligently, to reexamine all the associated problems, consequences, and prejudices relative to the use of this energy source, and to understand how to deal with them in a way that results in the least total consequence. It is also clear that there has to be a similar change in our approach to population control. New technologies of birth control continue to evolve, and societal factors will have to change to meet this challenge.

TOMORROW

If the failure of past predictions has taught us anything about predictions, especially about science and technology, it is that we cannot simply extrapolate our current understandings into the future. The interplay of science and technology with patterns of society, ethics, and history is far too complex for a simple extrapolation. Moreover, as scientific discoveries and new technologies add to older discoveries and technologies at an uneven pace, it becomes impossible to predict the end results. Each new technology poses new moral dilemmas, new economic challenges, and a series of personal and social crises. And our predictions must include not only the effects of technology on humankind but also its effects upon the earth itself.

My colleague Dan Kevles concluded in a 1996 essay, "So, what to think about claims for the future of science and technology? First, think with a mixture of respect, guardedness, and skepticism — respect, because in broad outline some of the forecasts are likely to be right; guardedness, because we will have to confront the impact of technologies that have not been predicted; and skepticism, because much of what is predicted will likely not come to pass, at least not in the way things are currently imagined."[14]

I characterized the course of science and technology in the 20th (and one-half) century with the title "Electrons, Genes, Society, and Nature." The reasons for the choice of electrons and genes is clear enough, but why "society and nature"? It seems abundantly clear to me that the evolution of science and technology will be dominated in the early part of the new millennium by its interaction with society. At some point however the evolution will be constrained by the natural limitations of the globe on which society lives.

There are moral, societal, and economic consequences to change. It is not clear whether society can accommodate itself to rapid change or will react by smothering the change as it has done with the promises of nuclear power. International, national, and personal diplomacy will have to rise to this challenge of a rapidly changing world. Only if society can address the problem of the distribution of technology can it ever hope to bring about the worldwide cooperation required to adapt to the fundamental limitations of the global atmosphere, the ocean, and the land before it is too late. The benefits of evolving technology must be distributed to the developing nations in return for the conservation and rational use of dwindling resources.

The greatest challenge to the technologists — scientists and engineers — in the new century will be the need to make their voices heard and to step up to new responsibilities of leadership. Technological evolution must be for society's sake, not for technology's sake.[15]

NOTES

1. Home Stretch, *Harvard Magazine,* 1998: 68–72.

2. David Patterson, "Microprocessors in 2020," in *Scientific American: A Special Issue* (New York: W. H. Freeman, 1996), 1.

3. National Science Foundation, *Science and Engineering Indicators — 1998,* NSB-96–21.

4. D. Goodstein, "The Big Crunch," *EOS,* v. 781(997), 329.

5. Board on Biology, National Research Council, *Trends in the Early Careers of Life Scientists,* (National Academy Press, 1998).

6. *International Space Industry Report, 2,* no. 17 (1998).

7. J. Bailey, *After Thought: The Computer Challenge to Human Intelligence* (New York: Harper Collins, 1996), 277.

8. *Business Week,* August 31, 1998, 5.

9. D. Plucknett, and D. L. Winkelmann, "Technology for Sustainable Agriculture," *Scientific American, Special Issue,* 133–38.

10. W. F. Anderson, "Gene Therapy," *Scientific American, Special Issue,* 55–60.

11. See K. J. Gabriel, "Engineering Microscopic Machines," *Scientific American, Special Issue,* 89–94; and E. Regis, *Nano-The Emerging Science of Nanotechnology* (Boston: Little, Brown, 1995).

12. "Visions of a Sustainable World," *Engineering & Science* 55, no. 3 (Spring 1992): 1–60.

13. See H. B. Gray, "Solar Fuel," *Engineering & Science* 60, no. 3 (1997): 28–33; and W. Hoagland, "Solar Energy" in *Nano,* 115–20.

14. D. J. Kevles, "The Shape of Things that Came — and Didn't — and How They Illuminate What's to Come," *Sigma Xi Forum,* 1996:21–31.

15. Over the last six months I have accumulated a stack of clippings from the Business Section and the Science File pages of the *Los Angeles Times*. I readily acknowledge that collectively these articles and notes have helped to stimulate my thinking about the future of science and technology. I must also confess that my reading of this essay suggests that I should acknowledge that my writing style and use of quotes seem to have come from many years of reading *Time* magazine.

INFORMATION SYSTEMS
IN THE YEAR(S) 2000 ± 50

The Two Cultures of the Information Age

Robert L. Ashenhurst

The term "two cultures" was introduced by C. P. Snow in 1959 to characterize the lack of understanding between scientists and humanists (he used the phrase "literary intellectuals"). His Rede Lecture at Cambridge University caused quite a stir, some of which is reflected in the "second look" he published along with the original essay five years later.[1] Here I adopt the two cultures metaphor to apply to those who design and implement computer-based information systems and those who look to such systems (hopefully) to support some worthwhile activities in the real world. It is common to view this as a disparity between the computer nerds and the technologically disadvantaged but, all joking aside, there are some serious issues here.

Stories of anomalies, glitches, and maladjustments, right up to catastrophic failures, of information systems are legion. The following concerns one of the few well-documented cases of the latter in what may termed the respectable literature:[2]

> In 1988, a consortium comprised of Hilton Hotels Corporation, Marriott Corporation, and Budget Rent-A-Car Corporation subcontracted a large-scale project

to AMR Information Services, Inc., a subsidiary of American Airlines Corporation. The consulting firm was to develop a new information system (IS) called CONFIRM, which was supposed to be a leading-edge comprehensive travel industry reservation program combining airline, rental car and hotel information. A new organization, Intrico, was especially established for running the new system. The consortium had grand plans to market the service to other companies, but major problems surfaced when Hilton tested the system. Due to malfunctions, Intrico announced an 18 – month delay. The problems could not be resolved, however, and three-and-a-half years after the project had begun and a total of $125 million had been invested, the project was canceled.

The article by Effy Oz from which the foregoing is the lead paragraph gives a coherent narrative account of the succession of circumstances leading to the final *denouement*. Left unexplained, however, is the fact that, although Intrico (the client partnership) expressed dissatisfaction right from the start with what AMRIS (the developer organization) was reporting, they nevertheless continued to pay (in monthly installments) millions of dollars to keep the project going. The $125 million mentioned in the article seems not to include the legal costs associated with the ensuing suits and countersuits, and although eventually AMRIS settled for a reported $160 million, the consortium partners ended up with no CONFIRM system. A later paragraph in the same article states: "Software development failures are not rare occurrences. According to one survey, an astonishing 75% of all system development undertaken is either never completed or the resulting systems are not used. . . ."

The tendency to pursue the technological with such enthusiasm as to neglect the organizational seems to blind many of those concerned, in both the cultural affinities. As one who has worked both with "techies" and "orgies" (pronounce, please, the "g" hard), I feel that the barrier is formidable for many reasons similar to those cited by C. P. Snow in discussing the scientist-humanist barrier. The applications-oriented do not understand the depths of the technology, and feel (rightly) that they should not have to. The systems-oriented think they understand the issues facing the organization, but fail to appreciate the finer points that are felt only through direct user experience.

THE MILLENNIUM BUG

In the context of the two cultures, and the difficulties this division causes for the effective and efficient development of information systems, it is hard to resist introducing a topic that is currently getting increasing attention, the Millennium Bug (a.k.a. the Year 2000 or Y2K problem). The use of "currently" in the foregoing sentence refers to the time I am writing, in the early months of 1999. Presumably you are reading it, however, in the year 2000, when the "zero date" 01/01/00 (a.k.a. January 1, 2000) is already past. As I write, predictions of what will happen with information systems all over the world on that date range from minor inconveniences to the disintegration of society as we know it (in which case, I suppose, you might not be reading this essay at all). If you are looking at me for a specific prediction, look away.

The problem, as most people know by now, is that in years past data processing systems carried dates in the form that programmers refer to as the MMDDYY (or in Europe perhaps DDMMYY), leaving the first two digits in the identification of the year to be understood as "19". So, for example, the date of the 1949 Harvard-Yale game (a day to remember—NOT) would be expressed as 111949. Note that the "19" here is not part of the year designation, but designates a day of the month (19th of November). If this date were to be represented (at all) in the European system it would be 191149. The 6–digit expedient was supposedly adopted for reasons of efficiency in the days when computer storage capacity was much more expensive than now—a date could be expressed with only six digits instead of eight (six because of the necessity of allowing two digits even for days 1–9 since 10–31 are possible, and even for months 1–9 since 10–12 are possible). The excuse for not anticipating that eventually the century would be 20 instead of 19 is that "nobody in their wildest dreams" could foresee that the massive transaction processing systems of the '60s and '70s would still be operating at the century interface. Well, anyway, that's the story—in fact, there were projects which took the end of the century into account, but the general software development industry ignored the problem.

The Millennium Bug is not really a bug, of course, but a massive manifestation of stupidity and shortsightedness. In any case, however it turns out, the Y2K situation illustrates a problem that permeates the entire computing industry, and extends to organizational activity generally. The CONFIRM project result, by contrast, illustrates a failure in a particular information systems development project. Although system problems can be attributed to a variety of causes, it appears that a breakdown of adequate communication between those who need systems for their organizational applications and those who produce the systems for them can often be assigned as a root cause. Miscommunication can be attributed to lack of understanding of the culture of each group by the other. To see what might be done about this, to remedy the situation, it is instructive to look at a bit of history.

IN THE BEGINNING

It is convenient, especially for purposes of this essay, to date the information age from the year 1950. At that time data processing for large-scale applications was carried out with punched-card equipment, and the use of stored-program computers for such tasks was just starting to be proposed seriously. In the summer of 1950 I obtained a position in the Harvard Computation Laboratory. I do not recall my official job title, but my work was essentially that of one who would later be termed a "programmer/analyst." The applications then were numerical solutions of mathematical problems arising in science and engineering, the original role envisioned for large-scale automatic computing machines. My qualification for this post was a Harvard A.B. degree with concentration in Physics. My knowledge of computing machines was solely that obtained from Edmund C. Berkeley's 1949 book *Electronic Brains, or Machines That Think,* the main supporting reference for a paper titled "What About Robots?" that I had written for Kirtley Mather's Social Sciences 113 course.

The Harvard Computation Laboratory grew out of a wartime project in automatic computation directed by Howard Aiken, then on leave from Harvard to the U.S. Navy. The Mark I machine (large-scale and automatic, but not electronic) had started operation in 1944, and subsequently the Marks II and III, of progressively more advanced design, had been built and shipped to the Naval Proving Ground in Dahlgren, Virginia. In 1950, planning was underway for yet another machine, designated (guess what?) Mark IV, to stay at the Computation Laboratory.

After some breaking in as a Mark I programmer I got involved in the Laboratory's research program, which at that time was mainly centered on computer system design. Graduate courses already were being introduced, however, dealing with what would now be called Computer Science, in the Division of Engineering and Applied Physics (ESAP). This enabled me to enroll in graduate study and work toward a Ph.D. degree while still employed full time.

The Computation Laboratory in those days was a remarkable place, not the least for the attitude that prevailed about the wide variety of disciplines that were relevant to computing, and vice-versa. I still have in my possession a Harvard publication[3] making an announcement most unusual for its time: "The Division of Applied Science and the Department of Economics of the Graduate School of Arts and Sciences, recognizing the pressing need for further education and research, will introduce in the fall term of 1954 a new program in Data Processing, leading to the degree of Master of Science. The program has the further support of the Graduate School of Business Administration."

The following paragraph indicates the program's philosophy:

> ...it is clear that computer techniques may be applied to a variety of operations involving the storage and the processing of data. A few examples of practical applications already realized or under active consideration are automatic inventory control, customer billing for utilities, filing of abstracts from professional periodicals, language translation, and the automatic control of machine tools, wind tunnels, and chemical plants. Although computer techniques may be applied to the general field of data processing, each particular field presents its own special problems and in most cases a great deal of research and development will be required before a practical solution can be obtained. In spite of the great interest shown both by suppliers and potential users of computing equipment, development in fields other than scientific computing has been slow. One reason for this is that the application of computing machinery is a field requiring knowledge of engineering, circuit design, and mathematics, as well as of the problems of the particular field of application. The number of people with the requisite experience is therefore very limited; in business applications, for example, few accountants have the necessary knowledge of the technological possibilities and few engineers have accounting experience.

Here already is reflected the notion that the development of information systems needs two different areas of expertise, the organizational and the technological. The implication that the requisite levels of expertise in both could be embodied in a single individual, however, was probably an impossible dream, even when that individual possessed a Master's degree from Harvard. Thus the basis for the two cultures metaphor introduced above.

OVER THE YEARS

In 1956, having achieved the S.M. and Ph.D. degrees in Applied Mathematics, I received an appointment as Instructor on the Harvard faculty (at a cut in pay from what I was then making at the Computation Laboratory as Research Associate). About then I became a member of what was at the time the only professional society for computer types, the Association for Computing Machinery (ACM), founded in 1947. Although at the time I thought I would stay at Harvard as long as it would have me, an offer from the University of Chicago came along in 1957, and I became an Assistant Professor in the Graduate School of Business there.

Several serendipitous factors were at work here. The School at Chicago was undergoing a rebirth and was hiring faculty in disciplines thought to be important for business education, even though how they fitted in was not exactly clear. The broad notions of the applicability of computing that I had acquired from the Computation Laboratory made this seem a reasonable proposition, although had I known more about the difference in cultures between an arts and sciences faculty and that of a professional school, I might have thought more about this.

I was influenced also at the time by a tale recounted by my grandfather, Robert Morss Lovett, Harvard Class of 1892. In his autobiography which appeared in 1948[4] he described how he had been doing a post-graduate year at Harvard when he received an offer to join the English Department faculty of a recently established educational institution in the Midwest:

> President Harper invited me to visit the University of Chicago, and as the Columbian Exposition of 1893 had just opened I accepted the opportunity to see the university and the fair. I was a good deal impressed by both, and by the city which had already begun its cultural progress with the establishment of the Art Institute, the Symphony Orchestra, and Hull House. Nevertheless, I

was not convinced and returned to Cambridge, so far as I knew to stay. I told Professor Marsh of my decision and boyishly revealed my romantic attachment to Harvard and my feeling that all my future was bound up in remaining in and of it. He listened with an expression of extreme distaste. "For God's sake," he exclaimed, "get away. Go anywhere." It was revealing. In a flash I knew that he was right. . . .

My grandfather served on the Chicago faculty from 1893 until 1938, when "three years beyond the age of retirement" he left to become Government Secretary of the Virgin Islands. His taking up residence in Chicago was of course the reason (on my mother's side) that I had grown up in that city, but the idea of "coming home" did not really seem important to me in 1957, although since then I have found that it has some advantages in life. It pleases me, however, to think that his position there 1893–1938 and mine 1957–1999 cover most of the 107–year history of the University of Chicago, which both my parents attended.

The university in question is famed for, among other things, allowing "interdisciplinary" activities to go on. Although my primary appointment there has always been in the Business School, I also participated in the programs of two entities in the Physical Sciences Division: the Institute for Computer Research, founded in 1958 under the directorship of Nicholas Metropolis, and a subsequent offshoot, the Committee on Information Sciences.

Under the aegis of the Institute I helped in the design and construction of the Maniac III computer, one of the last of the breed of such university projects, Metropolis having overseen the development of Maniacs I and II at the Los Alamos Scientific Laboratory. The Maniac III was intended primarily for scientific applications, and in this connection had in its arithmetic unit a novel approach to the way computing error buildup was tracked. Subsequently, the Institute embarked on the MISS project, for networked support of campus-wide laboratory computing (the acronym stood for Minicomputer Interfacing Support System, and the networking was essentially the currently popular client-server architecture ahead of its time).

The Committee on Information Sciences offered a graduate program similar to that of the Computer Science departments that were just being formed at other American universities. But, as the name may suggest, Information Sciences tried to incorporate the points-of-view of both of the two cultures, and had faculty with joint appointments in other units of the University, not the least with the Graduate School of Business.

Never let it be said that the lot of an interdisciplinary activity in a university is an easy one. Although both the Institute and the Committee were in many ways successful in their mission, both fell by the wayside of academic politics in the 1970s. Ten years after the demise of the Committee, the University of Chicago created a Department of Computer Science which emphasizes the theoretical side of the discipline but is much more like conventional departments everywhere, dealing mainly with the scientific and mathematical areas.

Meanwhile, in the Graduate School of Business, efforts to build up the organizational side of the computing discipline, which many business schools were starting under the designation Management Information Systems (MIS), did not flourish either. The School at Chicago emphasizes economics and statistics as basic disciplines, finance and accounting as applied disciplines, and is preeminent in all these. The academic role of computing seems to be regarded, however, mainly a tool for research in the aforementioned disciplines, rather than as the basis (via an application-oriented Information Systems approach) for an important aspect of the conduct of business and organizational functioning today.

The ACM, which periodically tries to eliminate the "Machinery" in its name as reminiscent of clanking gears and engineers, has tried to make room for the application side of the two cultures, as well as the system (hardware/software) side. In 1968 an ACM Curriculum Committee on Computer Science (C³S) worked on recommendations for curricula in the newly emerging discipline. While I was peripherally involved in that activity, I was an active participant in a later effort of the ACM Curriculum Committee on Computer Education for Management (C³EM). In its 1972 report[5] this committee tried to spell out a basis for programs in business schools, industrial engineering departments, and computer science departments (if the latter would pay heed). A balance of the organizational versus the technological appropriate to each of these academic venues was set forth.

Both the ACM Curriculum '68 and Curriculum '72 recommendations were influential in the field as a whole, and were revised and extended to higher and lower educational levels as well. Meanwhile, however, the growth of the uses and abuses of computing in all phases of business, government, and life was proceeding by extraordinary leaps and bounds. Not only have university educational and research programs had difficulty in "keeping up," but there are factors in information technology that could be branded anti-intellectual.

The technological achievements of the first half-century of the information age have been truly remarkable. Not the least of this has been due to developments which make possible enormous increases in speed and capacity of computing devices, at enormously decreased cost. But less evident to the ordinary public are the conceptual developments affecting how computer hardware and software can be organized and used. For hardware, beyond the original stored-program idea of von Neumann, the successful development of techniques for handling concurrency and coordination among processing units is of prime importance. For software, the notion of higher-level programming languages was an early phenomenon, but this has been extended to a larger concept of languages oriented not to programming but to the applications that are programmed. Finally, the extension of "computer technology" to encompass "communications technology" has profoundly effected both the nature and the style of computing and information systems applications. My colleague Anthony Oettinger (Harvard '51), the only one of our Computation Laboratory "old bunch" still at the mother institution, perceived the promise of this marriage early on, for which he coined the term "Compunications."

WITH THE CURRENT

Among the buzzwords and hype of contemporary information technology, the two cultures problem still rears its ugly head. Fifty years into the information age, massive failures of information systems to fulfill their intended objective, or indeed to fulfill any constructive objective, still occur (and, for obvious corporate reasons, are not very well documented for the public). These failures often, though not invariably, can be linked to the failure adequately to express and control the requirements of the application. It would be nice to say that this is because the field is still young, and these are just growing pains. Unfortunately there is not much evidence that these problems are gradually taking care of themselves.

For some time there have been attempts to characterize as a profession a discipline of Software Engineering, and have it recognized and accredited as one of the engineering disciplines that have a long and influential history in the industrial age. Recently the Texas Board of Professional Engineers has admitted software engineering as a licensable professional specialty, the first such state board to do so. Meanwhile, the academic societies whose interests are basically in computing are mounting projects to lay down professional requirements and a body of knowledge, supported by suitable university curricula, for this new form of engineering. Should these place within the purview of the software engineer only the design, implementation and operation phases of information systems development there would be little reason to question. The efforts seem to claim, however, that the application analysis and information requirements specification should be carried out by the software engineer, with only consulting support from the organizational users. Recall that the 1954 Harvard program sought optimistically to combine analysis and design, but the intervening years have served only to accentuate the notion that two very different cultural approaches are required.

A reasonable view would seem to be that the software engineer should be acquainted with the techniques for application analysis, and be able to organize the effort of specifying detailed informational and operational system requirements, but that the production of same be in the hands of a group familiar with the application as well as the techniques. The customary procedure when the organization people are only used to "make suggestions" for overall requirements and then "sign off" on the detailed specification produced by the technologically-oriented development team is unsatisfactory, as shown by the CONFIRM project failure described earlier.

In recent years there have been two developments in the system modeling area which perversely increase the likelihood that technological expertise will be taken to encompass the objectives of informational modeling. These are: first, the so-called Relational paradigm, which affords a systematic approach to the formation and manipulation of data in tabular form; and second, the Object-Oriented paradigm which allows data and processes to be handled in a way that results in cleaner and more efficient technological design. Computerized "tools" for designing and implementing hardware/software data processing systems in these terms are available from a wide variety of vendors. The related hype, replete with numerous buzzwords, is such as to bewilder the organizationally minded person assigned to an information systems project. At the same time, some real conceptual advances in informational modeling, the Entity/Relationship paradigm for representing organizational logistics, or the Dimensional paradigm for analyzing aggregate organization statistics, are treated as rudimentary appendages to the technologically oriented methods for systems design in the development process.

In its issue of January 3, 1983, *Time* magazine deviated from its customary Man (Person?) of the Year award feature to name "The Computer" as Machine of the Year. The issue was filled with coverage of the dawning of the new age of the Personal Computer (PC), also known as the Home Computer (or, perhaps perversely, as "The Homeless Computer"[6]). It might be thought that this would mark the major memorable watershed of the information age. Although in public perception this is probably true, the technology which enabled the PC to emerge has had perhaps an even larger impact on the way information systems are integrated into organizations, only now coming into full flower.

Specifically, computer hardware/software configurations can now be modularized to permit the realization of the client-server style of organizational computing (remember the MISS Project referred to earlier). Here both the client and the server are not humans but computing modules by which a user can request services of the client module, which then delivers them through its network connections with appropriate server modules.

None of this gets at the problem of cultural dysfunction between the techies and the orgies. Even when system faults seen to be purely on the technology side, the fact that their possibility was not envisioned and a warning mechanism not built into the system can be considered as a failure adequately to provide for application exigencies. A colleague, Peter Neumann (Harvard '54), has provided a compendium and classification of "mishaps and oddities related to computer technology," listed as an ongoing collection on the Internet Risks Forum, and presented in a book, *Computer Related Risks.*[7]

At issue here is not the use of computing to support the humanities, arts, and education. Rather it concerns the tools generated and adapted as products. In 1969 Tony Oettinger published a study of "the interaction of educational technology with society" *Run, Computer, Run.*[8] Much of what is there concerning the uses and misuses of computing in an educational setting probably still applies, although I will leave it to educational specialists to judge how much progress there has been. Chapter 4, "Educational Technology: The Devices," clearly needs updating in view of technological advances since 1969, but I am sure its author would agree with me that these by themselves do not solve the educational problems that abound.

INFORMATIONAL MODELING

A modern information system can be viewed as a man-made artifact which embodies three "personalities" simultaneously:

1. An information/knowledge system that supports organizational or other societal activities;
2. A data processing system defined in terms of data files and processing procedures that apply knowledge to information so as to accomplish the effect described in (1);
3. A computer hardware/software system that automates the data processing described in (2).

Here "information" and "knowledge" are used to mean, roughly, particular "facts" and general "laws" (or "rules") applying to the real world, while "data files" and "processing procedures" refer to the factors and functions involved in symbol manipulation without regard to real-world meaning. The bankers of Florence in the sixteenth century invented (1) an information/knowledge system for accounting (double-entry bookkeeping), that could be effected by (2) entering figures in rows and columns, headed appropriately, and calculating with them. Finally in the "information age" of the twentieth century, such systems are automated by (3) technology associated with computers, performing automatic data processing.

To oversimplify only slightly, every computer application is an information system, and every information system is simultaneously an application and a hardware/software system. The two important development activities, application analysis and system design, respectively emphasize these two aspects.

The techniques used in the two areas should be different, for understandable reasons. Application analysis must involve reference to the application, and requires a *representation* of the "subject matter" with which the application is concerned. System design must involve reference to the hardware/software system(s) on which the information system is ultimately to be implemented, and therefore specify a *realization* of the representation. To distinguish the two, the characterizations *informational modeling* (i.e. specifying an information/knowledge representation) and *data modeling* (i.e. specifying a data/process realization) are conveniently introduced (although in the development world, much widely varying terminology is rampant). From the earliest days, however, system design has been divided into logical design and physical design, the former expressing the hardware/software system in explicit but not finely detailed terms, without reference to specific vendor products and data/program formats, etc. that the latter involves. The unfortunate result of this is that those who think primarily in technological terms tend to blur the distinction between the (application) analysis representation and the logical (system) design realization. Hence the question of application analysis versus system design becomes directly relevant to the two cultures issue set forth earlier.

The representation/realization distinction is illustrated by a homely or, actually, workaday example which figures in many commercial information systems. Business organizations often need to deal with information about, and knowledge concerning, identified customers. In the real world these are individuals or organizations having characteristics and behaviors that can be embodied in an information/knowledge representation. This in turn is realized in files and programs, giving rise to system operations such as "accessing the customer record." Typically this record contains a number of data-items, one of which is the customer address. Well and good, most if not all customers have a "legal address" at which mail may be received. To the system designer the record *is* the customer and the customer address *is* of a form that can be used to produce mailing labels. Just thinking about the recorded information and the conventional form of mailing addresses, however, may produce a logical design but not suffice for the desired uses of the information system. All sorts of questions worthy of consideration arise from thinking about real customers and real addresses. Most obvious, perhaps, is that individuals usually have just a home address and an office address, while organizations, in contrast, may have a headquarters address and many branch addresses. But further, some individuals may have a legal address but also other addresses where they habitually spend extended periods of time, such as vacation addresses. Whether these variations need to be taken into account, of course, depends on the uses to which the information system is to be put.

Now, the way the address information is to be used also raises questions about how the representations are to be specifically realized. If the only purpose of customer address is to support mailing, the breakdown into number/street, city, state and zip code is not important. If, however, addresses are to be used in marketing studies and the like, provision must be made for extracting the zip code as a separate information item, and perhaps capturing geographic information by comparing number/street with census tract or neighborhood designations.

The point is, although all these alternatives perhaps could be anticipated by thinking of the customer and the associated customer address simply as information, they are more likely to get into an appropriate system design if they are thought of as pertaining to real customers with real addresses. Hence the analysis stage of information systems development should produce a representation expressed in terms of real world concepts and related information/knowledge. This paves the way for informational modeling techniques that produce a representation which not only conforms to the real world of the application, but also is translatable more or less systematically into a logical design which corresponds to it. The translation is not just routine, for there are a variety of technological expedients to be considered, in order to render the information system efficient as well as effective. An apt characterization of the contrasting objectives here is that information analysis is to "do the right thing" and system design is to "do the thing right." These are of course not totally independent objectives, since "the thing" in each case is the same, the primary support role of the information system in the organization.

For the present discussion, a small side question can be asked concerning the Y2K problem: is this an error (or anomaly, etc.) in the (information) representation of calendar dates, or in the (data) realization of same? Since the whole mess is laid at the door of the technically oriented types, the answer to this question does not tell where to point the finger, but merely says what kind of consideration should have been given in the development process ("Nobody ever told us that the century mark would be reached" or "This is the way a lot of people write dates in everyday practice, so let's do likewise, to save file space").

Clearly standing as a representation mistake, however, is the fact that many programs which deal with calendar dates do not incorporate the "400 years" correction into them. By this, while 1700, 1800 and 1900 did not have a February 29 in them under the "100 years" rule (although they ordinarily would have been leap years by the "4 years" rule), the years 1600 and (gasp!) 2000 reverse the reversal. Not recognizing this arises from insufficient attention to the calendar reform edict of Pope Gregory XVIII in 1582. Interestingly enough, a program which recognizes neither the "100 years" rule nor the "400 years" rule will give correct results for the year 2000, a leap year.

For the last several years my work has been to synthesize an overall approach to the informational modeling discipline. The SCRIM methodology (the acronym stands for Structured Characterization of Reality for Informational Modeling) is based less on technology and more on the study of the nature of the application world, as set forth in analytic philosophy (ontology and epistemology). Some remarks on the nature of informational modeling, as I see it, are presented in an essay entitled "The Nature of Informational Modeling," to be included in a book honoring Nicholas Metropolis on his seventieth birthday, *Essays on the Future*.[9] A more detailed (and weighty) introduction to the subject is presented in an article "Ontological Aspects of Information Modeling," appearing in a 1996 issue of the journal *Minds and Machines*.[10]

WHAT'S IN STORE

Assuming that, as you read this, Y2K has not brought about the disintegration of society as we know it, what about the next 50 years? In its wisdom the Essay Committee, in inviting these essays, stated that the theme for all should be "Yesterday, Today, and Tomorrow." The "2000±50" in the title is intended to pay lip service to this desire, and I am tempted leave it at that. After all, yesterday today was tomorrow. Predictions about the future of computing made over the years have tended to be ridiculously wide of the mark, whether they promised only more of the same ("The market domination of Big Blue will continue to predominate") or extremely radical change ("By the turn of the century nothing will be set down on paper anymore"). In 1997 ACM celebrated its 50th Anniversary, and put out a book *Beyond Calculation: The Next Fifty Years of Computing*.[11] In twenty essays by distinguished authors, a fair amount of space is devoted to discussing the failure of past predictions to come true.

At the century ends, the age of the Net and the Web is dawning. Most are aware of the Internet, a network of subnetworks through which any user may be connected to any other user or to a variety of services anywhere. Less perceived (and perhaps regarded by some as a typo), however, is the "intranet" concept, that of a proprietary network set up by a single organization to coordinate its widely dispersed activities. And while most people's main use of networking is the ubiquitous "e-mail," other services are now being developed in client-server mode. The most universal of these is the emergence of the World-Wide Web, at present mainly an application running on the Internet which allows individuals or organizations to distribute "web pages" to anybody and everybody through servers to browsers, using a language called HyperText Markup Language (HTML). But, just like the net concept, the web concept can be expanded. The notion of the Object-Web, realizable through a language called Java, gives the possibly of allowing organizations to completely rework their information systems, and to incorporate features pertaining to individual users as well as the protocols required by the organization of the whole.

This technological development, then, can affect the information systems activity of organizations great and small. But the achievement of this goal, needless to say, depends on the increased introduction of effective informational modeling methods, so that the synergy between systems and users is maximally coherent. And such a goal cannot be achieved through technology alone, without integrating with organizational factors.

Again in connection with ACM's semicentennial, the February 1997 issue of *Communications of the ACM* consisted entirely of a set of short pieces on the theme "The Next 50 Years." In the lead article, Larry Press outlines his hopes "not . . . for technology, but for the implications of technology," along with the caveat "hopes are not predictions."[12] So my look at the next fifty years is a hope rather than a prediction. The considerable brouhaha resulting from the original two cultures proposition presented by Snow lasted for about five years, 1959–1964. During that time there were many attacks and defenses, and at least one suggestion of a middle ground, the social sciences, in an article by Lloyd Fallers "C. P. Snow and the Third Culture."[13] After ten years a reasonable perspective on the whole thing could be presented, as in the book by William Daven- port, *The One Culture*.[14] The two cultures of information systems need to be bridged, perhaps by yet a third, as the social sciences were envisioned as bridging Snow's two-culture gap. But it would seem that if the gap is left unbridged that information systems will con- tinue in the mode "you can't live with 'em, but you can't live with- out 'em." It remains to be seen what kind of a professional specialty will emerge in this connection. After all, tomorrow today will be yesterday.

REFERENCES

1. Snow, C. P. *The Two Cultures: and a Second Look,* Cambridge Uni- versity Press, 1964.

2. Oz, E. "When Professional Standards are Lax: The CONFIRM Failure and its Lessons" *Communications of the ACM,* v. 37, no. 10 (Octo- ber 1994) pp. 29–36.

3. Brochure *Graduate Program in Automatic Data Processing,* Harvard University, 1954.

4. Lovett, R. M. *All Our Years,* Viking Press, 1948.

5. Ashenhurst, R. L. (ed.) "Curriculum Recommendations for Graduate Professional Programs in Information Systems" *Communications of the ACM,* v. 15, no. 5 (May, 1972) pp. 363–98.

6. Ashenhurst, R. L. "The Homeless Computer" in the *Britannica Book of the Year,* Encyclopedia Britannica, Inc. (1986) pp. 286–87.

7. Neumann, P. G. *Computer-Related Risks,* Addison-Wesley, 1995.

8. Oettinger, A. G. *Run, Computer, Run: The Mythology of Educational Innovation,* Harvard University Press, 1969.

9. Ashenhurst, R. L. "The Nature of Informational Modeling" in *Essays on the Future,* Birkhäuser (in press), 1999.

10. Ashenhurst, R. L. "Ontological Aspects of Information Modeling" *Minds and Machines,* v. 6, no. 3 (October 1996) pp. 287–394. Errata due to imperfectly produced figures in the original appeared in v. 7, no. 1 (February 1997) pp. 159–69.

11. Denning, P. J. & R. M. Metcalfe (eds.) *Beyond Calculation: The Next Fifty Years of Computing,* Springer-Verlag (1997).

12. Press, L. "Technology in Bloom: Implications for the Next 50 Years" *Communications of the ACM,* v. 40, no. 2 (February 1997) pp. 11–17.

13. Fallers, L. "C. P. Snow and the Third Culture" *Bulletin of the Atomic Scientists,* v. XVII, no. 8 (October 1961) pp. 306–10.

14. Davenport, W. H. *The One Culture,* Pergamon Press, 1970.

THE BIG CHANGE

Fifty Years of the Press, Television, and Politics

Charles W. Bailey

On Commencement Day, 1950, who would have thought that by the end of the century we would have:

- fought two major wars (Won 0, Lost 1, Tied 1)?
- watched men walk on the moon and float in space?
- seen five Presidents and would-be Presidents of the United States killed, wounded, or shot at?
- elected, by a landslide vote, a movie actor as President of the United States?
- re-elected him — by an even larger majority?
- heard one President say (with a straight face) that he was not a crook?
- heard another President say (with a straight face) that fellatio is not a sex act?

By now you will have gotten the point: the half-century since our class left Cambridge has produced astonishing changes in American politics, driven by even greater changes in the way we communicate with each other and with the rest of the world. The principal agent of that change was television, which has become not only the dominant purveyor of news but also the most powerful weapon in the arsenal of politics.

Indeed a central fact of American politics in the second half of the twentieth century is the revolution in the electoral process driven by television. We should expect even greater change post-millennium — change that will reinforce the trends in media and politics that have marked the five decades since we left Cambridge.

Television's impact on our politics has not been benign; it has cheapened the content and at the same time raised the cost of our electoral process. But however much we may deplore it, that's the way it is.

OLD SOLDIER, NEW WEAPON

The first presidential election after we graduated — Dwight D. Eisenhower vs. Adlai Stevenson in 1952 — was also the first in which television played a substantial role. The Republican campaign managers wanted to take advantage of their candidate's charisma, and a helpful advertising executive showed them how in a memo to Eisenhower's staff:

> A big advertiser . . . puts on a one-hour television show. It may cost him $75,000. . . . Immediately after, another big advertiser follows it with another big expensive show. . . . These big advertisers spend millions — with top talent and glittering names — to build a big audience. But — between the two shows — comes the humble "spot." If you can run your advertisement in this "spot," for a small sum you get the audience built at huge cost by other people.

The idea appealed to the Republican leaders, so the photogenic "Ike" became the star of the first political spots. They purported to be question-and-answer exchanges between the candidate and average citizens, but in fact, candidate and citizen never met. They recorded their parts in separate TV studios and the parts were then spliced together to give the impression of a face-to-face chat. Eisenhower didn't like the idea: "To think that an old soldier would come to this," he complained to his brother. But, ever the good soldier, he recorded the spots. Stevenson refused to match them, saying, "This isn't Ivory Soap versus Palmolive." He may have been right, but he lost.

In the same year, television also worked for another Republican. When Richard Nixon, the vice-presidential candidate, was accused of unethical behavior, he used the new medium to defend his personal honesty, telling a national TV audience that his wife wore a "respectable Republican cloth coat" and that his daughters had been given a dog named Checkers — which, he said, they were going to keep. The coat and the pup made the speech a hit with Republican politicians and the public; it saved Nixon's place on the ticket. It also convinced Nixon that TV was a valuable political tool.

And so it turned out to be. One can trace its rise in the hierarchy of political weapons in simple terms:

Phase I: Television shows candidates alive, breathing, moving, shouting, smiling, sweating. In this phase the politician is seen as a real person for good or ill.

Phase II: Television is used in a calculated and controlled way to show the candidate as he wishes to be seen. This phase includes the spot, which is now sometimes shrunk to as little as fifteen seconds, and such fakery as the "town meeting" in which the candidate fields softball questions tossed at him by carefully selected "average citizens" and/or "undecided voters."

Phase III. Television is used as an attack weapon — to depict the candidate's opponent as the candidate wants him to be perceived by the voter. When these negative ads begin to backfire, a campaign can switch to "issue" ads — TV spots that don't openly boost a candidate but rather focus on an issue on which the candidate and his opponent differ. Sometimes this works; sometimes it doesn't — as Newt Gingrich discovered in 1998.

As anyone who watched television through the last few decades knows, we are deep into Phase III. Presidential campaigns no longer consist of cross-country train trips, balloon- and bunting-bedecked rallies and ticker-tape motorcades. Today the candidate is barely visible in person, relying instead on TV to carry him and his message into the nation's homes — while he crouches in a hotel room wearily trying to raise money to feed the ever-more-expensive television monster.

Two phenomena have contributed mightily to the rise of television as the determining force in the politics of the millennium: the decline of the major national parties and the steadily increasing role of public-opinion polls.

THE PARTY'S OVER

There is no questioning the fact that the national parties, which once played a dominant role in the electoral process, have been marginalized. The only question is why — and again the answer is television. In the old days, national party chairmen tended to be leading political figures in their own right, men like Mark Hanna and Jim Farley. Today they are essentially mendicants, begging for alms to pay those huge TV bills (and making a half-hearted effort to keep track of how all that money is spent). The national nominating convention, once the place where candidates were chosen and major policies hammered out, has become another TV sitcom.

Where once the television networks boasted of "gavel-to-gavel" coverage, they now grudgingly grant the politicians one hour on each of three convention evenings. And even those few minutes are subject to network review, resulting in minute-by-minute scripts that prescribe not only the timing and content of the night's political entertainment, but also which politicians will be seen on national TV. That calls to mind an unintended consequence: television in effect *created* the modern convention by providing the required technology — the cross-country cable that allowed the broadcast of an event "live" to the whole nation. Now the money-driven imperatives of the television industry have destroyed the very institution it had created.

The same effect could be seen in the changing content of campaign coverage. As new technology came on-line, it first increased, then trivialized and eventually minimized the reporting of presidential campaigns. In this case the key technological advance was the shift from film to videotape, which greatly reduced the time required to get images on the air, and thus inevitably led to more emphasis on images and less on words. One need only recall George Bush wrapped in a flag or Michael Dukakis in a tank (or Willie Horton in the revolving jailhouse door) to comprehend both the potential and the perils involved. There was no question that this change would occur; the iron law of technology — if it can be done, it will be done — guaranteed it.

POLLS COUNT

Television's domination of the political process has been enabled by another device that was legitimized in the half-century now ending. In 1950, political public-opinion polls were highly suspect — a legacy of the 1948 election, in which all the major surveys had forecast that Thomas Dewey would beat Harry Truman. But the pollsters refined their techniques, and they are now as central to the strategy of a campaign as television is to its delivery. For better or worse (mostly the latter) the political campaign is now based almost entirely on television and polls.

In the decade of the '90s, in fact, poll results have been used by candidates and office-holders to guide them in policy decisions. President Clinton is notoriously addicted to this practice, but he's not the first chief executive to be so stricken; Lyndon Johnson seemed always to have the latest Harris or Gallup results in his pocket.

Such fixation on poll results can lead to self-deception. Professional researchers are among the sharpest critics of over-reliance on poll data. "Our measures have replaced reality," one network political director said. "To much of America, our research is reality." And a leading commentator, E. J. Dionne, put it this way:

> The normal curiosity about who would win an election
> had become an obsession of such proportions that it
> threatened to overwhelm any meaningful discussion of

the problems that actually engaged the voters. Voters were no longer the subject of politics, democratic citizens deciding the fate of their country. They were objects to be counted, studied, and counted again. The proliferation of polls had allowed almost any newspaper or television station in the nation to measure the feelings of any population. Measurement, not democratic debate, was becoming the stuff of American politics.

Of course the real stuff of American politics today is money. Money pays for all those expensive polls and all that expensive television. And all those expensive consultants who tell you to spend more money on polls and television. The entry fee for the millennial presidential race of 2000 was estimated at $20 million — and all that bought most presidential wannabes was a chance to find out if they could raise millions quickly enough to pay for television ads in the so-called "early" states whose primaries and caucuses may well have determined the nominees five months before the national conventions in late summer.

Another unintended consequence of television's pivotal role in politics has been the election to public office of TV personalities, including journalists. This should not surprise anyone; as the *Washington Post* noted on October 30, 1998, "A bad TV persona can be ruinous. TV journalists are in the business of cultivating trustworthy, on-screen images, which become natural assets when entering politics." And of course a candidate with TV experience comes already equipped with an internal clock that enables him or her to effortlessly deliver those fifteen- and thirty-second "sound bites" that have become the lingua franca of political debate.

TELEVISION TRIUMPHANT

Television not only plays the leading role in the American political process, it has come even more to dominate the entire business of communication. Consider some of the milestone events of the five decades since the Great Middle Class left Cambridge:

1952: First TV spot used in a presidential campaign: You can fool some of the people all of the time.

1954: First example of a demagogue's committing political suicide on national TV: Senator Joseph McCarthy challenges President Eisenhower and the U.S. Army in televised hearings.

1960: First national TV debate between presidential candidates: Kennedy vs. Nixon. This event was also the first example of a candidate's losing an election because beads of sweat formed on his upper lip on national TV.

1961: First presidential press conference live on TV: Kennedy showed how it should be done. None of his successors have come close.

1963: First example of the power of TV to move a nation: broadcasts on national TV of Alabama cops turning fire hoses and attack dogs on civil rights marchers.

1963: First time a whole nation spent four consecutive days and nights watching a live TV broadcast of a national tragedy: the death of President John F. Kennedy.

. . . And so on, to a climax in 1968, when, in the span of a single year, Americans watched black and white leaders being shot to death; urban ghettos burning; a war lost in the streets of Saigon, and a presidential election lost in the streets of Chicago. It was the watershed year of the American century, and for most Americans it was a story told on TV. And that would be the case from then on. Television had replaced the newspaper as the dominant mass medium.

Meanwhile a series of revolutionary technological advances, such as the computer, the cellular phone, the laptop, and satellite transmissions, strengthened television's pre-eminence in the untidy, fast-growing, dynamic bundle of devices and techniques that has come to be loosely labeled as "the media."

THE DECLINE OF THE DAILY

The half-century now ending has been marked by a sharp decline in the number of independent, locally owned newspapers, and a concomitant rise in the size and power of large media chains. The trend was to some degree inevitable; the ascendancy of the electronic media has compressed the news cycle from days to hours to minutes, making it almost impossible for a newspaper to maintain its traditional role of gatekeeper, at a time when the volume of information threatens to overwhelm us and the editor's task is more important than ever. The shrinkage in the number of newspapers has also been driven by inheritance taxes, which make it difficult if not impossible for a newspaper owner to pass his paper to his children, and by simple greed. Many family members with a stake in a paper but no interest in working for it want it sold so they can cash out their holdings — and the growth-obsessed chains will often pay a premium price. After such a sale the local editor is usually replaced by someone who has never lived in the community and whose career success depends on bottom-line results, not editorial excellence or the well-being of that local community.

The loss of the mass-circulation franchise has forced newspapers to re-examine their role. The few first-rate dailies — the *New York Times*, the *Washington Post*, the *Wall Street Journal*, and two or three major regional papers like the *Los Angeles Times* — chose to be what they have been all along: the principal purveyors of serious news to the nation. Most other publishers either have their heads firmly in the sand of status quo or are trying to imitate *USA Today*, the newspaper from nowhere, hometown paper of the nation's airports and motels.

Some newspaper companies seem to think the answer is to slaughter the faithful old cash cow and start over again with a different animal. Here's how it was explained in a memo to the staff of the *Minneapolis Star Tribune:*

> The goal is to change Minnesotans' perception of the *Star Tribune* from that of a newspaper to "the brand of choice for information products.". . . We need to move as far away as possible from the newspaper as the point of reference and focus on a product that's the most different from the newspaper. . . . And work will be done to

create a personality that is positive, contemporary, and appealing to our customers.

All too often that kind of thinking leads to a cheapening of the product, so that people who do want serious news have to search even harder to find it. (It may also help explain why the *New York Times* now finds it feasible to offer daily home delivery in Minnesota and more than forty other states.)

This is particularly unfortunate because it comes at a time when the quality of television news is in deep and apparently permanent decline. There are a couple of reasons: first, TV networks and local stations discovered that news could be a profit center, so they increasingly replaced traditional news programs with "soft" news, feature stories which masquerade as truth but are in fact mainly fiction, and endless talk shows long on opinion but short on facts. Nowadays most TV newsrooms seem to base their news judgments on the maxim that "if it bleeds, it leads." Sad to say, that also seems to be increasingly the rule at networks, where the news staffs have been cut and cut again, and regional and overseas bureaus closed in response to pressure for more profits.

That pressure, and the degradation of television news that inevitably follows, was greatly increased by the takeover of the networks by big corporations: for example, the purchase of NBC by General Electric and of ABC by Disney. The bottom-line pressure increased when networks were sold to corporations that regard news as just another commodity, like soap, or soup — or politicians.

L'ENVOI

Half a century ago, most of us who went into the newspaper business did so because it looked like fun. You got to travel a lot at the boss's expense; you got to meet the most interesting people; and, if you were lucky, you got a free, front-row seat at great events, from world war to the World Series. But our generation of journalists was serious about its work: we prided ourselves on our professionalism, and for the most part managed to maintain that quality in our reporting, writing, and editing.

By and large we did not seek, and certainly did not obtain, celebrity. That has changed. Today the journalist seems often to be a participant rather than an observer, a dispenser of opinion rather than a collector of fact. Today's journalists too often confuse who they are with what they merely represent: if booze used to be the bane of the newsroom, today the number-one ailment in those precincts is surely hubris.

That's too bad, because the information revolution is deluging us with so many facts and factoids and fictions that we need more help than ever in sorting out the important from the trivial, the honest from the fraudulent. Good journalists have always done that, but they will not be able to do it if they lose their credibility because some of them abused their privileged position in our society. Every time that happens, it gives the bean-counters in the head office one more excuse to cut the news budget; and when it happens again and again, the cumulative impact is devastating.

That is happening in our time, and it must be stopped, for a free and muscular press is an essential underpinning of a free society. Our system of government, despite its recent failures and follies, remains the best and most durable so far devised by the mind of man or woman.

So we must repair our media before we can salvage our politics. That will be a large and difficult task, and a painful one. If it were easy and pleasant, it would have been done long ago. The issues are so complex and the bad habits so ingrained that some suggest there is no way out of the present mess. I don't believe that: most newspapers would still earn a decent return even if they spent a lot more on news coverage. The same is even more true of television networks. All it takes is money — and a willingness to invite critical and continuing study of media performance by outsiders.

The money is there. Some two dozen studies are currently being funded by foundations, and there's more where that came from. The need for ongoing scrutiny is more controversial, but it is absolutely necessary. The journalists can't do it by themselves. They have forfeited their credibility by dumbing down and tarting up their publications and programs, and by increasingly adopting almost-anything-goes policies on the handling of news. So the journalists must stop stonewalling, which merely heightens public perceptions of the media as arrogant and irresponsible, and enlist in their support the very people who are currently most unhappy with their performance — their customers, their critics, and the public at large.

There are any number of ways to bring public scrutiny to bear on media performance. Maybe it's time for another Hutchins Commission, to bring that seminal 1947 study of the press into the Internet Age. Maybe it's time for the resurrection of the National News Council, that noble experiment that was suffocated by the bitter opposition of the *New York Times* and other major news organizations. Certainly it's time for many local and state news organizations to propose and support local news councils. And it's past time for many newspapers and television stations to create an ombudsman's position on their staffs.

We can choose from any number of remedies. But one thing is certain: if the media don't figure out how to clean up their act, someone else will do it for them — and it won't be a pretty sight.

A WITNESS TO PUBLIC EDUCATION

Robert Coles

In my junior year of college I had the great good luck to study with
Perry Miller, whose American literature courses and seminars
taught us so very much about this country. He wanted to get to
know us and invited us to his Widener study. I recall getting into a
spirited conversation with him once about Emerson and
Thoreau — I was taken aback, actually, by the moral energy he dis-
played himself as he spoke of the moral energy those two
Concordians possessed. I also remember talking with him about the
tutoring I was doing in Boston as part of my work at Phillips Brooks
House. I was trying to be of assistance to high-schoolers who were
having trouble with their school lessons. I helped students as they
struggled with their grammar and spelling, and their math. I also got
to know them as young men and women who had no interest, by
and large, in attending college. They told me they aspired to be car-
penters, electricians, plumbers, steam-fitters, nurses, or secretaries. I
remember noticing the academic ability of a particular youth,
encouraging him or her to think of college, only to be turned down
with the shake of a head or a look of surprise meant to give me
pause, second thoughts. I also remember discussing such experiences with Professor Miller. I kept speaking of the "potential" in one

or another youth, the considerable and evident intelligence, the untapped "promise" — and once he, in turn and unforgettably, remonstrated with me wryly, quietly: "It's quite possible to be bright and not want to go to college." I had, of course, been pushing that outcome with my tutees and, on their behalf, with Miller; and he had clearly decided with that remark to initiate a discussion with me — which we had at some length, and which I've never wanted to forget. In essence, a distinguished Harvard professor was reminding me of "class" and its relationship to the outlook of young, midcentury Americans. He was also, by indirection, commenting on the dangers of a smug parochialism and, too, a condescension masked as ostensible good will. He wanted me to realize that because I happened to be in college, and was brought up to want to get there, was no reason to assume that such a hope, such a destination or outcome, was "normal" or "natural" or expectable or desirable.

He saw how puzzled I looked as he gave voice to such observations; and, as a consequence, he amplified his remarks, gave me a disquisition (I can hear his voice, see his gestures and mannerisms) on the "working class world," in England (when it then reigned supreme) and in this country — on the pride and dignity, the feisty spirit of such a world. He wasn't romanticizing a segment of our 1950s nation, nor was he gratuitously critical of me for wanting "more" for my tutees, for (as he put it) "aspiring on their behalf." He simply wanted me to understand the complexity of a particular human involvement — what I brought out of my life to those young people, what they believed and felt out of their experiences at home and in a neighborhood. Once, memorably, he put the matter this way: "You're trying hard to teach them — but let them be your teachers, too."

That plea for a certain humility, for a willingness to subordinate one's own thinking life to that of others, was not easily heard, I fear — indeed, Professor Miller was the first to understand the difficulty his advice posed for someone like me, and for some of his other students as well. Again and again, in his "Classics of the Christian Tradition" course, he reminded us of the provocations to be found in the New Testament, as in, "The last shall be first, the first last" — an unsettling message for young ones quite pleased to be where they were, in that famous Yard, and at a time when their nation's power was triumphant.

I tried to remember my teacher's counsel, but really slipped into the habit of exhorting the high-schoolers I was tutoring; if they worked harder and did better in their classroom work, they, too, could be like me, a college student — but they were as little inclined to hear me as I was to hear my teacher, Perry Miller. Once, one of my most promising students, a young man named Hank, whom I remember well for his outspoken candor as well as his intelligence, turned the tables on me, let me know that he was quite happy with his future prospects (he wanted to be a carpenter, like his father), and decidedly uninterested in "going beyond high school," as he put it. I recall that phrase, frankly, because what followed it in explanation proved unforgettable. "I'm happy with my life — I know where I'm headed and I'm glad." This same youth had also told me how much he liked to go to the library, to browse through magazines and books. Surely with that strong inclination, he was a fit candidate for college — so I suggested. But he objected — and again, he put the matter in such a way that I had a hard time, in turn, putting his words out of my mind: "I like to read a book and enjoy it, but in school they make it into a big deal, and it's not fun anymore."

I had yet to know much, at least academically, about human psychology, nor was Professor Miller especially interested in psychiatry or psychoanalysis, but I did tell him about Hank and his comments with some sense that they had struck a significant chord or two in my mind, and he most forcefully and explicitly let me know what he made of what had transpired. I myself was having a lot of trouble figuring out what I wanted to do with my life — especially so because I was in the pre-medical school science course, and it was rife with fierce competition, to put it mildly. Moreover, I didn't like the way a particular English professor was dealing with the novels we were reading. He gave us frequent spot quizzes on "name identification," and he offered the densest kind of explication, interpretation, which we, then, had to offer back when we took the hour exams and the final. Professor Miller had heard me sing of my woes in both those respects, and so (without the mannerisms of the clinic, thank God) he tactfully let me know tersely and trenchantly, that "the fellow [Hank] may be a step ahead of us." Again, a moment that remains fixed in my head — a shrewdly knowing teacher who was willing to link himself with his student, and acknowledge on their joint behalf a measure of irony, at the very least.

I've often harkened back to those particular experiences, moments of awareness — for me, they are the college education I was lucky to receive: a professor who himself resisted the temptations of complacent smugness, of self-satisfaction, and who let a student know about certain hazards that go with trying to learn about others and to help them. A decade later, finally out of school myself, a child psychiatrist in the military, in accordance with the "doctors draft" that had all of us physicians give two years to our country (I sure was reluctant then; I now think it was the best thing that ever happened to me) I stumbled into Ruby Bridges, a six-year-old girl in New Orleans who was just starting her experience with school. In fact Ruby had to fight her way past a mob every day to get to a classroom, where she studied on her own because all other children had been withdrawn by their parents. This was the start of school desegregation in the Deep South — a great ordeal for public education in our nation. I would end up observing that ordeal for years; I got to know the African-American and white children who went through it and, too, their teachers, and learned thereby a little of what happens in schools when the world in which they belong makes new and serious demands on them — in this case, the initiation of a complex kind of human relatedness hitherto outlawed: the classroom as a color-blind scene. As I kept trying to learn how those children in Louisiana (and later in Georgia and Mississippi and Alabama and North Carolina) all managed under stressful circumstances, to say the least, I only gradually learned to stop imposing my own educational experiences and the assumptions they had prompted in me, in favor of a more tentative kind of watchfulness, worthy of what Professor Miller had suggested. In fact I went back several times during the early part of my seven-year stay in the South to visit this important teacher in my life (he died in 1963) and told him what I was seeing and hearing in the South's public schools. In 1962, thoroughly unsure of what to make of an exceedingly complex social and racial landscape, and of the psychological ironies and ambiguities that were hard to fathom, I was about to throw my hands up in surrender and return north. But I was told this in a Widener Library study:

> You're getting an education about education! I think you are trying too hard to get a fix on a research project. You keep telling me about what you're trying to find out about these kids, all their "problems," all the psychopathology. Fair enough — but I think they've got you confused, and that's a good thing. Your ideas aren't adequate to them, to the whole story of their lives, which you've yet to learn. Why don't you give some thought to what you are trying to unearth in this "research" of yours? Why don't you make those children and their parents and their teachers your colleagues — better, your professors? Ask them what they think is important, really important, for you to know."

By then I was tape-recording conversations in schools and homes — even the one I had with my former college professor. I thought I had figured out a so-called "methodology," a manner of doing my work: the use of children's drawings and paintings to get at their inner life, as well as, of course, interviews with them and "direct observation," as Anna Freud put it, of their school and home life. But Professor Miller's comments prompted me to make a shift in the way I conducted those interviews — I began to share some of my thoughts with the children; I began to ask them for their thoughts on schooling, on the racial tensions in their communities, putting emphasis on their social and cultural perceptions rather than on an exclusive interest in their psychology. I began to learn from these boys and girls (and their parents and teachers) throughout

the South, in a time of social upheaval, what happens in our public schools for the good and the bad.

The results of that research (it was extended to rural as well as
urban school children, for example, the sons and daughters of
migrant farmworkers and Appalachian families, and those who
attend schools on our Indian reservations and in Alaska) were a surprise to me: some children (especially those under the worst stresses)
often enough mustered an impressive quality of mind and heart, if
given half a chance, and thereby did far better educationally and
psychologically than I expected. For years, actually, I tried to understand the reasons for such an outcome, until, one day, the girl who
had experienced, maybe, the most fearful time of it, with her very
life at stake for a while, looked back (she was eight) at what she had
experienced a couple of years earlier:

> It was bad, yes, a lot bad; but I had this goal to outlast
> those folks screaming; and I had the teacher, giving me
> plenty to do, and you know, at first I had her all to myself.
> I wanted to learn the best I could, so I wouldn't disap-
> point my folks, and my people here in New Orleans [its
> African-American citizens]. I knew everyone was watch-
> ing, and that's why I kept saying to myself: let them see
> what you can do — you show them! It was tough, but
> when you win and it's been a long battle, then you're
> proud. My mom says, if things come too easy, you don't
> get as much out of what you're doing! I'd come home,
> and I did extra work so I could keep ahead, and no say-
> ing "I told you so, she just can't make the grade." I hope
> I'll keep on moving up, and I hope I'll be able to prove
> Judge Wright right [J. Skelley Wright, the federal judge
> who ordered school desegregation to begin].

She smiled as she considered the rhyme of Wright/right; she
wrote out both words for me — thus showing me what I already
knew, how well she was doing at spelling. But, in fact, she had in
her own unprepossessing, beguiling way given me a full educa-

tional textbook in those few sentences. She had pointed out what others call the "variables" or "factors" that go to make a successful public education, even one pursued under the most threatening of conditions. She may have met mobs on her way to and from school, but she had a lot to keep her going while there: a teacher who worked closely with her; a sense of purpose and direction; and a sense, also, of achievement measured daily by her willingness and ability to persist, no matter the difficulties confronting her. Moreover, her family and the neighborhood where she lived rallied around her — for many this child was a hero, applauded as a brave pioneer. For such a child, for others like her across the South during the 1960s, school attendance became a closely observed, highly sanctioned effort as well as a perilous and much-opposed one. No wonder these children by and large did so well both academically and personally. Vulnerable with respect to their background and their daily situation as participants in a controversial political and racial, as well as educational, initiative, these students were nevertheless given respect, attention, support, even acclaim. They faced angry crowds, but they were not by any means lost; quite the contrary: they received the kind of individual assistance in their studies at home and at school (from those who supported what they were doing) that any quite well-to-do children can take for granted in private schools.

Eventually I came back to my native New England to teach at Harvard, first in Erik H. Erikson's course, and then on my own, at the College and at the Medical School. At that time, the early 1970s, Boston also experienced an educational crisis not unlike, in certain respects, the ones I'd watched across the South where African-American parents were determined to find more adequate schools for their children. I rode on a bus for a year with some of those boys and girls — they were leaving Roxbury for a less-crowded, better-equipped school in the Back Bay. Now I was getting into the midst of an educational struggle that wasn't prompted by segregationist defiance, but rather, by the workings of class as well as race in a northern city known, ironically, for its long-standing abolitionist history. Now I was talking with children who weren't being individually celebrated as protagonists of progress, but who were regarded by themselves and others as victims of a flawed educational system — one whose inadequacies (and worse) had to do with the way our social and economic system works: those with money and power find thoroughly adequate schools, public or private, for their sons and daughters, whereas those who are poor, no matter their skin color, are far less able to command such an outcome for their children. In time, I concluded my "study" of northern children going through their kind of educational crisis and settled into a different relationship to such young people — I started working as a volunteer teacher in an elementary school (named after Martin Luther King) right near Harvard and in high schools in Boston (the Jeremiah Burke and Brighton High School). So doing, this past decade and more, I have been a witness to public education and its well-known and persisting problems as they, alas, help shape the lives of countless children who live in Cambridge and Boston, not far from many important colleges and universities. I often meet young people who strike me as intelligent, alert, knowing in many ways, yet indifferent to school work, even scornful of it. I meet others who don't know how to do their lessons very well, who need encouragement and assistance that, for the most part, is not forthcoming. I meet still others, in high school, who actually pose a threat to their classmates, not to mention their teachers. I also meet, I'm sorry to say, teachers who have long ago lost the enthusiasm and dedication that are needed to keep a class going well, especially under the circumstances that prevail in many urban schools. Yet there are more hopeful moments, and they are truly memorable.

Even in the toughest high school classes there are always — yes, always — some youths who are really trying to grab hold of that proverbial ladder and climb their way out of the ghetto life they have known so long. Often I wonder what makes for the difference: why are some in my classes so unruly, so provocative, or so bored and indifferent and sullen, or so irritable and restless and smart-alecky, whereas others are quietly industrious, respectful, anxious to learn, eager to take part in the various projects I try to initiate? I wish I could answer such a question in a clear-cut psychological and sociological manner, the approach I myself for so long have assumed to be the correct and desirable one. Always, that is, I have tried to understand the children in those classrooms as troubled because of this or that aspect of their home life, their street life, even their previous school life; or alternatively as the beneficiaries of one or another set of experiences or influences that have favored them as students, members of a classroom. Such an observation is, of course, true — yet the complexity of things, the constant presence of irony, has to be mentioned. That is, I know youngsters who are bright, who have received some valuable encouragement (and love) at home, but who have turned out to be rowdy troublemakers in and outside of the school building. Conversely, I have marveled at certain students before me — they have had a devastating time of it, day in and day out, since their earliest years, and still they have somehow found the capacity and will to take hold as students, to give an educational life a chance, and as a consequence, to improve mightily their prospects.

As I search for the explanations we all understandably crave, I come back again and again, to what George Eliot emphasized in *Middlemarch* — the impact of luck and chance and circumstance upon young lives, their susceptibility to fateful moments, for the good and the bad alike. Put differently, I have met schoolchildren whose destinies have been decisively affected, if not determined, by particular encounters, experiences, events — accidents and incidents that have figured importantly in the way they have lived their lives in and out of the classroom. Here, for instance, is a tough, intimidating gangleader who was for awhile disruptive in my tenth-grade English class, and who one day came to see me after class in hopes that we would "rap" — and so we did, several times, whereupon this declaration:

> Since my cousin lost his legs [in a shooting that caused hemiplegia], I've stopped myself from hanging out with the guys. I go to the movies in the afternoon and sometimes I don't watch the show, I just sit and think. I used

to hate being alone. Now that's the best time — you're able to figure out stuff, and you're not being pushed to get lost by falling in with someone who has himself a knife and a gun and a big mouth and some dough and some buddies to stand by and guard him. While the people in the movie do their thing, I "weigh things," that's what my cousin thought he was so good at, but he wasn't: he got cut down. I think I'm going to start school and be serious at it. See what I mean?"

I told him I did — I saw on his face his "meaning," his fear and his melancholy, and his consequent intent to shift his mind's angle of moral vision. He didn't become, overnight, a successful student, nor did he altogether surrender his swagger, his truculent, dismissive "cool" that, often enough, caused me irritation or frustration or fear or anger, or all the above. But he gradually did become a more-or-less participating member of the class, as opposed to a looming, scary, antagonistic presence in it — and by the end of the year I could honestly feel that he was really learning in the class, and glad that such was the case. On the last day of the school, ever so poignantly and tersely, he thanked a couple of us teachers for "showing up," and then added another thank-you: "I guess I should thank my cousin, too. [If it] wasn't for him I'd be walking down a different road for sure."

His head was lowered, and twice he shook it. I saw him then as the immensely hurt and worried youth he always was — now without the posturing and braggadocio meant to hide from others (and not least, himself) the great objective and subjective jeopardy of his young life. I recall thinking that his name was legion — that here, before me, in a particular life, was an educational story of America at the end of this century, this millennium: our inner-city youth in all their marginality, vulnerability, discontent, but also with the possibilities and potential capabilities that bespeak their humanity. No question, our schools will not in and of themselves rescue many of our troubled youth — especially because resources, including human resources, have a way of gravitating toward wealth and power, and so those most in need of small classes and the best-trained, most experienced teachers are least likely to get them. Indeed, when I go into some schools and take note of the number of children in the classrooms, and the equipment and reading material in those rooms, I get all too quickly discouraged. Still, as I well know from sitting in the classes of other teachers, and occasionally from my own teaching, there are plenty of young people, even in tough neighborhoods and understaffed, inadequately supported schools, who manage to take good advantage of the education offered them. Many more, though, are doomed by the life they bring to school, and by no means rescued from that downward tug once inside a room of students and teachers.

So often, I hear this or that teacher think aloud — say that it could be otherwise: with more money and with more and better teachers, more students could be reached, touched, connected in mind and heart to the intellectual and moral energy generated in a given day-to-day educational life. As I listen to such expressed hopefulness and idealism, often tentatively or wistfully rendered, I go back in my mind to my own college years — when, for instance, "The Quiet One" was made, a film by James Agee and Helen Levitt that told of a Harlem boy's slow transformation, by earnest psychological understanding on the part of his elders in an institutional setting. Now, alas, we have learned to be less hopeful about such children, and not without good reason.

Hope, actually, requires a commitment of time and money if it is to be translated into a continually felt social reality — something there, awaiting those in distress or danger. In "The Quiet One" a writer and a cinematographer dared to dream of a future when hurt children will be accorded the disciplined, wise commitment of a cadre of alert, lively, self-aware and idealistic adults, willing to guide and teach by word and deed, by constant example. All our recent knowledge notwithstanding — all our educational techniques, newly acquired and touted, neurobiology, "social engineering," and important technological breakthroughs — the way to the waywardness of the children I meet in our public schools is, finally, through their minds and hearts: they can be stirred and touched by teachers and athletic coaches and counselors and school nurses — by us grown-ups who are part of the world of children, and are able to offer various talents and skills to these young fellow-citizens so much in need of them. Come the next century, that will still be what will spare many of our country's youth one or another kind of educational, social, psychological perdition: the human connection that little Ruby in New Orleans and others have known to matter so very much.

INVESTING IN TODAY'S FAMILIES FOR OUR COMMON FUTURE

Nicholas Cunningham

This essay is a composite view of the family: close ups of my own family, social anthropologic aspects, historical definitions, a convenience sample of demographic and parenting data (neither exhaustive nor exhausting), pathologic features, child outcomes, societal responses, new findings, proven interventions, a diagnosis, and finally a few unpalatable prescriptions from an old pediatrician, new grandfather, and veteran observer of family foibles.

CLOSE UP VIEWS

My own family like so many American families is hybrid: half Boston, half New York; my father was born in Brookline, my mother in Brooklyn. My brother and I are fourth-generation Harvardians; my children's education was largely paid for by a Lawrence family trust fund. Amos Lawrence and his brother Abbott built the family wealth in textiles, saved it frugally, and spent it selectively: helping Kansas resist slavery, supporting higher education, and investing in their families. Next came Amos A. Lawrence, who had similar habits; the trust fund set up by his widow Sarah only terminated a century later after the death of her last grandchild at age 104.

My mother's father was penniless and lacked higher education, but he made a killing on the stock market a century ago. With this he bought land and built a farm on Lake Otsego in upstate New York. Besides this farm, we inherited clocks, portraits, musical instruments, books, and aspirations. Of his seven daughters, five lived to be ancient; their great-grandchildren continue to enjoy the place. This is what "old money" and a family that saves it can do. U.S. society is enriched and enhanced by personal and social investments by the Lawrences, Guggenheims, Rockefellers — but how much of the philanthropy of these robber barons was from altruism, from pride in the family name, from religious guilt, or related tax laws? This is worth considering when observing the disparate social behavior of today's tycoons, for example, Bill Gates and George Soros. Do today's first families invest in their descendants and in posterity in the same way?

Since the religious mores of wealthy families prevail far less than formerly, we might ask how today's families from all social strata are faring in terms of meeting the needs of their children and our democratic society.

Starting with my own family: last year at seventy, I finally became a grandfather. My pediatrician daughter and her psychologist husband both work full time. They both know the value of exclusive breastfeeding, and she planned to stay home awhile, study Spanish, fix up the house, and carry out a number of projects. My grandson is healthy; his mother gets huge support from his father and both families; there is zero hardship of any kind. To her surprise, however, she finds that the baby is 100% in charge; she's tired all the time and, besides breastfeeding, can do almost none of what she had planned and needs all the help she can get. And then she thinks about all the single mothers with housing, marital, and money problems, several children and little or no support. How do they cope? I think about my grandparents, their thirteen children, and the many servants who helped raise them, either directly or by taking over all the household chores.

Clearly things are different today, in many ways because of our freedom to choose: my Episcopalian, Bostonian father married an agnostic New Yorker; the children were brought up outside the church. I met my wife in the civil rights movement. We married in Togo, after our Peace Corps service, and our children are half black and half white. We raised them on the upper west side of New York City, far from the segregated suburbs. After many years of effort, the marriage ended when the youngest was fifteen. The divorce was mediated, the adjustment to it long and difficult. Nonetheless, I married again and after fifteen years of hard work and some professional help, we rebuilt our family for ourselves and our five children. It sprawls but it works.

ANTHROPOLOGY/HISTORY

We humans consider ourselves social animals, sometimes comparing ourselves to wolves (in packs) or sheep (in herds). The reason wolves are more relevant (as pointed out by my cousin Susie Allport) is not that they are more aggressive (as we are), or that they organize around alpha males (as we tend to), but because they are altricial: their babies are born helpless and require a huge investment to survive. Primate babies, especially humans, require so much care for so long that our societies tend to be built around the family. So, whenever human society seems not to be working so well, and especially now that global prospects seem threatened, "we" (including even those of us without families or who eschew reference to "family values") might ask ourselves: Does the made-in-USA family work? Is it competitive? Will it last? Will the rest of the world again follow us down this path?

To respond we might start by trying to answer four other questions: How does today's U.S. family differ from the families of the distant and immediate past? What difference does this make to how we live, who we become, and the shape of our democratic society? Who could, should, do something about it? What might improve things?

DEFINITIONS

The *Encyclopedia Britannica* eleventh edition came out in 1911, the year my father graduated from Harvard, and is said to be the last attempt to collect everything worth knowing. What was "worth knowing" was thought to have originated in ancient Greece and Rome. The codification of the family is traced back to 450 B.C. and the publication in Rome of *Lex XII Tabularium,* and thence (according to Livy) to Solon, from whom the twelve laws were supposedly derived. The Vth of these laws codified family relations, giving complete power and ownership of the wife and children to the husband and, at his death, to his male relatives or descendants. However, this Vth Law also codified an important Roman practice: that of "free" marriages in which wives, while giving up some of the formal marriage rituals, could retain their property and independence.

While there are vestiges of the former, the modern U.S. family tends toward these latter arrangements. Perhaps because of our immigrant, frontier origins (codified by innumerable "Westerns") the nuclear family with the wife as an essential and responsible (especially for the children) partner is considered the norm. And for the past half-century, thanks to Rosie the Riveter and her ilk, wives are now also seen as part of the breadwinning partnership. This begs questions about the role of the male partner in family life.

Recently, when consulting on a near fatally shaken (battered) baby from an observant family from Yemen, I learned that that community, even when residing here, tends to give the man, backed (actually today ruled) by religious leaders, just about total power within the family, even to beating a wife or daughter to death. Lesser forms of male domination and machismo prevail widely in the U.S., particularly in self-segregated communities (and in professional sports?). We are still struggling to create families with parents as partners . . . see below.

The *Britannica's* eleventh edition also classifies families by degrees of estimated consanguinity, pointing out that many societies use clan names to clarify these arrangements — that is, to ensure exogamy and avoid Oedipus-Jocasta and other such incestuous events. Whether promiscuity/incest pre-existed the formation of the human family is left in doubt for, as Darwin points out, "Promiscuous intercourse in a state of nature is extremely improbable. . . . The most probable view is that man originally lived in small communities, each man with a single wife or, if powerful, with several whom he jealously guarded against all other men. . . ." But the eleventh edition also points out that "to guard women jealously would mean constant battle, at least when man became an animal who makes love all year around." So Darwin postulates that "younger males . . . expelled and wandering about, would, when at last successful in finding a partner, prevent too close interbreeding within the limits of the same family." Family totems are recognized as protective against incest among societies without name inheritance (which doesn't explain why in some cultures, names like Smith, Carlson, Park, or Cohen were allowed to prevail so widely). Matriarchal and patriarchal societies are then compared, with the achievement of the latter being identified as "progressive and in fact essential for the formation of the family system of civilized life"! This was the era of *The Autocrat of the Breakfast Table*!

More recently, the *Oxford English Dictionary* (the two-volume, micro-print tome) includes eight separate definitions for the family, the first being "the household . . . of servants" and the last being "the thieving fraternity." Thirty years ago, the *American Heritage Dictionary* defined the family as "the most instinctive fundamental social or mating group in man or animal, especially in the union of man and woman through marriage and their offspring; parents and children," or simply: "one's spouse and children."

In West African traditional societies, I saw extended families living in compounds and merging indefinably into the society of the village, the hierarchy of the chief and the elders. Children did not belong to their biological parents but rather to the extended family. Nowadays these families have lost control of their children. Mortality dropped so much faster than fertility that children spilled out of the system, and rogue males, in gangs, armed and dangerous, are destroying whole societies.

At home, the family is also being rapidly redefined into: the reconstituted family; the same-sex family; the foster family (professional or amateur); the group home; the senior center; and finally the childless Florida community. And for some runaways we have street-gang families. Analogously, in East Africa, AIDS, like the plagues of the Dark Ages, leaves in its wake the parentless family. Conversely, the extended family has resurfaced in name only in the form of huge periodic gatherings of people, many of them strangers but with a common (man's) surname.

As a pediatrician, I espouse the concept of the family, in its procreational and nurturing aspect, as fundamental to the future of (Wo)mankind. Therefore, let us focus on the family's principal role: the early care of society's children, particularly since most societies (especially the former Soviet states but also Israel) have turned away from entrusting this function to the state or commune. Is the family still set up to do this job?

DEMOGRAPHY

Whatever we think of our own family, the U.S. family today is unrecognizable compared to what it was forty to fifty years ago.

	1960	1990	1994	2000 (est)
1. Far fewer parents marry				
Proportion of out of wedlock births	5%	29%	32%	> 33%
2. Half of the fathers leave home				
Population of children in fatherless families (1/4 of these fathers provide only partial child support, 1/2 pay nothing)	19%	–	–	60%
3. Divorce rates have tripled				
First-marriage divorce rates (Second marriages fare even worse)	16%	–	40%	>50%
4. Most mothers now work				
Proportion of working mothers	19%	–	–	60%
5. More families are poor			1997	
Proportion of children ages 0 – 6 living in poverty	15%		24%	

CHILDCARE

These factors combine to degrade family life and deprive American children, rich or poor, from conception throughout childhood. But, whereas better off families can buy help of some sort, poor families are more often without such support. Data on U.S. children demonstrate significant deprivation of the poor as compared to the better-off. This deprivation starts before birth:

1. For U.S. families below the federal poverty line, 25% of babies are unwanted as against 8% among the better-off (>200% above the poverty line)
2. Poor mothers are 25% less likely to get adequate prenatal care.
3. One of every twenty U.S. babies is exposed to illicit drugs prenatally — ten times the rate twenty years ago; but poor babies have higher rates: in some public hospitals, 42% of babies are tox-positive at birth.
4. 19% of all babies are exposed to alcohol prenatally (this is *not* associatedwith poverty).

After birth there are other problems:

1. Less than 5% of newborns get post-partum visits, which are routine in most European countries and help new mothers get off to a good start.
2. With most mothers now working, only 28% of zero to three year olds are in licensed day care. Many are in family day care, about which little is known. We do know that half of all child-care centers were judged mediocre, and 40% poor, in 1995. This contrasts with excellent state-subsidized early childcare in France and other European countries.
3. Only half our preschoolers are in preschools, many of which are inadequate and understaffed.
4. At home, parents are stressed out: 97% spank their children (illegal in Scandinavia), 3% beat them with a stick or belt, 3% are (under-) reported annually for child abuse/neglect. One quarter of U.S. parents abuse each other, usually in the

presence of the children, which is emotionally abusive but rarely reported.

RESULTS: HOW CHILDREN ARE AFFECTED

Association doesn't prove causality, but the data suggest that American children, especially the 25% who are poor, are not thriving:

1. One in fourteen babies is born underweight especially if the mother is poor. In New York City babies from poor districts are twice as likely to be born with low birth weight as those from well-off districts.
2. Half a million U.S. children were in foster care in 1996 — 25% more than in 1986.
3. Three million families are reported and 1,300 children die annually from abuse; children in poverty are six times as likely to be maltreated.
4. U.S. infant mortality is also higher than in all European countries except Portugal. In New York City, babies from poor districts are exactly twice as likely to die as babies from affluent sections.
5. Survivors are slowed down: poor babies are twice as likely to be physically or mentally handicapped and twice as likely to have learning disabilities as preschoolers. In New York City, 12% of all children end up in "special education."

SOCIETAL RESPONSES: DENIAL AND DYSFUNCTION

Denial

How is it that the most powerful and affluent nation finds so many of its children in this deprived, unhealthy, stressed-out state? There are many answers, but I believe it's mostly denial: we the people and our government have not acknowledged, accepted, or acted on the established fact that today's families, especially poor families, can't give their children what they need without outside help.

The U.S. government doesn't provide that help, or wraps it in so much bureaucracy that it is largely inaccessible. We are not the only country with a wide gap between rich and poor families, but the U.S. stands alone in how little we do to help the poor. The Luxembourg Income Study (1995) shows this. In eleven of the eighteen countries surveyed, child poverty is at least halved by government welfare measures. Poor families are as prevalent in France and the United Kingdom (25% and 30%, respectively) as in the U.S. (25%), but after government tax and transfer benefits, these rates are reduced to 7% and 10%.

Here at home, after subtracting for the value of government support, one in every five children (21.5%) remains in poverty. As Lisbeth Schorr wrote in 1997, "The notion that every family should be able to care for its own, with outside help, has made the U.S. the only industrialized country in the world without universal preschools, paid parental leave, and income support for families with young children."

We just don't do enough. For example, the Federal Head Start Program, by far the best U.S. program for young children, and the sole bipartisan survivor from the '60s "War on Poverty," enrolls less than 40% of those eligible. The only "advanced" countries that come close to our societal child negligence are Canada and Australia — also largely immigrant societies with that "pioneer" do-it-yourself spirit. The "cowboy" mentality got a new lease on life, after ambitious New Deal and Great Society initiatives, from our two most western presidents, Nixon and Reagan.

Nixon killed legislation to increase child care, saying that women should stay home (ignoring the fact that they'd already left to go to work). Reagan said, "We fought a war on poverty and poverty won," despite the fact that Medicaid, Head Start, WIC, and Community Health Centers, though cut back to finance the war in Vietnam, produced dramatic changes for poor families in health, education, and quality of life. Both presidents seemed to believe that government couldn't or shouldn't help young families but that tough love, forcing parents to stay home, was the only solution.

This final solution has now been rendered even more final by welfare reform: putting single parents back to work. The step was predicted twenty-five years ago in a book called *The Family — Can It be Saved?* (co-authored by Harvard Professor T. Berry Brazelton); and by relieving the dependency and stigma of welfare, it might conceivably help. So far, without concurrent enrichment and expansion of day care, it's hurting children.

Dysfunction

Meanwhile our society leads the world in child runaways, teen pregnancy, drug abuse, violent crimes (especially by juveniles) and incarceration (especially of poor people).

- 451,000 children run away each year.
- U.S. teen pregnancy rates (about 13% of all births) while slowly dropping, are double that of England and eleven times that of Holland.
- One of every sixteen Americans abuses drugs; all told we spend about $40 billion a year on illegal drugs (only 1/5 of that on pot) and while the crack epidemic has peaked, the rate of drug use by adolescents doubled from 11% in 1991 to 21% in 1995.
- We specialize in violence; while our cities grow safer, juvenile crime in the U.S. has quadrupled in the past twenty five years; school children across America no longer feel safe; 3,000 teenagers are murdered annually, compared to 300 for all of Europe; American 15– to 24–year-old males murder at six times the rate of any other developed country; they also lead the world in suicide.
- Our response? Prisons: there are 1.8 million Americans in jail today; one of every twenty babies born in the U.S. today will spend part of its adult life in state or federal prison. Since it costs more than $100,000 a year to incarcerate a

juvenile, California now spends more on criminal justice than on higher education.

WHAT CAN WE DO TO PROTECT OUR CHILDREN?

With the arrival of the baby, most families come together, dream of the future, plan for the present, and vow to do their best. Often, they don't know much about what's required. In his recently published *The Growth of the Mind and the Endangered Origins of Intelligence,* Stanley Greenspan makes many important points, among them that marriage partners or lovers tend to marry others at the same developmental level. For parents whose upbringing has been deprived, this may mean that they are not capable of meeting their children's emotional needs without help.

Greenspan (former chief of infant studies at the National Institutes of Mental Health) then lists the seven irreducible needs of childhood:

1. "Every child needs a safe, secure environment that includes at least one stable, predictable, comforting, and protective relationship with an adult. . . ."

    Comment: It doesn't have to be the parent, nor do education or wealth matter, but the person must have the time, maturity, and long-term commitment. In fact, young couples often change baby sitters before attachment can occur.

2. "Consistent nurturing relationships, including the primary one, early in life and throughout childhood. . . ."

    Comment: Home visitation programs often end or taper off after age one; day care facilities provide low pay, low status jobs, and have high turnover; foster parents often "insulate themselves from the pain of repeatedly 'falling in love' with youngsters they know they will have to leave."

3. "Rich, ongoing interaction. . . . Love and nurturance, though essential, don't suffice."

Comment: Day care frequently provides minimal interaction — nurseries can be worse. Family day care may include six to eight daily hours of TV. With high ratios of children to caretakers, each child's individual needs just can't be considered.

4. "Each child and family needs an environment that allows them to progress through the developmental stages in their own style and their own good time. . . ."

Comment: Each family starts from a different place and each child develops at his/her own pace; on-the-cheap day care ignores these individual differences and pushes for uniform staging, which often destroys self-confidence and denies opportunities for individuation and special talents. Programs like Head Start which involve the parents in the care, are more likely to meet this need and help the parents to do likewise at home.

5. "Children must have opportunities to experiment, to find solutions, to take risks and even to fail. . . ."

Comment: This requires maturity from caretakers and time. Many programs encourage passivity and helplessness by removing decision-making from the individual child's hands' — usually because there are too many children and the harried teachers just can't cope.

6. "Children need structure and clear boundaries. . . ."

Comment: This is often what I find most lacking in the abusive family; there are no boundaries, no limits, family life is punctuated by acting out behaviors, castigations and whippings. Many of these parents lack personal discipline and flexibility due to their own experiences as children and adolescents. If helped in time, they can do better.

7. "To achieve these goals, families need stable neighborhoods and communities. . . ."

> Comment: A study (by Elmer) many years ago compared the lives of abused children with control children from the same deprived area of inner-city Pittsburgh. The controls turned out to be in almost as much trouble as the reported children. Conclusion: that part of Pittsburgh was unfit for any child's healthy development.
>
> Permanently confining our poor (mostly minority) families in old, run-down neighborhoods or new unsafe projects deprives our children of what they need.

How hard is it to meet these seven needs? New parents approach the task with enthusiasm. First they make love and learn to love each other. After conception, genes are transmitted, hopes developed, and a nest prepared. At birth, the baby takes over and the family is transformed. What Selma Fraiberg called "the first love affair" (think of Della Robbia madonnas gazing at their infants against azure skies) sets the tone. The father provides security. The baby attaches. Later, the toddler lets go to individuate, vacillate, and separate. Siblings used to provide the next (socialization) stage. Now, with smaller families, it's mostly school and playmates. Meanwhile, family lore, culture, beliefs, limits, and values are transmitted. The foundations of personality and an outlook on life are laid: safe-unsafe, intellectual-physical, visual-auditory, dichotomous-inflected, empathetic-narcissistic.

Now, if we compare the seven needs and the outcome data listed above, we can see the widening gap between the ideal and our so-called "real world." Obviously many factors are involved. Genes play a major role, influencing intelligence, emotion, personality. First-borns may become more responsible, single- or last-borns more adventurous (at least according to Frank Sulloway). Parental chauffeurs either encourage or deny opportunities for music, dramatic/martial arts, sports, and outdoor exploration. The family teaches society's young how to listen, relate, cope, enjoy, and about what's safe and what's important. By age six, TV, school teachers, and peer groups strongly impinge on the family's influence (as stressed by Judith Harris in her eloquent but biased 1998 book *The Nurture Assumption*).

But the most astute observers of child development, Spitz, Winnicott, Bowlby, Ainsworth, Klein, Mahler, Miller, Brazelton, Fraiberg, Lief, and Stern all agreed that while nature and nurture interact throughout childhood, the first three years are crucial. They have told us this for decades but we didn't believe it.

Winnicott went still further, saying that the democratic society "derives from the working of the ordinary good home. . . . Of a true democracy one can say: In this society at this time there is sufficient maturity in the emotional development of a sufficient proportion of the individuals that compose it for there to exist an innate tendency towards the creation, recreation, and maintenance of the democratic machinery. . . . Ordinary good homes provide the only setting in which the democratic factor can be created."

NEW FINDINGS — THE GAP BETWEEN WHAT WE KNOW AND WHAT WE DO

We are slow learners and skeptical of social science findings, but *finally* we have some hard data. A scientific revolution has taken place and is being documented in an outpouring of publications about babies' brains. A good summary is *Rethinking the Brain, New Insights into Early Development*, by Rima Shore (New York: Families and Work Institute, 1997) (Website: http//www.familiesandwork. org). Using Positron Emission Tomography and Magnetic Resonance Spectroscopy, we have learned how a baby learns by receiving early, frequent, and positive reinforcement. Animal and human studies demonstrate that there is a crucial period for this programming and that for babies getting inadequate or adverse stimulation during the first two or three years, later catch-up can only be achieved by huge effort and is likely to be incomplete.

Babies are born with one hundred billion or so neurons. Each neuron develops 15,000 synapses or connections. Pathways are established and reinforced by outside stimulation, or by what Ainsworth called Contingent Responsiveness. Conversely, pathways not reinforced (by excess TV for example) or reinforced negatively (i.e. by shaking) eventually shut down. Causality between early child maltreatment and later problems is hard to prove in the absence of prospective studies, but it has been estimated that 22% of learning disabilities, 53% of juvenile arrests, 38% of adult arrests, and 38% of violent crimes are attributable to early abuse or neglect. Thus, the human environment can either enhance the pathways of competence and sociability or lead to reduced cognitive function and/or deficits in social functioning.

Here is a positive example. My colleagues and I studied the effects of carrying babies in Snuglis (soft baby carriers). In a randomized trial we showed (I believe for the first time) that carrying in the first months of life significantly strengthens attachment, as measured at one year.[1] The baby learned that he/she mattered, was worthwhile, that someone was listening and responding, and that the mother cared. And of course this also reinforced the mother's behavior. This is just one example of a general principle:

> How individuals function from the preschool years all the
> way through adolescence and even adulthood hinges to
> a significant extent on their experiences before the age
> of three. Researchers have thoroughly documented the
> importance of the pre- and post-natal months and the
> first three years, but a wide gap remains between scien-
> tific knowledge and social policy.[2]

Now, just five years later, because of the new science, the gap is wider! We now know that babies have twice as many neurons as we do, and that the connections are being formed from day one of life (and even pre-natally). By age ten, they start being pruned. The first three years are crucial. We need new social policy to reflect new knowledge. Helping parents and pre-school teachers to use this knowledge in the first three years is the key to maximizing each child's potential and protecting society from the consequences of ignoring it.

Sheperd and Farrington summarized the argument in 1995:[3]

> The best way to prevent crime and violence seems to be by family support, training parents, pre-school education, and modifying opportunities for crime (situational prevention). Interventions that have been shown by randomized experiments to produce long term benefits have targeted single parent, low income and poorly educated families of pre-school children.

It's not just to stop spanking or beating. It is treating children with respect, listening to them — responding to them and stimulating them positively. All parents need to learn this, but working parents and poor families especially need help to be able to do this. This is what creates character and empathy in the child as described in the following quote from the 1994 Carnegie Task Force on meeting the needs of children:

> Empathy appears to exist in newborns, who make distress cries in response to the cries of other infants. Children
> - by age two or three show emotional distress and intervene when others are suffering;
> - develop a sense of helping rather than hurting or neglecting, respecting rather than belittling, and supporting and protecting rather than dominating or exploiting others;
> - by age three have begun to be aware of the thoughts, feelings and experiences of others.
> Children's capacity for empathy grows in the context of secure attachments and the example of caring adults: toddlers, for instance, imitate their mothers in helping other children. This growing sense of connectedness and social

responsibility — together with the development of self-confidence, intelligence, language, physical and mental health, social relations, and empathy — makes the first three years of life critical for the individual and for society.

Of course solid attachment is followed by separation, and this requires even more understanding and patience by parents and/or parent helpers. Protecting children and setting limits while allowing them to explore, individuate, and develop competence is particularly hard for working or stressed-out parents. Yet, most parents can be "good enough" (in Winnicott's phrase) *if* they receive support and help.

PROVEN INTERVENTIONS

Two social programs have been shown to work:

1. post-partum home visits, by visitors trained to support parenting and recognize risk factors, and continuing for as long as necessary depending on need, and

2. quality pre-school education, like Head Start and Early Head Start, where children (and if necessary infants) and the parents (part-time) find the kind of day care that provides a home-like nurturing and stimulating environment.

Together, these two kinds of programs can provide a continuum of in-home and out-of-home family support which should be available to *all* families, on a voluntary basis, i.e., for all those wanting or needing this kind of help. Unfortunately, even today, the U.S. does not routinely provide these services.

Do these things work? Yes: recent reports demonstrate the long-term efficacy of both programs.

CAN WE AFFORD THESE THINGS?

Emphatically, yes, mainly because the costs of *not* doing anything are so high. According to the American Humane Society, foster care costs us $1.9 billion a year, while caring for juvenile offenders previously maltreated costs us another $1.9 billion. In-patient mental health services for abused children cost $2.8 billion. Child protection services cost us another $0.7 billion and hospitalization of abused children and family counseling add another $1.6 billion, for a total of $9 billion.

Annual costs for providing home visitation for all new parents are estimated at about half that amount or $4.7 billion annually, with costs dropping later as the population of new parents declines. The costs of quality early child care (five days a week) range from $10,000 to $14,000 per preschool child per year, while social savings are estimated at $88,000 to $100,000 per child, mostly from reduced eventual spending on special education, welfare assistance, and juvenile crime.

In any case, these costs for helping families seem reasonable when compared to what our government spends on Medicare and Social Security ($6 billion), veterans ($19 billion), and the military ($267 billion).

Lisbeth Schorr has summarized what we know and what we must do:[4]

> Individual parents cannot meet their responsibility in our complex world without support from outside. . . . Our society is in jeopardy because not enough of our arrangements for providing these supports are in place and working. . . . (This) requires us to think about how government can function effectively, often in partnership with the private sector to enable parents and communities to function effectively . . . . If government doesn't work, it must be made to work . . . .
>
> We may have to reorder our spending priorities because we dare not write off any of America's children, families, and inner city communities.

DIAGNOSIS

My primary diagnosis of the American family is *parenting dysfunction* due to ignorance and inadequate support from community and society.

TREATMENT

My prescriptions are therefore for the family but also for all of us:

1. For both parents, love and nurturance to be administered daily to each other in person, by phone/fax, by e-mail, and, where that fails, counseling by a skilled mental health professional.

2. For every family, professional outside support to be administered:
   - Before nuptials: marital counseling.
   - Before childbirth: prenatal care including preparation for breastfeeding and infant care — monthly.
   - Post-partum: home visitation/support as needed, daily if necessary.
   - Throughout the early years of life: group therapy as needed to learn and practice appropriate child care.

3. For every child:
   - Designated caretaker one to two per child: to provide warm, consistent and contingent care as needed to establish attachment (preferably by the mother to establish breastfeeding until age three).
   - Designated "medical home" e.g. a pediatrician: to monitor child's growth and development every two or three months and advocate for what each child needs.

4. For every community, quality, universal childcare:
   - Administered via certified well paid teachers: one per three to four children ages two to three, and one per five or six children ages three to five.

5. For every citizen, political action to be taken regularly as needed and applied to movers/shakers, to move national

priorities until families and children have found their rightful place — #1 — in social policy.

NOTES

1. N. Cunningham et al., *Child Development* 61, (1991):1617.

2. K. T. Young et al., "Starting Points," *Report of the Carnegie Task Force on Meeting the Needs of Young Children* (Waldorf, MD: Carnegie Corp. of N.Y., 1994).

3. Sheperd and Farrington, "Preventing Crime and Violence," *Br. Med. J.* 310 (1995):270.

4. L. B. Schorr, *Common Purpose, Strengthening Families and Neighborhoods to Rebuild America* (New York: Anchor-Doubleday, 1997).

THE CONDUCT OF AMERICAN DIPLOMACY

William C. Harrop

Between 1945, when World War II ended, and 1991, when the Soviet Union disintegrated, we lived in a bi–polar world. Since 1991 the United States has been the only superpower. Remarkable opportunities open to a nation with global reach, but with the opportunities come responsibilities and burdens. Diligent leadership from the global power proves essential to maintaining international order, resolving crises, and enabling human progress. And the problems have become more complex and less tractable. This essay will sketch the world America faced in 1950 and the world it faces at the millennium of 2000. It will examine the performance of the American people and their government at those two junctures, and will speculate on what the next half-century may bring in the foreign relations of the United States.

INTRODUCTION

There has always been a thread of self-sufficiency in the American character, a preference for remaining independent of other nations, uninvolved in other peoples' problems. George Washington's farewell address of 17 September 1796 is often cited:"It is our true policy to steer clear of permanent alliances with any portion of the foreign world."

Self-absorption is not surprising in a population of immigrants who abandoned other continents to find their own new lives. For 150 years Americans were preoccupied with advancing their frontiers across a continent. The Atlantic and Pacific oceans provided natural barriers. When you can travel 3,000 miles speaking English, foreign languages and foreign countries seem less relevant.

The American market became so huge that American producers were hard pressed to supply it, and American manufacturers lagged in adapting products to the tastes and needs of overseas customers. As late as the 1970s, while Japanese automobile manufacturers captured more and more of the American market, Detroit still resisted building cars for export with the steering wheel on the right. Only in the last thirty years has production for markets abroad become of central importance in the American scheme of things.

Historically the trauma of war has reinforced America's intuitive tendency to keep to itself. The United States resisted involvement in World War I for as long as it could and then, after the war, demobilized rapidly and turned inwards, rejecting participation in the League of Nations that its own president had sponsored. The high tariffs of the Smoot-Hawley Act of 1930 insulated American industry from the stimulus of foreign competition and limited the access of American consumers to inexpensive foreign goods. The United States seemed to prefer isolation.

America remained aloof as Hitler advanced across Europe. Defeat of the democracies would have imperiled the United States, but year after year Americans equivocated and delayed, until their hand was forced by the Japanese.

When World War II ended in 1945, the United States demobilized urgently, turning with relief to domestic concerns, and was at first inattentive to the impending Soviet threat. There were 12.1 million Americans in uniform in 1945. One year later, this number had dropped to 3 million and it continued rapidly to decline, while the Soviets maintained their far larger armies. But the aggressive behavior and unmistakable expansionism of the Soviet Union obliged the United States to change course.

During nearly half a century of Cold War, the United States set aside its inclination to stand apart from the world in order to compete vigorously with the Soviet Union. Political partisanship, normally inherent in a two-party democracy, was largely suspended in regard to foreign policy and national security. Now, as the twenty-first century begins, both the international agenda and the circumstances of international relations have changed dramatically. American engagement in world affairs, and steadfast American leadership, are even more necessary than they were during the Cold War.

In the absence of a clear foreign threat, however, and without robust leadership in Washington, the old American predisposition to concentrate upon problems at home, and to allocate resources to domestic needs at the expense of international matters, has re-emerged. This is a troubling phenomenon. How long it persists will bear upon the international position and the welfare of the United States in the next fifty years.

THE UNITED STATES AND THE WORLD AT MID-CENTURY

Between the Yalta Conference (February 1945) and the invasion of South Korea (June 1950), the United States, already the world's largest economy, transformed itself from a reluctant participant in European affairs into a committed global power and the leader of the free world. These five years — 1945 to 1950 — were a watershed in American history, comparable to the periods 1776 to 1789 and 1861 to 1865.

A generation of great American leaders — Roosevelt, Stimson, Marshall, Acheson, Truman, Eisenhower — had learned from their experience following World War I, when the Allies' harsh punishment of Germany had contributed to the collapse of the Weimar Republic and the rise of National Socialism. The League of Nations, ill-designed and without American support, had failed.

Protectionism had impeded economic growth. Even in the midst of World War II, Americans were seeking ways to prevent a repetition of the earlier errors.

In the Moscow Declaration of October 1943, the United States, the United Kingdom, the USSR, and China called for a new and stronger world organization to replace the League. The United Nations Charter, negotiated in San Francisco in the spring of 1945, became effective in January 1946. In response to American leadership (and the generosity of John D. Rockefeller, Jr.) the UN was seated in New York.

Similarly, at the Bretton Woods Conference of July 1944, which prepared for the International Monetary Fund and the World Bank to be established in Washington the following year, the American delegation under Dean Acheson worked for an open and global economic system. They believed — correctly — that this would benefit the United States. Three years later, the General Agreement on Tariffs and Trade (GATT) established a standing mechanism to reduce trade barriers.

Franklin Roosevelt, at Yalta and then during the two months of life remaining to him, closed his eyes to mounting evidence of Soviet postwar intentions. He was determined to maintain grounds for cooperation with his wartime ally and, despite repeated warnings from Winston Churchill, believed he could work with "Uncle Joe." Harry Truman, although indignant about Soviet duplicity over Poland, apparently felt the same after his first meeting with Stalin at the Potsdam Conference in July 1945. Truman learned while at the conference that America had successfully tested the atomic bomb and immediately informed Stalin. From Potsdam, Truman authorized use of the bomb against Japan, ending the war three weeks later.

By mid-1946, in light of Soviet actions and the deep concern and mistrust expressed by American diplomats (particularly Averill Harriman and his deputy George Kennan in Moscow), American opinion began to harden against Soviet expansionism, the harsh domination of satellite countries in eastern Europe, and Russian manipulation of Communist parties further to the west.

In early 1947, the British informed the United States government that they could no longer afford the military and economic backing essential to prevent Greece and Turkey from slipping under Soviet control. On February 27, Truman called Congressional leaders, including notably Republican Senator Arthur Vandenberg, to the White House, where Marshall and Acheson explained the nature of the crisis and the likelihood that if Greece fell to communism other countries would follow. There was bipartisan support for the defense of democracy and freedom. This thesis became the Truman Doctrine, and Congress voted the substantial appropriations requested.

Events moved rapidly. At the Harvard Commencement in June 1947 General Marshall proposed his plan for the reconstruction of Europe, involving a massive expenditure of $17 billion. Congress approved after long debate in April 1948. The Soviets, although nominally invited to participate, declined, hardening the East–West split. George Kennan's "X" article in the summer of 1947 in *Foreign Affairs Quarterly* advocated determined, systematic containment of Soviet expansionism, a doctrine that in essence was to guide the United States for the next four and a half decades.

In July 1947, Congress passed the landmark National Security Act that established a unified Department of Defense, the National Security Council system, and the Central Intelligence Agency. These reforms were to prove crucial to effective American prosecution of the Cold War.

When the Soviet Union imposed a blockade of surface access to Berlin in June 1948, the United States responded with the brilliantly successful Berlin Airlift. The United States was now determined to stand up to the USSR. The North Atlantic Treaty and the establishment of NATO were ratified overwhelmingly by the Senate in July 1949. This completed the alliance system which, under firm American leadership, would permit the West to prevail in the coming forty-two years of Cold War. One other achievement of this remarkable era should be cited: the Foreign Service Act of 1946, which assured a professional, disciplined, and effective American diplomatic service.

Thus, by 1950, five tumultuous years of events and decisions had forged a United States unified in its determination to block the expansion of Soviet power; braced to allocate the resources needed; comfortable with the ideological underpinning of its strategy; equipped and able to lead the free world in a sustained test of strength and diplomacy. America had overcome, at least for a time, its inborn preference to remain aloof from international contention. When North Korea invaded South Korea in June 1950, the United States was prepared to remobolize, and it worked skillfully through the United Nations to legitimize its stand against Communist belligerence.

FROM THE COLD WAR TO THE YEAR 2000

The Berlin Wall fell in 1989, and in 1991 the Soviet Union simply broke apart, much as George Kennan had expected would happen if the West could hold firm to a policy of containment. The United States breathed a sigh of relief and, once the Gulf War was over, turned its attention to domestic problems. Politicians debated how best to apply the budget savings of disarmament, which were termed the "peace dividend."

Most American forces overseas in Europe and Asia were brought home. The defense budget was reduced by a third in a few years' time. Unfortunately, appropriations for the conduct of foreign relations were cut even more. Between the height of the Cold War in the mid-1980s and 1995, there was a reduction of over 50% in constant dollars in the Function 150 Account of the U.S. Federal budget. These are the appropriations allocated to the State Department, the Foreign Service, our overseas embassies, public diplomacy, arms control, foreign aid, the Peace Corps, the Export-Import Bank, and payments to international organizations. As of Fiscal Year 1999, the budget projections of both Congress and the Clinton Administration will force a further reduction of 12% in these resources over the next five years.

The result has been a retraction in American official presence abroad; in the recruitment and training of Foreign Service officers; and in the basic infrastructure of American diplomacy. Between

1992 and 1997, the United States closed thirty-six overseas embassies and consulates.

Unlike multinational corporations and the Department of Defense, the State Department and embassies abroad — although their work is grounded upon information and communication — lack up-to-date information technology: teleconferencing capability; enciphered e-mail systems; ready electronic access to key information and databases in foreign countries. A report on the advocacy of U.S. overseas interests by fourteen distinguished Americans, including Frank Carlucci, Warren Christopher, Carla Hills, Max Kampelman, Ralph Larsen, Donald McHenry, Sam Nunn, Phil Odeen, Colin Powell, Condoleezza Rice, George Shultz, Robert Strauss, Cyrus Vance, and John Whitehead has recommended an urgent appropriation of $400 million to redesign and modernize the nation's diplomatic information technology and communications systems.[1] While inadequate resources are the central problem, the Department of State has not been well managed. In the second half of the twentieth century, the only Secretary of State to pay sustained attention to the organization and infrastructure of American diplomacy was George Shultz.

National security is supported and defended by our diplomatic corps, our intelligence assets, and our armed forces. Their interlocking functions make up a system analogous to the meshing of land, air, and sea components within the military services. Diplomacy is prevention, our first line of defense. If we can resolve international differences through discussion and negotiation we do not have to send our forces into battle and risk their lives. If diplomacy is weak, or inadequate, troops may have to be deployed prematurely. Yet the international affairs (diplomacy) budget is treated as a domestic appropriation and as part of discretionary funding, which will remain the essential target for cuts as long as entitlement programs are not touchable and defense/intelligence are addressed separately under the "National Security" rubric.

The State Department, for budget consideration, is linked with the departments of Justice and Commerce, and so must compete with the domestic political constituencies of small business, the judiciary, law enforcement, the war on drugs, and so forth. Small wonder, in the absence of the sort of life-and-death threat earlier posed by the Soviet Union, and without strong Presidential leadership, that appropriations for the conduct of diplomacy have plummeted since 1992.

Meanwhile the world becomes more and more interdependent, and diplomacy is as involved with economic and social issues as it is with national security. Financial markets are intertwined, as we learned from the Asian crisis of 1997–1998. The United States is the world's largest trading nation. Exports now account for a third of America's real economic growth and have created one million new jobs in this country over the last few years. Overseas markets are pivotal for cereal and soybean producers of the Midwest and Plains states. American consumers benefit from a diversity of foreign products; manufacturers depend on the timely arrival of components produced abroad. Cyberspace does not know national borders. The overseas travel of American businessmen, students, and tourists continues to increase (although there are no longer American consulates to support them if needed in, for example, Lyons, Bordeaux, Genoa, Porto Allegre, or Palermo).

The timing is bad for a decline in America's diplomatic readiness. As we enter the new millennium, American foreign policy seems less manageable than it was during the Cold War. The Soviet threat was a yardstick against which to measure each issue. Whether the challenge arose in Cuba, Vietnam, the Congo, Central America, the Middle East, or Afghanistan, we knew what we had to do. Advanced American technology, and dominant American military and economic power, were normally relevant to the task and could be deployed effectively. We sought, but were rarely dependent upon, the support of allies.

How has the international agenda of the United States changed? A new list of issues and problems has replaced the nuclear stand-off of the Cold War. These include:

- The proliferation of weapons of mass destruction;
- Trade and investment (American access to foreign markets and sources of raw materials);

- Enforcement of trading rules (intellectual property rights, dumping, non-tariff barriers);
- Terrorism;
- International crime, especially traffic in drugs;
- Regional conflicts, often ethnic or religious, causing displacements and, frequently, appalling bloodshed;
- World environment (population growth, global warming, pollution, exhaustion of natural resources);
- Maintenance of international financial and economic stability;
- Democracy and human rights, including the role of women and minorities;
- Regulating hundreds of international activities in the age of globalization (telecommunications frequencies, air traffic control, food and drug standards, health, immigration, taxation, etc.).

Such questions seem rather more complex than the deployment of American economic strength and defense capability to block Soviet expansion. The new agenda of problems cannot be solved unilaterally by one nation, even the world's only superpower. They require communication with other peoples; building coalitions of concerned governments; working together with others to address issues that ignore national borders. In short, they demand diplomacy.

Because the United States is the only global power, it must engage and lead. Other governments tend to wait for the superpower. For over two years we stood back and urged the Europeans to come to grips with the deteriorating situation in former Yugoslavia. They could not do so, and progress was made only when the United States finally convened the parties in tough negotiation in Dayton. A forceful American lead was prerequisite to addressing financial crises in Mexico in 1995 and in Brazil in 1998. This does not suggest that the United States can always succeed in persuading others to follow, but without clear American involvement not much is likely to happen. In Madeleine Albright's words, the United States has become "the indispensable nation."

A global power should be represented in every world capital, if only by an embassy of two or three people in the smallest countries. There is no telling when a vote in the UN may prove crucial; where key minerals may unexpectedly be uncovered; where terrorists may find a haven; when access to a particular airfield may be essential; when an American tourist or an American company may desperately need help. The cost of such representation is minimal. But at the end of the twentieth century, for lack of resources, the Department of State is closing United States embassies.

Some argue that, in a global economy with modern telecommunications, with the internet, e-mail, and CNN, we no longer need embassies. This is quite wrong. True, the President or the Secretary of State can telephone any foreign leader directly, but he or she badly needs the advice of trained Americans on the ground. Experts who speak the language, understand the history and culture, know foreign leaders personally and can explain their values and the political pressures they are under, can suggest which arguments — or what public statements — will be effective.

In curtailing resources devoted to foreign relations, the Administration and Congress are reflecting a public sentiment that since the Cold War is over the United States can save money on defense and foreign affairs. The President knows better. He should be educating the American public and Congress about where national interest lies, not adapting to public opinion polls.

Actually, in national budget terms, economizing on the conduct of relations with other countries saves little money anyway. International affairs, including foreign aid, the State Department and Foreign Service, embassies abroad, the Arms Control and Disarmament Agency, public diplomacy and the Voice of America, payments to international organizations, all together represent approximately 1.3% of the federal budget. We spend 0.15% (3/20 of one per cent) of our Gross National Product on development assistance. We are in last place, number twenty-one out of twenty-one, among the leading industrial nations by that measure. Austria, Italy, Great Britain, even Portugal spend twice what we do relative to their GNP, Canada three times, France four times, and Sweden six times.[2] And the United States, which has benefited more than any other power from the United Nations, is by a wide margin the farthest in arrears in payment of its dues. A demeaning picture.

Thus, at the close of the twentieth century, Americans live in a world so interdependent that the notion of isolationism as historically defined seems incongruous. International issues have become more varied and more ambiguous, demanding the steady involvement of the only global power. Terrorism, weapons of mass destruction, epidemic disease, regional confrontations, environmental destabilization — all remain dangerous, although the truly existential threat of the Cold War is past. In these circumstances, the United States, lacking strong Presidential commitment, appears to engage intermittently in foreign policy. Americans have, in a sense, withdrawn into their own prosperity. Distracted, they have allowed their government representatives to deny adequate resources to the conduct of American relations with other governments and peoples.

In late 1998, following a desperate public appeal by the Joint Chiefs of Staff, the Administration and Congress began to reverse the exaggerated reductions they had made since 1991 in the national defense budget. A similar correction for the relatively deeper cuts in support of diplomacy does not seem to be on the horizon.

A FORECAST FOR THE MID-21ST CENTURY

Predictions about the international scene fifty years into the future are of dubious value, given the acceleration of change and technological innovation in our times. The best we can manage are some educated guesses. Of interest for this essay is whether the United States is likely still to be the world's dominant power, how international issues may evolve, and how Americans will relate to and communicate with other peoples.

We are ending what has been called "the American Century." There is reason to believe that the United States will still be a superpower in 2050, but not the only one. Europe, and probably China — assuming transition to an acceptable form of democracy can be achieved without protracted disruption — will have attained comparable status. India, by then with the world's largest population, will be a significant factor. However, national governments, including "superpowers," will have less capacity to determine events in an environment altered by the march of globalization and much will hinge upon what proportion of humankind is not yet a part of that global society.

A discussion of trends apparent at the end of the twentieth century may suggest some future directions:

- The United States is not only the largest economy at present, it is the most dynamic and most productive, the clear leader in defense technology as well as information and communication technologies (the dominant sector in the age of globalization). The United States is well situated to maintain its strong position.

- Census Bureau projections for the year 2050 place the United States at 394 million, the European Union (current members) at 343 million, China at 1,322 million and India at 1,707 million. Japan is expected to decline to 101 million and Russia to 122 million, probably not levels from which either could project influence globally.

- Building a united Europe has proved a gradual process (the Treaty of Rome was signed in 1957), hindered by strong nationalist sentiment and a somewhat confusing overlap with NATO. It has thus far included little coalescence in foreign policy, but the process goes forward. The advent of a common currency in 1999 should provide a major and, within a few years, probably a decisive stimulus to political unity.

- As stressed earlier in this paper, much of the new international agenda will not respond to military or economic power, but only to communication, persuasion, and shared commitment among nations. Now, however, when the United States, as the lone super-power, exerts its influence for a cause it believes to be in the common interest, it may be criticized for arrogance and resisted for behaving like a hegemon.

- Thus, it is becoming more difficult for the United States to shape events (even when it does engage fully); smaller powers or entities can threaten the global power with terrorism or by developing weapons of mass destruction, or can frustrate it by refusing to cooperate (Sadam Hussein's Iraq, Indian and Pakistani nuclear capability, the Arab/Israeli peace process, wars in Central Africa, narcotics production and trade, global warming); terrorism is a pointed example — since the end of 1998 the United States, confounded by serial bomb threats, has felt constrained with increasing frequency to close various overseas embassies temporarily.

- Professor Francis Fukuyama, formerly a member of the State Department's Policy Planning staff, wrote nine years ago that the great ideological debates which had marked mankind were at an end as the entire world was moving toward liberal democracy.[3] Fukuyama may have been premature (as well as melodramatic) but he had the direction right. At the close of the twentieth century, there are major hold-outs — the Islamic countries generally, China, some other parts of Asia and most of Africa — but the weight of history does seem on the side of democracy and the open market economy.

- Globalization — the term no longer requires quotation marks — and the headway of technology will vastly change the world in the first half of the twenty-first century: the routine operation of large corporations across borders and continents; the increasingly inter-dependent global financial system; personal (and portable) telecommunication capability; the expansion of the internet and of transnational communication links among individuals and groups with common interests; the growth of multinational, nongovernmental organizations pursuing defined political, social, or economic objectives; more rapid and cheaper transportation; the increasing international mobility of labor as well as capital; perhaps also the dissemination of English as the world language. This evolution will make it more and more difficult to sustain authoritarian regimes insulated from the relatively open world system; globalization will also challenge and almost certainly diminish the authority of governments and could reduce the likelihood of war between developed nations.

- The gap between rich and poor countries is widening, and the poor countries lag behind in sharing benefits of the global economy; despite the scourge of AIDS in Africa, the population of the third world continues to expand rapidly while that of the industrial world contracts (the U.S. Bureau of the Census projects that, between 1998 and 2050, the population of Africa will grow from 760 million to 2 billion while the continent of Europe declines from approximately 500 million to 400 million); extreme poverty and overcrowding will inevitably generate suffering and conflict; the resulting demand for humanitarian aid and peacekeeping deployments will be costly: this underlines the myopia of America's niggardliness toward development assistance and aid for family planning.

- Outer space and medical/biological technology are outside the scope of this paper. However, genetic engineering in particular, and the cloning of human beings (which appears to be imminent), could have vast and unpredictable consequences for international relations, as it will for human society altogether.

- A final and daunting trend must be cited. The United States — through its scientists, military and intelligence officers, and diplomats — will continue to lead a concerted international effort to contain the proliferation of weapons of mass destruction. This operation has been surprisingly successful for fifty years, but it becomes more and more difficult. Most of the advances of modern technology are generally available. Sooner or later, probably well before the year 2050, terrorists, international criminals, or rogue states — perhaps all three — will be in a position to threaten the use of these weapons, and to use them in fact.

★ ★ ★

Well, here we are in the middle of the twenty-first century. The unification of Europe has advanced to the point that the European Union, with a consolidated foreign policy, is now a global power. The wisdom of U.S. policy since World War II of support for the integration of Europe (despite obvious economic competition) is confirmed, since the United States is now joined by another powerful democracy with a major stake in global stability. Heretofore, the United States has been frustrated by the disinclination of European governments, whether through NATO or the European Union, to share the burden beyond their immediate region. The United States is no longer the only "reluctant sheriff."

China will have been able to attain superpower status only if successful in the transition to democracy. For that reason China as a superpower, notwithstanding its profound cultural dissimilarity to the United States and the European Union, may well prove more partner than adversary.

In 2050 the great bulk of international transactions are effected electronically among individuals, organizations, and companies without respect to governments. Financial cross-currency operations are especially hard to track. The nationality of most giant global corporations is unclear, and individuals relocate frequently across national boundaries. Multinational non-governmental organizations pursuing a wide variety of environmental, social, economic, and political purposes, are well funded and powerful. In the industrialized world, but to far less extent in the developing world, there is interdependence approaching homogeneity among manufacturers, service industries, communications and transport companies, in education, medicine, and other professions.

Under these circumstances the authority of national governments has been circumscribed. For example, the difficulty of tracing cross-border economic transactions and currency movements complicates the implementation of fiscal and monetary policy, to put it mildly. By 2050, most governmental regulation of economic activity has been supplanted by international agreements and organizations, in which it is not always easy to obtain the cooperation (often absolutely essential) of smaller countries. In fact, a new breed of sophisticated diplomatic experts must manage the heavy agenda of international discussion and negotiation as well as staff international regulatory authorities.

But the greatest problems of the mid-twenty-first century stem from the contrast between the developed (globalized) world and the less developed (essentially unglobalized) world, which comprises most of Africa and parts of the Middle East, Asia, and Central America. In the less-developed countries, the paucity of skilled human resources and the still relatively inhospitable business climate restrict investment. Poverty and high population density breed malnutrition, instability, ethnic conflict, and refugee movements. The migration of people from poor to rich societies, legal (because of the demand for labor) as well as illegal, have aggravated the social tensions from immigration already evident in the last quarter of the twentieth century in Western Europe and the United States. Cultivation and trade in narcotics have increased, not abated, during the twenty-first century.

The earth's environment has continued seriously to deteriorate from deforestation, the depletion of fisheries, and the refusal of the developing world to share in the economic costs of reversing global warming. Human population pressure has sharply affected biodiversity; for example, the extinction of major species of African wildlife (reinforced by the growing insecurity of travel) has caused the loss of important tourist revenue to East and Southern Africa.

Effective communication between the global powers and developing governments is crucial to addressing the sobering problems suggested above, and to accelerating economic development so as to facilitate wider participation in the global economy. American diplomats must as before be expert in cross-cultural communication, but also trained in relevant technologies. Ambassadors must be leaders able to coordinate the contribution of non-governmental organizations, business corporations, and private citizens as well as governments in seeking common objectives.

Thus, diplomacy will continue to be central to achieving United States purposes in the twenty-first century. But the quality of American national leadership will be the most important single factor, as it was in 1950. Superb leadership at the middle of the twentieth century equipped the United States for a long, arduous, and ultimately victorious struggle in the Cold War.

At the year 2000, American leadership in international matters is less certain. The United States is not fully exerting the role it could and should exert — in its own self-interest and in the world's interest. If, in the two decades before us, the American political system can produce another generation of competent, decisive leaders, capable of convincing the American public and Congress that the United States must be fully engaged internationally and must allocate substantial resources to support the political and economic development of the poor countries, then world conditions at mid-twenty-first century need not look so bleak as has been outlined above. But that is a large "IF."

Unfortunately, even the finest leadership will lack the means to ensure that nuclear, chemical, and biological weapons not fall into the hands of disaffected zealots.

NOTES

1. F. Carlucci et al., *Equipped for the Future: Managing U.S. Foreign Affairs in the 21st Century* (Washington, D.C.: The Henry L. Stimson Center, 1998).

2. See U.S. State Department, Bureau of Public Affairs, *The International Affairs Budget,* October, 1995.

3. Francis Fukuyama, "The End of History?" *National Interest* (Summer 1989).

100 YEARS OF EVOLUTION FROM "SEPARATE BUT EQUAL"

1950–2050

John Dwight Ingram

BEFORE JUNE 1950

The Early Years

Ever since the first slaves were brought to North America in the early 1600s, Black people (I use the word "Black" because it is widely used and recognized; during my life we have gone from "colored" to "Negro" to "Black" to "Afro-American" to "African-American" to "people of color") have faced serious, and often fatal, discrimination. Although the legal status of Blacks in the United States has changed dramatically from the days of slavery, the controversy about the legal status of Blacks has always been a focal point of United States politics and legislation. Beginning with President Lincoln's Emancipation Proclamation of 1863, which declared that all slaves "shall be then, thenceforward, and forever free," federal authority began to expand. In 1865, the Thirteenth Amendment to the Constitution ratified and expanded the Emancipation Procla-

The valuable contributions of my very capable Research Assistants, Jennifer Stewart, Lisa Santos, and Jennifer LaMell are gratefully acknowledged.

mation. This important landmark in federal law prohibited slavery and involuntary servitude in the United States and, very importantly, granted Congress the power to enforce it "by appropriate legislation." However, the formal abolishment of slavery was insufficient to change the real status of southern Blacks. The Civil Rights Act of 1866 was an attempt to make the Thirteenth Amendment effective against the challenge posed by "Black Codes"; it granted Blacks all of the rights of White citizens. With the addition of the Fourteenth and Fifteenth Amendments, more rights were afforded to Black citizens, helping to ease the discrimination.

Plessy v. Ferguson — "Separate But Equal"

We are all aware of the 1896 landmark case of *Plessy v. Ferguson* in which all but one member of the United States Supreme Court gave approval to a Louisiana state law that required separation of Blacks and Whites in railway passenger cars. The court said such segregation was constitutionally permissible so long as the separate facilties were equal. Neither the word "Black" nor the word "equal" were defined by the Supreme Court, or by the segregation statutes of various states. Plessy, though his ancestry was $1/8$ Black and $7/8$ White, was deemed to be legally "Black," and he would undoubtedly be so classified today both legally and socially. If a person had any Black ancestry, he (when the gender for a personal pronoun can be either male or female, I use the masculine pronoun generically, from habit and because of my masculine personal orientation; I trust that female authors will balance the scales on the other side) was "Black."

Early Years of "The Great Middle Class" — The 1930s and 1940s

Mostly Separate and Mostly Unequal. We who grew up in the 1930s and 1940s can clearly remember that, to a large extent, Blacks and Whites were separated in most aspects of life — education, employment, housing, etc. — often *de jure* but, if not, usually *de facto.* There was very little contact between members of the two races, especially not in an atmosphere of equality. Racial discrimination by Whites against Blacks (of course discrimination by White Anglo-Saxon Protestants on the basis of ethnicity, religion, and national origin, as well as race, goes back to the earliest colonial times) was so widespread that it was largely taken for granted and rarely questioned. And despite the apparent mandate of *Plessy* that public facilities and opportunities must be "equal," they rarely were, and that too was seldom questioned and rarely challenged successfully.

Early Attempts at Integration. Perhaps the first government attempt at affirmative action was a 1941 Executive Order by President Roosevelt, which required "the federal government, as an employer, to take "affirmative action" not to discriminate against any worker on the basis of race, creed, color, or national origin."[1] The purpose of this order was unquestionably to stimulate wartime employment of minorities, but similar orders were issued thereafter by Presidents Truman and Eisenhower. As we well remember, however, we left college to enter a still heavily segregated environment.

THE CIVIL RIGHTS MOVEMENT

In *Brown v. Board of Education* in 1954, Chief Justice Warren, speaking for a unanimous Supreme Court, held that segregation of children in public schools on the basis of race deprived Black children of equal protection of the law, even if the physical facilities and other tangible factors were equal (which they rarely, if ever, were). Whereas the *Plessy* Court had refused to recognize any stigma which might result from the segregation of Black schoolchildren, the *Brown* Court held that such separation "generates a feeling of inferiority as to the [children's] status in the community that may affect their hearts and minds in a way unlikely ever to be undone." Because of this stigma, segregated facilities were "inherently unequal."

Brown came along in the early years of the Civil Rights Movement of the 1950s and 1960s and provided strong impetus and support to the efforts of Martin Luther King, Jr., and others. The political atmosphere was changing, and a political coalition was emerging with more interest in and support of equality for Blacks than had existed at any time since Reconstruction. The civil disturbances, mass demonstrations, marches, urban violence, sit-ins, and vigils of Dr. King and other leaders drew increasing support in all parts of the country. This change in public opinion inspired President Kennedy to urge Congress, in 1963, to enact "legislation aimed at the elimination of the economic disparity between Blacks and Whites in America."[2]

AFFIRMATIVE ACTION

President Kennedy did not live to see his proposed legislation become law, but the shock of his assassination was undoubtedly a major factor in the passage of the Civil Rights Act of 1964. This statute prohibited racial discrimination in any program receiving federal assistance and in places of public accommodation, and included important provisions dealing with school desegregation. Soon thereafter President Johnson issued Executive Order 11.246, which mandated that federal contractors take "affirmative action to recruit, hire, and promote more minorities." This reflected the belief of Harvard alumnus Senator Joseph Clark of Pennsylvania and others that "[e]conomics is at the heart of the racial situation. The Negro has been condemned to poverty because of a lack of equal job opportunities. This poverty has kept the Negro out of the main stream of American life."[3]

From that time on, there has been widespread disagreement about the meaning of "affirmative action." Some people feel that affirmative action should be used to remedy all past discrimination; others would limit affirmative action only to instances of present, intentional discrimination.[4] For the purposes of this essay, I will use the phrase "affirmative action" in a broad sense to include any program that actively seeks to increase minority representation in employment, education, and government contracts.

While affirmative action initially merely prohibited discrimination, within a short time federal regulations were established which required affirmative action by means of "goals and timetables," clearly requiring a good faith effort to achieve the stated goal. As time went by, affirmative action came to mean preferential treatment in the form of quotas and other efforts that made race (and often gender and national origin) a determining factor in employment, school admissions, and contracting decisions.

During this same period, the Supreme Court was establishing strong precedents for race-based remedial measures through its decisions requiring busing to increase the integration of public schools. The Court's lead was soon followed by action in lower federal and some state courts to reduce or eliminate racial segregation in the schools.

It's interesting to note at this point that there are some racial and ethnic groups which have been discriminated against throughout American history, but have not been included among the minority groups to be favored by affirmative action and preferred treatment.[5] In fact, some of these groups have been subjected to quotas that limit their numbers, especially in higher education, in contrast to the quotas assigned to other minorities that assured them of a minimum number of places. Probably the two most glaring examples of this are Jewish and Asian immigrants and their descendants. Asians have acquired a reputation for being hardworking, studious, unassuming, thrifty, and are often portrayed as a "model minority." They are pointed to as people who are succeeding despite their minority status. In similar fashion, because of the success of a high percentage of American Jews, they not only received no preferences, they have often been subjected to limiting admissions policies at Harvard and other high-level schools.[6]

THE RECENT DECLINE OF AFFIRMATIVE ACTION

Quotas and Preferences

By the 1980s, however, there was increasing sentiment for the view that affirmative action had fulfilled its purpose and should be reduced or completely eliminated. It is fascinating to note that this view had been previously expressed in 1884 by Justice Bradley, writing for an 8–1 majority of the Supreme Court in the *Civil Rights Cases:*

> When a man has emerged from slavery, and by the aid of beneficent legislation has shaken off the inseparable concomitants of that state, there must be some stage in the progress of his elevation when he takes the rank of mere citizen, and ceases to be the special favorite of the laws, and when his rights as a citizen, or a man, are to be protected in the ordinary modes by which other men's rights are protected.[7]

It would not be surprising today to hear such a statement from Clarence Thomas and many others, a statement that would undoubtedly cause proponents of affirmative action to repeat the classic warning of George Santayana: "Those who cannot remember the past are condemned to repeat it." But whether or not historical retrospect should teach us that affirmative action is still necessary and desirable, the trend away from it in recent years is unmistakable.

A brief review of action by the federal courts and state governments since 1978 will suffice to illustrate this. The first sign of retrenchment came in the 1978 *University of California v. Bakke* case, in which the Supreme Court declared unconstitutional an admissions program at the University of California at Davis Medical School that each year set aside sixteen of the school's 100 new places for members of minority groups. The momentum really began to roll in 1986 when the Court struck down a school board's layoff of White teachers with more seniority to preserve the positions of junior minority teachers (in *Wygant v. Jackson Board of Education*). Soon thereafter, the Court found a violation of the Equal Protection Clause in a set-aside program that required the prime contractor on every city contract to subcontract at least 30% of the dollar amount of the contract to minority-owned businesses (*City*

·of *Richmond v. J. A. Croson, Co.*). The Court held that there was no valid basis for such a program in the absence of past or present evidence of discrimination by the city. A further limitation on affirmative action programs was added by the Court in 1995: a federal highway program provided for financial incentives to prime contractors for hiring "disadvantaged" subcontractors, with a presumption that minority-owned subcontractors were disadvantaged. The Court remanded the case to the lower court to determine if the program served a compelling governmental interest and was narrowly tailored to further that interest.

Voting Districts

In more recent years the Supreme Court has also considered a series of cases involving "majority-minority" legislative districts resulting from the redistricting of legislative bodies following the 1990 census. In the early '90s there were a number of attempts to create districts which contained a sufficient majority of members of a certain minority group (usually, if not always, Black or Hispanic) to assure that these voters could elect a representative of their choice. The tacit assumption was that most Blacks would vote for a Black candidate, and that most Whites would not, and similarly with Hispanics. Thus, a Black candidate could only be elected if he were given a constituency with a substantial Black majority. As I will discuss later in this essay, there is considerable evidence that minority citizens do not blindly vote along color or ethnic lines.

For many years there have been districts in which a majority of the residents were Black and the elected representative was usually, but not always, Black. The boundaries of these districts were usually drawn with reference to accepted considerations: compactness, contiguousness, political subdivisions, protection of incumbents, and advantage to the polititcal party drawing the map. There was seldom, if ever, any obvious attempt to disregard these traditional guidelines in order to increase the number of districts that would be likely to elect a Black representative. But after the 1990 census there were numerous attempts to draw maps for Congressional, state, and municipal districts to create more "majority-minority" districts. The establishment of such districts resulted in the election in Alabama, Florida, North Carolina, South Carolina, and Virginia of Black Representatives to Congress in 1992, for the first time since Reconstruction. In order to do this, the map drafters sometimes found it necessary to create districts so extremely irregular in shape that there could be no rational explanation other than a primary, and perhaps sole, purpose to put enough Black persons in the district to assure the election of a representative of their choice, presumably a Black person.

The first case to reach the Supreme Court challenging one of these districts was *Shaw v. Reno* in 1993. North Carolina adopted a map that was intended to create a second majority-Black Congressional district, stretching for about 160 miles along I-85 and for much of its length no wider than the I-85 corridor. The court held that the Equal Protection Clause is violated if a "reapportionment scheme is so irrational on its face that it can be understood only as an effort to segregate voters into separate districts on the basis of race. . . ."

Applying a similar analysis, the Court found in *Miller v. Johnson* in 1995 that an attempt by Georgia to create a third majority-Black Congressional district was unconstitutional. The proposed district joined metropolitan Black neighborhoods with coastal areas 260 miles away. The Court found that it was clear that race was the predominant and overriding force in the districting determination. Again, in 1996, in *Bush v. Vera,* the Court struck down a newly drawn Congressional map in Texas which created two new majority-Black districts and one new majority-Hispanic district, basing this action on the determination that the new district lines were drawn with race as the predominant factor.

The Illinois legislature created a majority-Hispanic district in Chicago, and in 1998 the Supreme Court affirmed, without opinion, the judgment of a three-judge district court panel, holding that the district furthered a compelling state interest by ensuring that the Hispanic electorate had a reasonable opportunity to elect a candidate of its choice. I can find no rational basis for the Supreme

Court affirmance. The district court's opinion is directly contrary to *Shaw, Miller,* and *Bush*. First, it found that racial considerations predominated in the configuration of the district. The court somehow found that the district was "reasonably compact and regular," despite the fact that it looks like a pair of earmuffs, one Mexican and one Puerto Rican, connected by a thin arc in which only 4.7% of the district's population lives. The court also held that the district needed this majority of Hispanic voters to counteract the effects of racial bloc voting and ensure that the Hispanic electorate had a reasonable chance to elect its choice of candidates. Of course this simply replaces the presumed bloc voting by Chicago Whites and Blacks with the presumed bloc voting by Hispanics. And finally, the court held that the residents of the districts were "politically cohesive," despite the fact that they share only the Spanish language (for most). The court did not even mention that Puerto Ricans are born United States citizens, while those of Mexican ancestry have much more in common with other immigrants and their descendants from Europe and Asia.

California Proposition 209

Perhaps encouraged by the Supreme Court's moves to limit affirmative action, but not satisfied that it had gone far enough, a majority of the California electorate approved Proposition 209 in November 1996. This amended the California Constitution to provide that "the state shall not discriminate against, or grant preferential treatment to, any individual or group on the basis of race, sex, color, ethnicity, or national origin in the operation of public employment, public education, or public contracting." The objective was clearly to close the door completely on any further affirmative action that was still permissible under the federal Constitution as interpreted by the Supreme Court. All state-sponsored affirmative action programs were eliminated. Minorities (and women) could no longer receive any economic or social benefit solely because of their race (or gender). California thus became legally color (and gender) blind. This new law was challenged in the federal courts. The Ninth Circuit Court of Appeals held that it did not violate the United States Constitution, and the Supreme Court denied a petition for *certiorari*. The change first clearly manifested its effect in higher public education. At Berkeley, the most selective public university in the state, the number of Blacks admitted dropped 57%; at UCLA, the drop was 40%. The acceptance for Hispanics dropped 40% and 33%, respectively. It is interesting to note, however, that when all University of California schools are included, acceptance for Blacks dropped only 18% and for Hispanics only 7%. A number of these minority students who in the past would have gone to Berkeley or UCLA went instead to other state schools for which they were qualified on the basis of non-affirmative–action standards.[8]

Hopwood v. Texas

In *Hopwood* (1996), nonminority applicants who were rejected by the state university's law school challenged the school's affirmative action admissions program, which gave substantial preferences to Black and Hispanic applicants. Cases similar to *Hopwood* have been filed challenging racial policies at the University of Washington School of Law and the University of Michigan at the undergraduate level.[9] The University of Texas Law School actually operated a dual admission system. Many Black and Mexican-American applicants were admitted with much lower "Texas Index" scores (based on college GPA and LSAT scores) than the scores of other applicants who were not deemed to be preferred minorities. Though there were no quotas as such, the two groups of applications were separated and were considered by two separate subcommittees of the admissions committee.

The Texas admissions program was upheld in 1994 by the United States District Court, which said that the law school could use race in admissions decisions to remedy the effect of past discrimination, and to maintain a racially diverse student body. The

Fifth Circuit Court of Appeals, however, rejected both of these justifications in 1996. First, the court said that sufficient evidence had not been offered to show the law school's participation in past unlawful discrimination. Second, the court held that racial diversity in the school was not a compelling governmental interest. While diversity of viewpoints might have value in a student body, there was no basis for "resorting to the dangerous proxy of race" and stereotyping applicants by imputing certain views to individuals because of their race. The result was quite similar to the changes that occurred in California at the same time. In 1997, acceptances for Blacks at the University of Texas Law School dropped from 65 to 5; for Mexican-Americans from 79 to 18. Not a single Black, and only a few Mexican-Americans, enrolled.[10]

Other Resistance to Affirmative Action

Court-ordered school-busing plans for the sole purpose of desegregation, which were widely adopted in the '60s and '70s, are quietly dying away. Many Blacks and Whites now agree that they haven't worked very well, and that the important thing is quality education, not integration *per se*. And as many of our cities become more and more Black, with large numbers of Whites either "fleeing" the city or sending their children to private schools, it becomes pragmatically impossible to racially integrate the public schools in any meaningful way.[11]

In the early '90s, in a series of cases, the Supreme Court seemed to invite the lower federal courts and school districts "to get out of the busing business."[12] In part this reflected the difficulty of determining when, if ever, past discrimination could be deemed to be sufficiently remediated. A perceptive observation by Linda Greenhouse, the Supreme Court reporter of the *New York Times,* brings us to the affirmative action environment at the close of the twentieth century: "The mood of the Court and the mood of the country on affirmative action are substantially in sync — closely divided, increasingly impatient, skeptical at best, and not persuaded that there is a single, easy answer to the questions posed by award-ing public benefits on the basis of race."[13]

WHAT IS OUR GOAL?

Most of us would subscribe to the goal so eloquently stated by Martin Luther King, Jr., when he told us about his dream that some day his children would live in a nation "where they will not be judged by the color of their skin but by the content of their char-acter." Some feel that the best way to reach this goal is for our coun-try to be legally colorblind. This approach has great appeal in a society that values individual liberty and would like to believe that individuals get what they deserve: those who work hard will suc-ceed even in the face of group handicaps that may temporarily remain as the result of discrimination. Yet others would argue that colorbindness ignores the realities of social and economic prejudice and discrimination, both that which is intentional and that which is unconscious.

Does "colorblind" mean that we must achieve complete inte-gration in housing, education, work, and politics? Should we go beyond that and seek to eliminate all social and cultural differences? How can we know if we've integrated without recognizing race?

Is our goal to be the traditional ideal of a "melting pot," where racial and other distinctions blend and fade away, or to be a "mosaic" or "salad bowl," where cultural differences are still recognized and even encouraged in social life? Our motto, "*E Pluribus Unum*," can be used to support either view, i.e., pursuing common ideals or drawing strength from diversity. But "equal protection of the laws" guarantees that race will have no *legal* significance, and that all cit-izens will have equal *opportunities* to all public economic and social benefits.

However we define the goal, most of us will agree that, while the status and opportunities of Black Americans have improved considerably in our lifetime, in overall terms Blacks are not treated as "equal" to Whites in many important ways. There is a classic illustration that makes the point very effectively, at least to me as a Caucasian.

Suppose I am standing before two doors, one marked "White" and one marked "Black." If I choose the first door I will remain White for the rest of my life. If I choose the second door I will become Black in physical appearance but will remain the same person in every other way. Would I go through the "Black" door if I were to be paid $100,000? $1,000.000? $100,000,000?[14] I would posit that, until the answer to this question is "zero," we have not achieved the kind of America I would like my grandchildren to live in, even though I don't expect to see it myself. I join in the vision of Justice Blackmun, concurring in part and dissenting in part in the *Bakke* decision:

> I yield to no one in my earnest hope that the time will come when an "affirmative action" program is unnecessary and is, in truth, only a relic of the past. . . . At some time, beyond any period of what some would claim as only transitional inequality, the United States must and will reach a stage of maturity where action along this line is no longer necessary. Then persons will be regarded as persons, and discrimination of the type we address today will be an ugly feature of history that is instructive but that is behind us.

AFFIRMATIVE ACTION IN THE NEXT FIFTY YEARS

Has It Helped Improve Our Society So Far?

For some, the civil rights revolution has gone too far; for others, it has not gone far enough. Most people will agree that there has been considerable progress in the past fifty years toward the goal of equal employment for all. Educational achievement for Blacks has risen dramatically, and, with it, their professional status. In 1970, only 4.5% of Black people age twenty-five or older had completed four or more years of college and beyond.[15] By 1980, this had risen to 7.0%, and by 1990 it was 11.9%. President Clinton stated in his commencement address at the University of California at San Diego on June 14, 1997, "[Affirmative action] has given us a whole generation of professionals in fields that used to be exclusive clubs. . . .There are more [Black] lawyers and judges, scientists and engineers, accountants and executives, than ever before."

Affirmative action has carried with it, however, a concern that it is based on stereotypes that inevitably stigmatize Blacks as inferior and polarize society. In her 1990 dissenting opinion in *Metro Broadcasting v. FCC,* which upheld FCC radio station licensing policies that manifested a preference for minority ownership, Justice O'Connor stated:

> [Race-based classifactions] may embody stereotypes that treat individuals as the product of their race, evaluating their thoughts and efforts — their worth as citizens — according to a criterion barred to the Government by history and the Constitution. Racial classification, whether providing benefits to or burdening particular racial or ethnic groups, may stigmatize those groups singled out for different treatment . . . .

Justice Kennedy, also dissenting, expressed similar concern:

> A plan of the type sustained here may impose "stigma on its supposed beneficiaries," and "foster intolerance and antagonism against the entire membership of the favored classes." Although the majority disclaims it, the FCC policy seems based on the demeaning notion that members of the defined racial groups ascribe to certain "minority views" that must be different from those of other citizens. Special preferences can also foster the view that members of the favored groups are inherently less able to compete on their own.

The same concern was expressed by Justice Stevens in 1980, in his dissent in *Fullilove v. Klutznick,* which upheld a provision for racial set-asides in government contracts:

> Even though it is not the actual predicate for this legislation, a statute of this kind inevitably is perceived by many as resting on an assumption that those who are granted the special preference are less qualified in some respect that is identified purely by their race . . . . That perception — especially when formed by the Congress of the United States — can only exacerbate rather than reduce racial prejudice . . . .

Clearly, affirmative action programs create at least the potential for stigmatization. Members of non-preferred racial groups often assume that *all* minority competitors are beneficiaries of affirmative action and are less qualified, though neither may be true as to individual people. Some minority competitors may assume, probably correctly, that non-minority competitors will question their qualifications. Since members of racial minority groups will usually not know whether or not they were beneficiaries of racial preferences, they may feel stigmatized, with a resulting loss of self-confidence.[16]

The danger of stereotyping and polarization was well expressed by Justice O'Connor in the context of the creation of majority-minority voting districts in *Shaw v. Reno* in 1993. The assumption that members of a racial group will "... think alike, share the same political interests, and prefer the same candidates . . . may exacerbate the very patterns of racial bloc voting [the legislature is trying] to counteract. It also sends to elected representatives the message that their primary obligation is to represent only that group's members, rather than their constituency as a whole."

The extent of the presumed polarization of voters along racial lines is exemplified by an April 3, 1998, article in the *Chicago Tri-*

bune headlined "Appeals Panel Urges Additional Black Ward." Here we have an express recognition by the United States 7th Circuit Court of Appeals that in the city of Chicago there are White wards, Black wards, and Hispanic wards, and it was perfectly proper to adopt a map with aldermanic districts based on this concept.

Can Affirmative Action Help Our Society Reach Its Future Goals?

There is no "official" or generally accepted definition of "affirmative action." It has been defined as "race-based governmental action designed to benefit . . . groups which have suffered discrimination in our society"; as "policies that provide preferences based explicitly on membership in a designated group"; and as "public or private actions or programs which provide or seek to provide opportunities or other benefits to persons on the basis of, among other things, their membership in a specified group or groups."[17]

Regardless of what the future may hold for racial preferences in employment, education, and contracting, there seems to be little opposition to one widely used form of affirmative action — outreach and recruitment. Broadening the pool of contractors, employees, executives, students, professionals, teachers, police officers, and so on to include more minorities will likely continue to be legally and socially acceptable, so long as race or ethnicity are not the basis for the decision to hire, admit, contract, etc. Outreach and recruitment programs have been largely noncontroversial because they are nonthreatening. The beneficiaries of such programs receive no advantage in hiring or admissions; they simply have an equal opportunity to compete for spots they might otherwise not know about or try for.

There also seems to be substantial support for measures taken to eliminate *present* racial discrimination. When Blacks are excluded from employment, housing, schools, etc. because of their race, there would seem to be ample justification for legal action to end this discrimination. Much more controversial is affirmative action used as a remedy to *past* discrimination, and it is here that a consensus seems to be developing on the Supreme Court and in society that we should be at or near the end of such practices.

Is Affirmative Action Justified as a Means of Promoting Diversity?

In *Bakke,* Justice Powell stated that the pursuit of diversity in higher education could constitute a compelling state interest. While that position has never been adopted as a majority holding of the Supreme Court, and has been considerably undermined in recent cases, it has been espoused and supported by many. Many businesses feel that a diverse workforce is needed to serve a diverse customer base in the United States and around the world. Diversity is also often deemed desirable in such areas as broadcast media, police departments, and education for both students and faculty.

Some of the strongest arguments for the need for diversity have been made in the field of education. President Neil Rudenstine wrote:

> The range of undergraduate interests, talents, backgrounds and career goals affects importantly the educational experience of our students, [because] a diverse student body is an educational resource of coordinate importance with our faculty and our library, laboratory and housing arrangements. . . . Such diversity is not an end in itself, or a pleasant but dispensable accessory. It is the substance from which much human learning, understanding and wisdom derive. It offers one of the most powerful ways of creating the intellectual energy and robustness that lead to greater knowledge. . . . Therefore affirmative action admissions policies contribute to educational values at the core of the mission of higher education.[18]

While it is undoubtedly true that a race-neutral college admissions process will reduce Black enrollment at the most competitive colleges, at least until more Black high school graduates are academically prepared to compete on an equal footing with their White and Asian counterparts, this does not necessarily mean that the enrollment of Black students will be reduced nationwide. Elimination of racial preferences will likely redistribute Black students down the educational hierarchy, as happened in California in 1998. Although this will have a large effect on "elite" institutions, it may be highly beneficial to others by increasing the size and quality of their applicant pools. While some young Black students will lose the prestige and benefits an "elite" institution may offer, they may be much better served by an education and degree from a less prestigious school for which they are well qualified academically. In recent years, 42% of Black students at Berkeley have dropped out, compared with only 16% of White students. It has been predicted that the number of Black graduates at the various University of California schools will *rise* by 19%. And if "elite" schools really feel that racial diversity is vital to their mission, they can simply be less academically choosy for *all* of their applicants.[19]

It has also been suggested that racial diversity is desirable in the ownership of radio and television stations. In *Metro Broadcasting v. the FCC* (1990) the Supreme Court held that the FCC had a legitimate interest in increasing the number of stations owned by minorities. The rationale was that this would not only "serve the needs and interests of the minority community but [would] also enrich and educate the non-minority audience." It would also foster "the inclusion of minority views in the area of programming."

The majority of the Court seemed to overlook the potential for polarization in having "Black" radio and television stations. It also failed to address the strong possibility that, if Blacks indeed had recognizable needs and interests as a group, these interests would undoubtedly be discovered by some radio and television stations seeking to profit from serving that market. One other place where a strong argument has been made in favor of promoting racial diversity is police forces. In *Wygant v. Board of Education* (1996) Justice Stevens wrote, "In a city with a recent history of racial unrest, the superintendent of police might reasonably conclude that an integrated police force could develop a better relationship with the community and thereby do a more effective job of maintaining law and order than a force composed of white officers."

A similar rationale was adopted by the Sixth Circuit Court of Appeals in *Detroit Police Officers' Association v. Young* (1979) in upholding an affirmative action plan aimed at recruiting and promoting more Black police officers:

> The argument that police need more minority officers is not simply that blacks communicate better with blacks or that a police department should cater to the public's desires. Rather, it is that effective crime prevention and solution depend heavily on the public support and cooperation which result only from public respect and confidence in the police. In short, the focus is not on the superior performance of minority officers, but on the public's perception of law enforcement officials and institutions.

What Should Be Included In Diversity?

If some kind of diversity is desirable in education, employment, and so on, we will still have to decide what factors to include. For purposes of this essay, and for resolving what is probably the most controversial issue relating to affirmative action, the key question is whether race should be allowed as a factor in achieving diversity. But perhaps we can better answer that question after we look at the various factors that are sometimes considered by those seeking to create a diverse student body or work force.

It is well known that for many years Harvard College has sought to admit a diverse student body. I do not know what factors Harvard considers in the selection process, and the factors probably change some over time. But I am sure the list would include all or most of: academic ability; race; ethnicity; gender; urban or rural; intended field of concentration; intended career; place of residence; special talents (athletic, musical, etc.); relationship to alumni; family wealth and contributions to Harvard; economic and other hard-ships overcome; work and volunteer experience; disability; immi-grant status; languages spoken; whether parents attended college; foreign travel or residence; and perhaps sexual orientation. Most of these factors may be used today, with whatever weighting the Admissions Office prefers, without any fear of legal challenge. If Harvard decides that diversity requires the admission of a 250–pound tackle with a high school GPA of 3.2 over a trombone player with a GPA of 3.9, the decision will be widely accepted and gen-erally approved. Will the new Crimson football player feel stigma-tized because he suspects that he is less qualified academically than some rejected applicants? I doubt it.

What about the children of alumni, often called "legacies"? I have read that in recent years Harvard admitted more Whites as legacies than the total of Black, Hispanic, and Native American stu-dents combined, and that in 1988 almost 200 students were admit-ted because of legacy preference who might well have been rejected otherwise.[20] Did these legacy students feel stigmatized? I doubt it very much. Did they add to Harvard's diversity? No, in fact they probably reduced it. Was their admission beneficial to Harvard? Undoubtedly. I assume that when I applied for admission to Har-vard in 1946, the Admissions Office knew that my father was a member of the Class of 1916; I also assume that was a plus factor for me. But at the risk of sounding egotistical, I have never felt that my "legacy" was needed for my admission. In 1946 Harvard was half empty; our entering class was about 2200, twice the normal number. I was fifth in my class at a top prep school, played three sports, was in theater and chorus, and lived in the midwest. Would I be readily admitted today? Perhaps not. Would I be ashamed if I were admitted only because of my legacy? I don't think so. I think I would feel that Harvard was enriched by the sharing of the Har-vard tradition between father and son.

If diversity is an important goal in creating the "best possible" student body, there would seem to be no end to the different factors one might consider: tall and short, fat and thin, red hair and blond, liberal and conservative, fundamentalist Christian and atheist Darwinian, neo-Nazi and orthodox Jew. If carried to the ultimate extreme, each student would be *sui generis.*

So now back to the main question: Should race be allowable as a factor in creating a diverse group? In the eyes of some, "The use of race, in and of itself, to choose students simply achieves a student body that looks different. Such [a] criterion is no more rational on its own terms than would be choices based upon physical size or blood type of applicants."[21] A Black person *may* offer a distinct perspective on the treatment of Blacks by the police or the role of welfare in the lives of Black people, based not on a stereotyped "Black" point of view, but rather on that person's personal experience. On the other hand, he may not.[22]

Yet there are those who feel strongly that race *is* a proper factor in diversity because it represents not mere skin color but also the consequences of the minority racial experience in America. Given more than 300 years of American social history, with so much depending on a person's racial identification, there is reason to believe that the experiences of racial minorities have diverged at least to some extent from the experiences of Whites. Those who subscribe to this view believe that the "simple matter of the color of one's skin so profoundly affects the way one is treated, so racially shapes what one is allowed to think and feel about this society, that the decision to generalize from this division is valid."[23]

How Do We Classify?

If race is to be a factor in diversity, we have finally the question of how to classify by race. Racial categories have been used by the federal government since the original census in 1790, and there has been considerable discussion about what racial and ethnic categories to use for the 2000 census. People have been classified racially over the years in a number of ways. The three most common are probably: (1) visual observation of a person's features; (2) documentary evidence, such as birth certificate indicating Black ancestry; and (3) the fact that the person or his family hold themselves out to be Black and are considered to be Black in the community.[24]

Historically, when there has been discrimination *against* Blacks, a person was classified as "Black" by the White majority if the person had "one drop" of Black blood. Now that one may be given a *preference* based on being Black, will many racially mixed people identify themselves as Black to get the benefit of the preference? As stated by Sally Rubenstone, a part-time admissions counselor at Smith College, "Kids are savvy enough about checking the minority box [on the college admissions application]. . . . It's hard to prove and colleges give them the benefit of the doubt. Any kid with an ounce of Native American blood knows how to fill out the box."[25]

There are probably few Americans whose ancestry is pure African. In the past there were large numbers of children born of slave mothers and slave-owner fathers, and since those days there has been a great increase in interracial marriages and relationships. There has, indeed, been a movement to have a separate census category for mixed-race people such as well-known golfer Tiger Woods. The five racial categories used in the 1990 census were: "White," "Black," "American Indian, Eskimo or Aleut," "Asian or Pacific Islander," and "Other Race." The "Other Race" category included people "providing write-in entries such as multi-racial, multi-ethnic, mixed, interracial . . . or a Spanish/Hispanic origin group (such as Mexican, Cuban, or Puerto Rican)."

2050

I think it is safe to say that no member of the Harvard Class of 1950 will see the year 2050. Yet our grandchildren will, and we want to help build for them the best possible environment in which they can live. One important decision in the creation of that environment is the role of affirmative action on the basis of race. If race is recognized as a factor in creating diversity in an institution, and diversity is important to that institution, the reason for recognizing race would presumably be because people of different races will bring different viewpoints to the institution. The courts might very well reject this as representing an incorrect and overly broad stereotype. But that would probably not be the case if the institution uses race as only one of many characteristics which may be indicators of the unique personal experience of the individual applicant.

I am convinced that there are at least some occasions when a person's experiences are affected by race, and that race can influence the way a person is treated, especially by government officials and by members of the dominant culture.[26] A commonly cited example is the case of a Black student, professor, or business executive who is stopped and questioned by police in a middle-class, White, suburban neighborhood near a college campus, for no apparent reason other than race.[27] There would not seem to be any race-neutral proxy for this experience. If someone is treated differently specifically because of race, that experience would not be shared by a White person merely because the latter is poor, or grew up in the inner city, and has struggled to overcome adversity.

If we're honest with ourselves, most of us have lived our whole lives surrounded by affirmative action, and many of us have profited therefrom, or helped others without regard to merit. A Harvard degree opens a lot of doors, without much concern for the actual "merit" of the alumnus. I've discussed legacies as a factor in admissions at some schools, but there are many more examples of helpful actions taken without regard to comparative merit. I often try to help my Research Assistants, and other students I know and like, in their quest for employment. While I only recommend those whom I consider well qualified, I will freely admit that they may not always be the "best qualified." People in business and professional life tend to hire people like themselves, and then to mentor them and help them up the ladder. Nepotism, without regard to merit, is frequently noted.

I am still an idealist, and hope that we can some day have a society that is truly colorblind in the best sense — where we can recognize our different skin colors as a physical characteristic like hair color, but where none of our governmental, economic, or social decisions are based on race. I think we've made some real progress toward that goal, but we still have a long way to go.

NOTES

1. Rebecca Smith, "Comment," in "A World Without Color: The California Civil Rights Initiative and the Future of Affirmative Action," *Santa Clara Law Rev.* 38 (1997):235.

2. Smith, "Comment," 237–38.

3. *110 Cong. Rec.* 13.080, 1964

4. See *Johnson v. Transportation Agency,* 480 U.S. 616.670, 1987. (Justice Scalia, dissenting.)

5 See, for example, the statement of Justice Douglas in *DeFunis v. Odegaard,* 416 U.S. 312, 339 (1974) that there is no "Western State which can claim that it has always treated Japanese and Chinese in a fair and evenhanded manner."

6. See John D. Lamp, "The Real Affirmative Action Babies: Legacy Preferences at Harvard and Yale," *Columbia Jour. of Legal and Social Problems* 26 (1993): 491.

7. 109 U.S. 3 (1883): 25.

8. See Steve Chapman, in the *Chicago Tribune,* Apr. 9, 1998, sec.1, p. 23.

9. See Steven Holmes in the *New York Times,* Dec. 1, 1997.

10. Michael A. Olivas, "Constitutional Criteria: The Social Science and Common Law of Admissions Decisions in Higher Education," *Univ. Colorado Law Rev* 68 (1997): 1065.

11. Mark Hansen, "A Road No Longer Taken," *ABA Jour.*, Feb. 1998:28.

12. Hansen. "A Road No Longer Taken."

13. "In Step with Racial Policy," the *New York Times,* June 14, 1995, A1.

14. See Tung Yin, "A Carbolic Smokeball for the Nineties: Class-Based Affirmative Action," *Loyola L. A. Law Rev.* 31 (1997):213, 247.

15. Emmanuel Margolis, "Affirmative Action: Deja Vu All Over Again?" *Southwestern Univ. Law Rev.* 1 (1997):65.

16. See Lackland H. Bloom, *Hopwood, Bakke, and the Future of Diversity Justification.*

17. *Adarand Constructors, Inc. v. Pena,* 1995; Randall Kennedy, "Persuasion and Distrust: A Comment on the Affirmative Action Debate," *Harvard Law Rev.* 99 (1986):1327, 1346, n. 1; James E. Jones, Jr., "The Genesis

and Present Status of Affirmative Action in Employment: Economic, Legal and Political Realities," *Iowa Law Rev.* 70 (1985): 901, 903.

18. Neil L. Rudenstine, "Harvard University, the President's Report 1993–1995: Diversity and Learning," quoted in "An Evidentiary Framework for Diversity as a Compelling Interest in Higher Education," *Harvard Law Rev.* 109 (1996): 1357.

19. See Chapman, in *Chicago Tribune,* 1998, and Bloom, *Hopwood, Bakke.*

20. See David Benjamin Oppenheimer, "Understanding Affirmative Action," *Hastings Const. Law Quarterly* 23 (1996): 921, 965; and Elaine Woo, "Belief in Meritocracy, an Equal-Opportunity Myth," *L. A. Times,* Apr. 30, 1995, A1.

21. *Hopwood v. Texas* 78 F.3d 932, 945 (5th Cir.), *cert. denied,* 116 S.Ct. 2582 (1996).

22. See Paul Brest and Miranda Oshige, "Affirmative Action for Whom," *Stanford Law Rev.* 47 (1993): 855, 862.

23. See T. Alexander Aleinikoff, "A Case for Race-Conciousness," *Columbia Law Rev.* 91 (1991): 1060, 1095: and Patricia Williams, "Alchemical Notes: Reconstructing Ideals from Deconstructed Rights," *Harvard C.R.-C.L.L. Rev.* 22 (1987):401, 404, n. 4

24. Leonard M. Baynes, "Who is Black Enough for You? An Analysis of Northwestern University Law School's Struggle Over Minority Faculty Hiring," *Michigan Jour. of Race and Law* 2 (1997): 205, 214.

25. *Chicago Tribune,* Apr. 29, 1998, sec. 1, p. 20.

26. See, for example, Derrick Bell, *Confronting Authority,* 1991; Cheryl I. Harris, "Whiteness as Property," *Harvard Law Rev.* 106 (1993): 1709.

27. See Paul Butler, "Encounters with the Police on My Street," *Legal Times,* Nov. 10, 1997.

A HALF-CENTURY OF CHANGE

Race, Admissions, and the Harvard Community

Frank S. Jones

The class of 1950 marked the opening up of a half-century of admissions at Harvard College. The subsequent fifty years of Harvard admissions and the University's policies on race are the subject of this essay.

When we came to Harvard over fifty years ago, our entering class was the largest in the history of the College. Also noteworthy was the quality of the entrants. In his report on that freshman year, Dean of Freshmen Delmar Leighton observed that the academic record of the class of 1950 was "outstanding." There was a marked excess of applications over available spaces, and Leighton noted with pride the high level of selectivity required to form the class.

Part of the increase in applicants reflected a phenomenon not unique to Harvard — a wave of World War II veterans anxious to begin or complete their education. With the passage of the GI Bill, many who otherwise could not afford higher education were able to do so. The United States armed services were segregated. Black

My thanks to Philip N. Alexander, Akosua Barthwell-Evans, Fred Glimp, Charles J. Hamilton, Kenneth R. Manning, George Mumford, and Nathaniel Ober for their assistance and support. I dedicate this essay to the memory of my father, David D. Jones.

units fought separately from white units. As units came home, veterans in search of educational opportunity filtered back into the segregated institutions that America had to offer, many contrasting their experiences in Europe with those in America. Whites gravitated to certain institutions, blacks to others.

The Harvard class entering in September 1946 numbered 1,645, including 896 veterans. Four of the veterans were African-American. I remember running into George Wilson at orientation, and later met Tom Roberts, John Rice, and Hugh Hill (later known as "Brother Blue," the famed street raconteur designated as the "official storyteller of Boston and Cambridge"). Jack Norman, who transferred in from Howard University, and Oscar DePriest were non-veterans like myself. Seven African-Americans were part of the class at one time or another during my four-year stay, carrying on a long-standing Harvard tradition of admitting a small number of blacks and other racial or ethnic minorities — at that point a passive, unconscious pattern disconnected from any formal, conscious notion of recruitment.

Meanwhile, life at Harvard was returning to normal. Living arrangements suspended during the war resumed beginning in September 1946. Freshmen lived in the Yard. The Union and Widener Library had reading rooms; Lamont Library was not open until 1949. Wilbur J. Bender had become Counselor for Veterans in July 1945, which made him responsible for advising interested veterans, and for interviewing as well as admitting them. The regular Admissions Committee, chaired by Richard M. Grummere, considered the non-veteran applicants. Bender became Dean of Admissions and Financial Aid in 1952.

I was among the four African-Americans entering as freshmen in September 1946. I had come by way of Phillips Academy, Andover, where I had "prepped" for three years. My brother David had preceded me there. After attending elementary school in Greensboro, North Carolina, I lived two years with my grandparents in St. Louis in order to prepare for the academic rigors of Andover at a better school than was available back home. My grandparents were both graduates of Berea College in the 1880s. When

I went on to excel academically at Andover, especially in Latin, I attributed this in part to my preparation in St. Louis. In fact it was my grandmother who first taught me Latin. My admission to Harvard, along with a number of other Andover students, opened a new horizon for me. My father and brother had both gone to Wesleyan University, and I was the first in my family to attend Harvard.

Not long after arriving on campus I encountered the other African-American freshmen. As I lived in Weld Hall at the center of the Yard, I ran into them frequently. Oscar DePriest lived in Massachusetts Hall; Tom Roberts commuted from his Cambridge home; I never knew where George Wilson lived. Even though there was no black student association, we managed to get together on occasion.

While Harvard offered a range of academic opportunities for its freshmen, it was football that attracted me, not as a player but as a member of the squad of managers. I was captivated by the opportunity that sports offered and went out as manager of the Harvard freshman football team. Few blacks had played in the Ivy League, and no black to my knowledge had served as manager. In many ways my talent for bringing people together and making things happen was not unlike the administrative skills I had observed in my father, David D. Jones, on a daily basis as President of Bennett College, a black women's college in Greensboro.

As a result of my auspicious start with the freshman squad, I was firmly in the running during sophomore year to be manager of the football team — a goal that I had set for myself early in the freshman year. I spent many days at the Dillon Field House learning the tasks of a manager trainee in the competitive hierarchy leading to the managership. With the exception of a single black, Chester Pierce, who later became a renowned psychiatrist on the Harvard Medical School faculty, the team was all white. I saw the managership as an opportunity to develop throughout the country a range of business and other influential contacts. In my junior year I was selected from among the competing trainees to become manager — the first black manager of the Harvard football team. The *New York Times* featured this accomplishment along with an announcement about Yale's black running back and first black captain, Levi Jackson — a remarkable player. Just the previous year, 1947, Jackie Robinson had joined the Brooklyn Dodgers and integrated professional baseball for the first time since the 1890s. President Truman issued an executive order on July 26, 1948, integrating the armed services. I was riding high on what was another symbol of progress in racial integration.

During the fall of my senior year, I was crowning off my term as football manager. I had reason to feel good about myself and about my Harvard career. I arranged the annual football banquet on no budget after perhaps the worst football season in Harvard's history. We lost to all but one team, morale among the players was low. As the first black manager, I felt intense pressure to pull the team from its morass, and when my father visited me that fall we worked out a scheme to insure that the traditional banquet would indeed be carried on as usual. I managed to persuade outside sources to underwrite the banquet at the Commander Hotel.

Perhaps as a result of this accomplishment, classmates selected me as second marshal of our class in the spring of 1950. Remember the others? Howie Houston was first, and Jon Spivak was third. The three of us were connected to undergraduate athletics in one way or another. One classmate suggested recently that we may have been selected as a ringing statement about diversity — a Roman Catholic (Howie), a Jew (Jon), and a black (me). If this was done consciously, then bully for the class of '50! May the class of '00 be as forward-looking.

In addition, I had received praise from fellow students and the athletic staff for devoted service — a true highlight, an emotional conclusion to my Harvard career. These accolades were as important to me as earning the highest academic distinction — *summa cum laude* — must have been to my classmate Oscar S. DePriest, III, who was a grandson of the first African-American from a northern state — Illinois — to be seated in the U.S. House of Representatives. Both Oscar and I could feel proud not only for our accomplishments, but also for Harvard's appointment in 1950 of the scholar Ralph Bunche to a faculty position in the government department. Bunche was the first African-American to ever be appointed a member of the Faculty of Arts and Sciences. The appointment made national headlines, but shortly thereafter Bunche won the Nobel Prize and chose an ambassadorial career. I remember being disappointed that Harvard had no African-Americans in its faculty ranks at that time.

After graduation I spent six months working at odd jobs around the Dillon Field House. Then came several years in the Army. I was posted to Germany and spent considerable time studying Russian. Since I was aiming for a career in business, I was fortunate to have chosen the path of football manager, as in the past there had been a tradition of team managers entering the Harvard Business School. It seemed not to matter that I was black. I was accepted to enter in the fall of 1955, following in the footsteps of football managers such as Dwight K. Nishimura ('49). A few years earlier, *Life* magazine had published an article observing that the experience gained by Harvard football managers was equivalent to completing one year of the Harvard Business School.

The decision to come to Harvard in the 1940s and 1950s was not necessarily one guaranteeing an African-American a leadership role in the larger community. In general, African-Americans could expect to assume leadership only within the black community and only on black issues. By choosing Harvard, or any other predominantly white university, we were sacrificing the opportunity for training and for developing contacts within the black community. I was no exception. Harvard had no leverage as such in the black communities of Greensboro, or New Orleans, or Atlanta. A degree from Morehouse or Fisk or Howard would have been a faster route to leadership in the African-American community. For example, although Oscar DePriest spent four years at the Harvard Medical School and served his internship at the prestigious Massachusetts General Hospital, his career and professional life played out at Howard rather than Harvard, Yale, or Columbia, and perhaps less gloriously than might have been expected. His successes at Harvard did not provide him with any special advantages later on.

As blacks at Ivy League colleges during this era we were

suspended between two worlds in several ways — unable to choose one over the other, uncertain about what opportunities existed to maximize leadership potential, and divided over where such efforts would best be exerted. The predicament was all the more ironic for us African-Americans at Harvard since Harvard has always been about producing leaders. As President Derek Bok observed in his 1982–1983 annual report, referring to an earlier period:

> A primary objective of the College since its founding in 1636 has been to educate talented people for roles of leadership, originally in the ministry and later in the professions and in civic life. Harvard had indeed produced a number of minority graduates who had distinguished themselves but their numbers were relatively small. Although a remarkable proportion of the country's most influential blacks, especially in the professions, were numbered among its alumni, the College had not succeeded, as it had with non-minority students, in attracting blacks in sufficient numbers so that they could exert substantial leadership in all sectors of society.

It is ironic, if not regrettable, that blacks as a group at Harvard did not put their imprimatur on perhaps the two most profound events of the last fifty years — the Supreme Court decision in the case of *Brown v. Board of Education of Topeka, Kansas* (Brown, 347 U.S. 483, 1954), and subsequent federal civil rights legislation in the middle and late 1960s. The legal work for both was carried out forcefully at Howard with little or no help from the Harvard Law School. Charles Hamilton Houston and William H. Hastie, two of the giants of the civil rights movement, had undertaken their legal training at Harvard (Harvard Law '22 and '30, respectively), but it was only through their subsequent connection with Howard that they functioned as pioneers. The driving spirit behind the civil rights legislation of the 1950s and 1960s was in many ways centered around Morehouse College, with Dr. King and others actively involved. My brother David was a Harvard law graduate who was neither connected with a black organization or institution nor a participant in the civil rights movement at the level of Howard law graduates. Of the Harvard law graduates, only William T. Colemen, Jr. ('46), it seems managed to make a contribution comparable to the Howard people without actually affiliating himself with the black community. Coleman finished first in his law school class and became the first black to clerk for the Supreme Court.

Prior to World War II, Harvard had adopted two programs that were intended to attract more able students from outside the Northeast. The first, put into practice under President Lowell in 1923, assured admission to any student whose school recommended him and whose academic record put him in the "top seventh" of his class. This offset frequent geographic obstacles to taking the required admissions examinations. The second, the program of Harvard National Scholarships initiated by President Conant in 1933 in recognition of Harvard's 300th Anniversary, sought to demonstrate Harvard's interest in students from all parts of the nation by offering special scholarships to students from Massachusetts and from all states south of the Mason-Dixon line and west of the Mississippi River. National Scholarships could be continued for study at Harvard graduate schools and had need-based stipends that were set high enough to obviate the need for earnings from term-time jobs. A young Wilbur Bender, working as an assistant dean at the College while studying for a Ph.D. in history, had helped work out the procedures for awarding National Scholarships before he moved to Phillips Academy, Andover, in 1936 to teach history.

After World War II, Harvard began framing diversification of its student body as an important goal. At first the focus of this effort was along the lines of veterans. The "special student" category was essentially closed to civilians during the late '40s in order to make room for veterans. Harvard was trying to pay a debt to men who had served their country, providing them with educational opportunity and integrating them into the college experience. This effort was explicit, reiterated again and again in Admissions Committee reports. It led to a way of formulating concerns along lines of diversity — the collection of relevant data to measure success; the posing of appropriate questions to ferret out the values of the institution. Staff and faculty comprising the Admissions Committee reexamined and reshaped diversity goals on a regular basis. In addition to veteran status, other factors given special consideration were geographic origin and disadvantaged background.

Although the admissions policy of the University has always been a responsibility shared by many individuals from the faculty to the president, the dean of admissions and his colleagues have shaped the selection of students for each "Harvard class." During the early 1950s, as a result of too many applications from qualified candidates, the Admissions Committee was forced for the first time to consciously shape the makeup of the student body, rather than simply selecting qualified individuals in a *laissez-faire* manner. The ensuing half-century of committee deliberations came under the stewardship of Wilbur Bender (1952–1960), Fred Glimp (1960–1967), Chase Peterson (1967–1972), Fred Jewett (1972–1986), and most recently William Fitzsimmons (1986–present).

While a student at Andover, I had known of Bender. As a faculty member engaged in a faculty colloquium on visions for the school's future, he had set the controversial goal of selecting half the student body from the pool of scholarship applicants, thus earning an early reputation for innovative thinking along lines of diversity. When Bender returned to Harvard to process the flood of applications from veterans, his interest in diversity was channeled into bringing veterans into the College. This effort required of him a broad vision of Harvard's role and accessibility, as well as a familiarity with broader trends and practices in American education. It also took place against the backdrop of *Brown v. Board of Education,* the landmark Supreme Court case that challenged the "separate but equal" doctrine and laid an essential underpinning for the entire civil rights movement of the 1950s and 1960s. No specific indication of Harvard's awareness of or response to the decision can be gleaned from admissions reports at the time.

Another noteworthy development at Harvard, although it had little if any relationship to the issue of race, was the changing of the presidential guard in 1953 — the year that Nathan Pusey succeeded

James B. Conant and, in the ensuing years until his retirement in 1972, waged a successful campaign to increase the College's endowment and to revitalize education in the sciences and in regional international centers.

Education in the United States had evolved in such a way that talented black youths were not easily identifiable by Harvard. Harvard and other Ivy League schools knew well only about a half-dozen high schools throughout the country with high black enrollments such as Dunbar High in Washington, D.C., and Sumner High in St. Louis. Any population of talented students from segregated schools in the South had virtually no chance for admission because Harvard simply had no tradition of contacts with these schools, contacts that ordinarily would have come by way of certain teachers or counselors. In any event, despite the dramatic events surrounding *Brown,* racial diversity seems not to have been paramount in the discussions of the Admissions Committee during the 1950s. The goal was more to reach out to students from disadvantaged socioeconomic backgrounds and to increase the number of all ethnic minorities: Jews, Irish, Italians, Poles, and others, as well as blacks, to draw more deeply from the public schools rather than from the old, standby prep schools such as Choate, Exeter, and St. Paul. Harvard realized that unless the schools and families of the applicants from disadvantaged backgrounds believed that the College was interested in them, that it would admit and give them aid, and that they would prosper here, recruiting efforts would have little success.

Usually fewer than a dozen — more like half a dozen — African-Americans matriculated at Harvard in any year in the '50s. Throughout the decade, blacks entered in small but steady numbers, graduated, and left to pursue various careers. Walter Carrington ('52) entered ambassadorial service; Mel Miller ('56) became a lawyer and later publisher of *The Bay State Banner.* The Howe twins, Arnold and Alan ('55) entered from Boston Latin and are perhaps the only African-American alumni twins. A few years earlier, Clifton R. Wharton, Jr. ('47), son of the first African-American to head a U.S. diplomatic mission in Europe, had embarked on what would become a stellar career in economic development, insurance management, and higher education administration.

But by the end of the decade there were still just a dozen or so African-Americans per class. I remember the country just beginning to grapple more intensely with racial discrimination in higher education. I had spent two years at the Business School and remained there an additional five years as a beginning administrator in the dean's office before leaving to take up an executive position at the Scott Paper Company in Philadelphia.

When I was at Harvard, black students looked toward the larger black community of Boston — especially Roxbury — for support and fulfillment. We often went there to church for spiritual reinforcement and sense of community; we went to Roxbury nightclubs for entertainment, and to Roxbury barbers, dentists, and the like for personal essentials. We also made friendships with the few other black students at greater Boston institutions such as Boston University and Wellesley College.

In 1956 I married Anna Faith Johnson, who was a Wellesley graduate and daughter of Mordecai W. Johnson, the first black president of Howard University. It was the time when renowned African-American Howard Thurman was pastor of Marsh Chapel at Boston University, and Martin Luther King, Jr., was working on his doctorate there. This pattern of community relationships — the forging of bonds between a precious few — continued into the 1950s and 1960s, and even beyond.

As freshmen at Harvard, African-American students were by and large assigned to each other as roommates. Even though the practice was not exclusive and not all black students in university housing lived with other black students, the record indicates that the placement was not accidental even if it did not rise to the level of a formal policy. The dean of freshmen was most likely responsible for conceiving and implementing the pattern, no doubt, in his mind, for the advantage of these students. Over the years, African-American alumni have mentioned to me that this practice was an observable and regrettable failure of their Harvard experience. Even so the dormitory situation during our day had progressed from the retrograde policy of President Lowell, under which black students were explicitly excluded from living in freshman dorms. It was not until 1923, late in Lowell's administration, that the President and Fellows modified it to state that: "up to the capacity of the Freshman Halls all members of the freshman class shall reside and board in the Freshman Halls. . . . In the application of this rule, men of white and colored races shall not be compelled to live and eat together, nor should any man be excluded by reason of his color." As a result, students in our day had a say in choosing a roommate. Just how much of the segregated patterns of freshman living was due to administrative practice or to the attempt of deans and others to accommodate our own wishes (and prejudices) is difficult to determine.

During the 1950s, Harvard was fast becoming the diverse national and international institution that it had set out to become under Bender, pouring even more resources into diversifying the student body along many lines, with a special emphasis on targeting and recruiting public school students. The Admissions Committee had the task of assembling a class in the context of many constraints and conflicts. Some of the frustrations involved in the process are illustrated by Bender's statement (President's Report 1959/60, p. 247):

> The regular Admissions Committee and staff, of course, have to act, have to make decisions about thousands of imperfect and imperfectly known individuals to meet a deadline. They cannot take refuge in neatly balanced generalities. They have to take more, or fewer, local boys; more, or fewer Harvard sons; put more, or less, weight on a variety of imperfectly evaluated non-academic qualities. They can award only the scholarship money that a tight-fisted Dean of the Faculty will give them and have no control over the endless, upward march of tuition, board, and room charges.

When Harvard was at the juncture of changing its admissions dean in 1959, Bender knew that he had brought the University only up to a point and there was still a distance to run. His success had been recognized and applauded, but he knew that there was a long way to go toward understanding what actually had happened in the past; how to continue the reforms he had helped put in place; and how to innovate and change for the future. He warned neophytes about jumping to conclusions before they had the facts or had done some serious thinking about these issues that he knew to be both profound and complicated. Nevertheless, in summing up his activity as Dean of Admissions, and turning over the baton to his colleague and protege, our classmate, Fred Glimp, Bender expressed confidence in the increasingly diverse Harvard student body: "I have more doubts about the ability of Harvard College under present conditions to give these men an education worthy of their quality than I have about them as men or scholars."

I had known Fred since we were undergraduates together in Lowell House. After graduation he had gone on to graduate school in economics and on many nights played poker with our mutual friend, Oscar de Priest. Our friendship deepened as he was beginning his new venture as Director of Admissions while I was commencing studies at the Business School. My interest in Harvard admissions could now be pursued through my contact with Fred.

When he became director in the fall of 1960, Harvard was headed into a new era of admissions. Former President Conant, a proponent of general education, had recently completed an extensive study and published a best-selling book, *The American High School Today,* that set the paradigm for curricula in American high schools. American education was being called into question as a result of the scientific and technical achievements of the Soviet Union, which had launched Sputnik — the first man-made satellite — into space in October 1957. Even though Conant may not have been initially motivated by the comparison of American education with Russian education or by the impact of Sputnik — as was claimed by John W. Gardner, President of the Carnegie Corporation, the sponsor of Conant's project — his book nonetheless

derived considerable notoriety from that event. Every superintendent, principal, and teacher began modeling school curricula on the
program outlined by Conant, and by extension, Harvard. Conant's
experience and research in writing the book took him to school
districts throughout the country (he did, however, refuse to visit
segregated schools in the South) and helped him to establish ties
and networks invaluable for Harvard admissions and the work of
Glimp and his office.

At the same time, Harvard began to broaden its efforts at
understanding the educational system of other countries. As a result,
a marked increase in the number of international students, especially Africans and West Indians, occurred around 1960, as the
Admissions Office developed methods of evaluating academic performance in systems unlike the American one. The Africans and
West Indians, more visible as a result of their numbers, added a fla-
vor of racial diversity to the campus. In fact, their presence may have
helped pave the way for a greater number of African-Americans.

During the early 1960s, the struggle for civil rights was
carried out within the context of organizations such as the Southern Christian Leadership Conference, the Congress of Racial
Equality, and the Student Nonviolent Coordinating Committee, as
well as at lunch counters and elsewhere, notably among African-
American students at historically black colleges in Atlanta and
Greensboro. Voting rights campaigns in Mississippi and other parts
of the deep South attracted the attention of certain politically
minded undergraduates at many northern colleges and universities
who themselves brought back to campus their concern about social
justice for African-Americans in this country, particularly in the
South.

When the federal civil rights bill passed in the summer of
1964, Harvard had admitted approximately twenty-five black students in the freshman class. There is little doubt that racial diversity
was assuming a more prominent place in the minds of admissions
people. A number of enrichment programs for gifted black students
at the high school level came into existence around this time,
including A Better Chance (ABC). Harvard was not among the

institutions that pioneered these programs, considerable credit for which goes to individuals like John Kemeny, a mathematician who became President of Dartmouth in the early '70s. But about this same time, Harvard began to articulate a long-standing practice that it had always implemented almost silently — the notion of the importance of the bottom quarter of the class. With Fred Glimp at the helm, the practice was expressed openly. It coincided with increased willingness on the part of the College to accept more African-Americans, and was linked with the cause of admitting more "disadvantaged" student to address "Harvard's serious interest in the problem." The concept itself is the signature of Fred Glimp and his tenure as Dean of Admissions, as illustrated in his admissions report for 1966–67:

> A[n} issue [that] I am particularly delighted the Admis-
> sion Committee takes seriously, is what we have come to
> call the "bottom-quarter issue." The essence of the issue
> is fairly clear. Because any student body has a bottom
> quarter and because students vary greatly in their ability
> to cope constructively with even a relative sense of
> "being below average," the lives and personal develop-
> ment of bottom-quarter students can be unduly affected
> in different ways. Some are challenged, but for some their
> self-respect is so greatly affected as to impede their per-
> formance in college and in their future careers. Hence
> the proposition: doesn't it make educational sense for a
> college to make a conscious effort to avoid having a bot-
> tom quarter made up of students who are likely to
> become disillusioned and defeated by their relative stand-
> ing there, and to have instead a "real" bottom quarter of
> students who are productive yet content to be there? We
> know from experience that many students for whom we
> predict bottom-quarter records do deal constructively
> both with the educational complexities of college life
> and with the effects of their own relative averageness.
> Some students respond so well to the challenge that their

development far outruns their bottom-quarter creden-
tials; in a sense they prove the case for the special rele-
vance of strong non-academic factors. In two of the last
seven graduating classes, for example, the man whose sec-
ondary school grades and test scores combined to predict
for him the lowest academic record in the class graduated *magna cum laude*. . . . Particularly with the greater
efforts at all levels of education to make it possible for disadvantaged students to realize their potential, and given
Harvard's serious interest in this problem, it seems likely
that Harvard can continue to attract some outstanding
men.

Glimp's view of admissions policy was shifting to encompass
more African-Americans, and at the same time he did not want the
College to accept only those who would end up with honors
or high honors. On the one hand he wanted to argue for the
reasonableness — even necessity — of favorable consideration for
the applicant in the so-called "bottom quarter," and on the other
hand he wanted to emphasize that conventional predictors of what
the "bottom quarter" would be were sometimes inaccurate. He had
seen, firsthand, students come in with predictors placing them in
the bottom of the class, but who had graduated at or near the top.
While the concept might seem like a stroke of genius, it did implic-
itly set up the bottom-quarter notion as part of the overall policy
to diversify the student body, in tandem with increased acceptance
of African-Americans.

Admission to Harvard represented an achievement in itself,
whether or not a student actually decided to attend. Certificates
were issued and those admitted came with a deep sense of accomplishment. The undergraduate years were thought to be an integral
and integrated experience, regardless of how bumpy the ride.
Digressions, disorganization, flexibility, and looseness seemed to be
interpreted favorably for the chosen few; withdrawals and time off
were viewed as contributing to the positive experience of being at
Harvard. The Admissions Office was clear in sending this message

to the faculty, administration, and the world at large. In fact, it was hard, if not impossible, to be a failure at Harvard, as Glimp laid out in his '69 admissions report:

> The many diversions here — the *Crimson,* the Loeb, even Radcliffe, and so on — can be important and con- structive. We surely cannot expect every promising man to be utterly effective and well organized at each stage of his life. The capacity for being carried away with unthinking zeal for an activity, even if it stands in the way of maximum or only adequate academic performance, is one of the harbingers of a significant life. What we should make of the drop-outs at all levels of ability is hard to say. More than half were voluntary withdrawals, and if past experience applies about half will eventually receive Harvard degrees. For many the leave will prove to have been a constructive experience.

This kind of thinking went against any notion that African-Americans as a group were more likely to fail than any other group. So, Glimp's concept carried with it two possible effects — the first due to its historical timing and association and the second due to its own essential definition. It was a double-edged sword. The con-ception equalized a pool of average performers in a Harvard class with no regard to race, ethnicity, or social and economic standing. It gave respectability to the "Harvard gentleman's C" (a status I had maintained as an undergraduate) And Fred and his office articulated the concept in the mid-1960s just as there was some effort to bring in more African-Americans. The concept was often laid out in a context that allowed its direct association with the enrollment of increased numbers of African-Americans.

During the mid-1960s — in the midst of great civil rights activity that for many reasons passed me by — more African-Amer-icans applied and were accepted to Harvard College, both because of recruitment efforts by Harvard and because of the earlier efforts of programs like ABC. One of my colleagues in later years at MIT, noted historian of science Kenneth R. Manning, recalls making his decision to apply to Ivy League schools during a Summer Study Skills Program in Knoxville in 1964. When Manning was accepted to Harvard a couple of years later, his mathematics teacher in the Summer Program, Frederick A. Parker (himself an early African-American graduate of Amherst College and recipient of an honorary doctorate from his *alma mater*), dissuaded him from choosing Yale. In Parker's view, Harvard had a tradition of working at being the best, whereas Yale had over the years assumed itself to be the best. Manning entered Harvard in the fall of 1966, exactly two decades after I had entered. Glimp, as Dean of Admissions amidst profound social and political change nationwide, continued to increase gradually the number of African-American students on the Harvard campus.

When I first took up an administrative position at MIT in 1968, Chase Peterson ('52), a Mormon and member of the Porcellian Club, had already succeeded Glimp as director of admissions, four years before yet another change in the presidential guard — Derek Bok succeeding Nathan Pusey in 1971. Efforts to increase the number of African-American undergraduates proceeded under Peterson's leadership. In the wake of political unrest at Harvard, including the takeover of University Hall in 1969, demands to recruit more blacks and to initiate a program in "black studies" were made by students and acceded to by the faculty and administration. The Committee on Admissions Report in 1968 is the first document in Harvard's history to present data by race. It was in that year that Harvard hired for the first time a black financial aid officer, John Harwell, who was assigned to admissions as well. In the next three years the number of black students doubled in the class, increasing from 4.24% in the class of '72 to 8.68% in the class of '75. African-American enrollment remained at that proportion well into the '80s.

A major concern among Harvard students during the late '60s centered on the lack of opportunity within the University for those interested in studying African-American culture. Black students wanted Harvard to make education more relevant to the experiences of black people, to hire more black faculty, and to increase the number of black students. On April 10, 1968, a few days after the assassination of Dr. Martin Luther King, Jr., the Afro-Am student group took out an advertisement in the *Crimson* issuing four demands to "*Fair* Harvard: 1. Establish an endowed chair for a Black Professor; 2. Establish courses relevant to Blacks at Harvard; 3. Establish more lower level Black Faculty members; 4. Admit a number of Black students proportionate to our percentage of the population as a whole." The demands were consciously linked. Dean Peterson met with Afro-Am to report a dramatic increase in black admissions in the class of '73, but the issue of black studies was a more complicated one involving faculty consideration and action. A committee chaired by Henry Rosovsky was appointed by Pusey to look into the students' demands for offerings in that area. Within months it reported that "the absence of course offering in many areas of Afro-American culture is emphatically a matter of more than academic or pedagogical concern to black students." The report went on to observe that "it seems likely that the absence of such offerings is the single most potent source of the black student's discontent at Harvard." Under the threat of violence from Harvard's African-American students, and with the alarm of a building seizure on the Cornell campus the day before, the Harvard faculty adopted on the evening of April 22, 1969, a proposal for an Afro-American Studies Program.

Concern also continued to focus on the recruitment of black students. Two years later, in 1971, Harvard brought in a black admissions officer, David L. Evans (currently the senior admissions officer), to help with the task of increasing the number of African-American students. The only other black administrator to that point outside of the Admissions Office had been Archie C. Epps, who was promoted to Dean of Students in 1970 after six years as an assistant dean. I witnessed similar concerns and trends regarding black recruitment at MIT.

While Chase Peterson continued to recruit more black students during his tenure, a landmark case was brought by Allen Bakke, a white student who had been denied admission to the University of California's medical school at Davis. The claim was that Bakke's qualifications exceeded those of some African-American students who had been admitted. The question put before the Supreme Court was whether race was a justifiable factor in the medical school admissions process.

When the Bakke Case was filed in 1972, Harvard was in a unique position to file an *amicus* brief using its own admissions practice as a model. The argument put forward was that Harvard's use of race as one of many factors was legitimate and necessary to achieve the overall diversity it sought, and that diversity itself was an asset in the process of young men and women educating one another. But race was only one of several factors or criteria cited, the point being that the admissions process was not a linear one in which a rank ordering was the desired end. Harvard had to assemble a class — somewhat as a director of an orchestra does, selecting the appropriate number of strings, woodwinds, and brass; oboe players always got special consideration. Harvard could make the argument with impunity since it had always been open about its other criteria, including preferences for children of alumni. It did not matter that preferences were often at odds with each other. The preferences for alumni sons, for example, could conflict with the desire to increase the number of African-Americans, since very few of the latter were alumni.

The Bakke Case triggered a concern that I had about the qualifications of incoming African-American students at MIT, and about their performance. In the spring of 1981, MIT's provost asked me to chair a committee to search for a director for the Office of Minority Education, which had been created in 1974. A summer study, directed by me, indicated that black and Latino students were not performing at the level of other students. I believed passionately that such students could perform at a high level, given appropriate support. After all, I had been born and raised on a black college campus where a single standard of excellence was stressed for all. This single standard is particularly important in the natural sciences, hence central to success at an institution like MIT. A little later, I ran into the black psychologist and Harvard alumnus Jeffrey

Howard ('69), who had similar data on a cohort of Harvard students. The same question was being raised at these neighboring universities, albeit in two totally different contexts.

The "gentleman's C" has little or no respect at MIT, whose primary focus on mathematics and science makes admissions data more reliable as predictors of college performance than would be the case in an educational setting not so focused. My concern was to make certain that adequate resources were put in place for an appropriate level of preparedness of admitted students. In no way did I want to retrench from recruitment efforts; I wanted to insure responsible implementation.

My views must be distinguished from those of an African-American professor at Harvard, Martin Kilson, as I understood them. Through his legendary letters to the editor of the *Crimson* in the late '60s and early '70s, Kilson publicly derided black students for their lack of academic performance. The issues seemed complicated and confused, and certainly provoked tensions all around. Kilson often seemed to be arguing against the enrollment of certain African-American students, unless they were Predicted Rank List I. Glimp's notion of bottom quarter for African-Americans was lost on him. I, on the other hand, could care less whether a black student was mediocre as long as the mediocrity blended in with that of non-African-Americans. I had no numerical goals as such for graduation rates for African-Americans, only that their rates be the same as for other groups. This seemed to be difficult to accomplish at MIT with its rigid standard of achievement for everyone.

Harvard's focus on attracting black students [later] developed into a program to draw minority students [of other backgrounds,] including Native Americans, Asians, and Hispanics. As more [and more] minorities entered, Harvard was confronted with the question of whether or not to set up special support entities to address problems of minority groups. Beginning in 1980, a student-faculty committee chaired by Peter J. Gomes, an African-American professor of religion and the first black [and youngest person] to be appointed minister in Memorial Church, was charged to look into the matter. The committee rejected the idea of focusing specifically on minority issues, however defined. Instead it played around with an old idea from the Rosovsky Report (1968) of "third world center," which [subsequently] materialized as the Harvard Foundation. The Foundation embodied a concept that was "more harmonious" with one of Harvard's fundamental principles, that "the responsibility for all students belong, and be understood to belong, to the College's mainstream." In the end, the Harvard Foundation was established as an organization "devoted to the improvement of relations among racial and ethnic groups within the university," rather than [one devoted] exclusively to minority students. Allen Counter, an African-American biologist was selected to run the Center.

My son David entered Harvard College in 1978. He came in the midst of ongoing concerns about recruitment of African-American students and affirmative action. There was no way for him to escape the attention placed on African-American students, or for him to escape the preference for alumni sons —though his own educational achievement, based strictly on quantitative data, would have made him an attractive candidate for admission. Tradition and legacy seem to accrue new dimensions in the context of Harvard.

My son Chris, on the other hand, entered the University of California, Berkeley, in 1985 in a similar atmosphere of efforts to diversify the student population, after having been denied admission to Harvard. While Harvard was perhaps his first choice, Berkeley was so close a second that no feelings of missed opportunities emerged. Chris developed as a person and a scholar on leaving the East Coast, away from family, on his own path to academic and personal independence. His later admission to the Harvard Business School may have been in part a way for him to connect with his brother (who had recently graduated) and me. Race, diversity, and excellence have been part of their legacy.

When Neil Rudenstine succeeded Derek Bok as president in 1991, African-American students were being admitted at a steady rate to the undergraduate level, even though many issues of affirmative action remained unsolved at the graduate and faculty levels. Both presidents had occasion to reflect deeply on the issues — Rudenstine, for example, selected "Diversity and Learning" as the focus of his President's Report (1993–1995), and Bok co-authored with William G. Bowen, former President of Princeton University, a study entitled *The Shape of the River: Long-Term Consequences of Considering Race in College and University Admissions* (Princeton: Princeton University Press, 1998). Also during the 1990s, Harvard Law School professor Derrick Bell protested at the small number of African-Americans on the law faculty. Faculty development became paramount throughout the University, but with not much success in my opinion. Intense publicity surrounded the appointment of Henry Louis Gates, Jr., as head of the Afro-American Studies Department and director of the DuBois Institute. The high-profile and entrepreneurial activities of Gates have raised as many questions as they have answered for many in the black community, especially about Harvard's commitment to real and viable scholarship in the area of Afro-American studies. A colleague at MIT, for example, in a recent op-ed piece, called to task Gates, Cornel West (one of the first black university professors), and the Harvard administration for making what he considered to be a mockery of a serious, scholarly field. Perhaps in time Gates will find an appropriate balance between scholarship and entrepreneurship. When that happens, dignity will accrue to those idealistic goals that African-American students espoused in the '60s and that few of us could plausibly hope for in the '40s.

The new millennium finds Harvard in a good position to utilize its resources, financial and otherwise, to help solve not only its own racial problems but those of the country as well. Harvard should lead the world in black faculty recruitment outside of the area of African-American studies. The Harvard faculty needs blacks in science and mathematics, Judaic Studies, and anthropology, for example. When the entire community of faculty, students, alumni/ae, and administrators feels equally at home on the steps of Widener looking toward Memorial Church, then we shall have made ourselves whole as a community. I expect it to happen sooner rather than later, and certainly before another fifty years have passed.

THE WORLD ECONOMY

Convergence and Conflict

George C. Lodge

GLOBAL CRISIS

The dawn of 1999 revealed a most fragile world. Treasury Secretary Robert Rubin warned that we were facing "the most serious financial disruption of the last fifty years." He along with Alan Greenspan, the governments of the seven leading industrial countries (the G-7), the International Monetary Fund (IMF), and the World Bank were trying to prevent a downward spiral into global depression.

During the past two decades a host of financial firms — commercial banks, investment banks, and hedge funds — had invested trillions in the so-called "emerging markets" of Indonesia, Thailand, Malaysia, South Korea, Russia, Brazil, and India. They sought big profits. Guided by the best and brightest financial wizards, whose computer-based models promised to quantify and diversify their risks, they could swiftly shift funds here and there with the flick of a switch. Some were attracted by the high interest rates offered by the poor countries; others saw gain in minute fluctuations of currency values and bond prices. If the past was "the age of innocence," one financier told the *New York Times*, the techniques of the future heralded "the age of excitement." And there seemed to be plenty to go around.

The world's stock of liquid financial assets had grown from $10.7 trillion in 1980 to an estimated eight times that or close to $80 trillion in 1998 (J. Fraser, in the International Finance Corporation *Impact,* Winter 1998). International bank loans more than quadrupled during the 1980s, and cross-border stockholding had doubled. Capital flows to "emerging markets" from G-7 banks and institutional investors increased five-fold from $40 billion in 1990 to more than $200 billion in 1996. Much of this was fast money, portfolio investment that could leave a country as quickly as it had arrived. By the mid-1990s foreign exchange trading totaled more than $1.2 trillion a day.

When things went sour, investors wanted their money back. The fear was that there wasn't enough. Suppliers of capital hunkered down to weather the storm and nervous investors ran for cover, searching for quality. Credit dried up in spite of soaring interest rates. As demand for goods and services declined, markets eroded and commodity prices fell — the price of a barrel of oil imported into the United States went from about $20 to $11. At the same time cheap exports from the ailing nations threatened the markets of the more prosperous. Competitive currency devaluations and protective tariffs were in the offing. In a speech at Rice University in 1998, Lee Kuan Yew, founder, former ruler, and currently senior minister of Singapore, quoted Charles Kindleberger's history of the Great Depression: "When every country turned to protect its national private interest, the world public interest went down the drain, and with it the private interests of all." The crisis, said Lee, whom Henry Kissinger called the world's smartest man, had raised "fundamental and complex issues about the architecture of the global financial system." He urged the United States to provide "enlightened intellectual leadership to address these issues."

Unfortunately, the United States itself was vulnerable. A $6 trillion public debt — stemming largely from President Reagan's breathtaking 1981 tax cut — scarcely any domestic savings, and twenty-five years of trade deficits had made our country the world's largest debtor. Japan and China were our largest creditors. What if they decided to put their vast holdings of dollars, earned from exports to the United States, elsewhere? And what if the United States was unable or unwilling to absorb the world's exports? U.S. companies were the most innovative and successful in the world, but many firms manufactured abroad; close to half of U.S. imports were from overseas subsidiaries of U.S. companies. So our companies were doing fine but what about the country? Some benefited from the soaring stock market, but real hourly wages were below where they had been in 1973. The gap between rich and poor was greater than at any time since World War II, and it was growing. Our education system was far behind that of our global competitors. To be sure, we retained a certain global preeminence as the world's largest economy, a reminder of what we could do as a nation if we had a purpose. But our military exploits, such as the Gulf War, depended substantially on the willingness of other countries to pay the bill.

What did the financial crisis of 1997–1998 signify? There is not space here to go into the long list of factors, but in general the ailing countries had borrowed too much, more in fact than they needed. Many had plenty of domestic savings; they were investing more than enough; they were running at or near full capacity. But they had been urged by Western economists in the IMF, the World Bank, and the finance ministries of the G-7 countries to open up their capital accounts and liberalize and deregulate their financial systems in order to reap the full benefits of a free capital market. Having done so, the lure of easy access to foreign funds was irresistible.

Perhaps it is worth noting that China sailed through the Asian storm with a sustained growth rate of roughly 8%, and a $40 billion dollar trade surplus with the United States. It resisted Western advice and actually tightened its capital controls in 1998, allowing its currency to be convertible only for trade and tourism. Hedge funds were not welcome. With $600 billion in household savings and more than $100 billion of foreign exchange reserves, China is destined within a decade or so to pass the United States and become the world's number one economic power. (The Central Intelligence Agency has estimated that China's gross domestic product will be $20 trillion in 2020 compared to $13.5 trillion for the United States.)

WHO'S IN CHARGE?

Gobalization has hit the world economy full force. The world's six billion people find themselves hooked by a degree of interdependence unimaginable in 1950. It is not just the flows of money. Trade and foreign direct investment have also soared, driven by communications technology and the intensification of global competition. (For example, in the past thirty years imports to the United States have grown from 5% of our gross domestic product to more than 15%.) And while capital moves easily, labor does not. So there is pain as well as gain, winners and losers among and within nations. (In the early 1990s, some 8,000 U.S. software engineering jobs moved to Bangalore, India, where labor costs even among the highly educated were a fraction of those in the U.S. The move was made possible by the Internet.) Globalization is also forced by a growing consciousness of environmental degradation: air, water, and the ozone shield transcend earthly boundaries.

Nations that can save, invest, and compete in the world economy — for example, Japan, Singapore, China, and Germany — retain substantial control of their destiny, although even they are dependent on world markets for the sale of their exports. Other nations must borrow and obey the rules of the lenders. When they can no longer borrow, the IMF moves in with its rules, which go to the very vitals of sovereignty. Mexico, for instance, had to abandon the promises of its revolution and welcome foreign ownership of its assets as well as commercializing the cooperatives (*ejidos*) Zapata had promised the peasants. Civil strife ensued. In Asia the IMF strictures were so severe they caused recession, unemployment, and violence. And unfortunately, while the IMF may temporarily restore the confidence of private investors in troubled economies, it does nothing to change fundamentally sick systems such as those of Mexico, Brazil, Russia, and Indonesia.

Who is running the world economy then? Increasingly it is a combination of multinational corporations, banks, and traders together with multilateral institutions like the IMF, World Bank, and the World Trade Organization. It may look like a conspiracy but it is more chaotic, although the decision-makers are mostly from the big seven industrial countries and, one must assume, are mindful of the group's interests. Whatever the advances made in the world economy under this leadership — and they have been considerable as trade and investment data show — there have also been failures. The financial debacle of the late 1990s is an indicator of such failure. Another is the astronomical escalation of world debt and more especially the burden of debt service that stifles the growth of so many developing countries. Brazil, for example, has a foreign debt of $240 billion and Mexico $120 billion. Africa south of the Sahara is submerged in a sea of debt. While it is hard to imagine that this will ever be paid off, just the interest payments cripple the ability of these economies to grow and to export. And, of course, unless their exports are greater than their imports these countries cannot earn the dollars that are required to pay the interest. It's a vicious circle and at the center are systemic defects that prevent the economy from operating effectively. There are many measures of such defects: low productivity, unemployment, corruption, illiteracy, gaps between rich and poor, and perhaps most of all, poverty.

The reduction of poverty is the stated aim of the World Bank and a host of development banks and governmental agencies. Although the bank has loaned more than $300 billion since its birth in 1945, more than a billion people are poor, living on less than $1 a day. Indeed, poverty in the world today may well exceed what it was fifty years ago. So whatever else globalization may have done, it has not reduced poverty.

This sketch of the world economy in 1999 reveals two central questions. The first concerns governance: How will the world govern itself to diminish the waste and suffering of financial crises and disasters — environmental, political, and social? What sort of institutional mechanisms are needed to augment or replace those that exist? The second concerns poverty reduction: What procedures will produce the changes that are necessary for "emerging" countries/communities to make the most of their capacities? I shall examine these questions later in the light of my own experience.

LOOKING BACKWARD

In June 1950, the embryo of some of what came to pass was discernible. Secretary of State Dean Acheson, who gave the Commencement address at Harvard that year, was shaping what became the North Atlantic Treaty Organization to combat Soviet imperialism. He reported that $10 billion had been spent under the Marshall Plan, begun three years earlier, to rescue Europe from economic collapse. At the same time, the *New York Times* in a series of six front-page articles reported a vast Communist operation to gain control of Central America. Six European nations merged their coal and steel production under a new, transnational authority. It was, according to the authority, "the first move to European unity." (Britain was "hesitant.") Harvard's President James B. Conant advocated two-year "community colleges." And the Supreme Court struck down barriers separating races in railroad dining cars.

In many ways, however, we in June 1950 could not have imagined today. (Some statistical comparisons are given in the Appendix.) So it is that we have been routinely surprised principally for two reasons: the explosion of technology and our ignorance of most of the world. As the century turns, we are thus in a kind of techno shock, victims of unpredictable innovation, breathlessly trying to cope. We cannot manage what we don't understand and understanding takes time, of which technology ruthlessly deprives us. A computer fifty years ago was an inscrutable oddity the size of a room, aglow with vacuum tubes. And in 1950 one could easily go through Harvard College, as I did, without hearing a word about Asia — or Africa, or indeed much about Latin America. We had defeated Japan in war and thought, I suppose, that that was that. Knowledge of the nether world came via the Cold War, a questionable teacher, as Vietnam was to show.

We might, of course, have read the seers who foresaw globalization long before the economists or anyone else. Perhaps the greatest of them was the French paleontologist and theologian, Pierre Teilhard de Chardin. More than fifty years ago he wrote: "Nothing, absolutely nothing — we may as well make up our minds to it — can arrest the progress of social Man towards ever greater interdependence and cohesion. . . . It would be easier, at the stage of evolution we have reached, to prevent the earth from revolving than to prevent mankind from becoming totalized." Long before the Internet was even imagined, Teilhard spoke of the "thinking layer of the earth," a "thinking envelope," a "collective global energy." He called it the Noosphere, and attributed this "phenomenon of growing consciousness on earth . . . to the increasingly advanced organization of more and more complicated elements."

Teilhard was an optimist; he saw virtue in convergence. Vaclev Havel in his 1995 speech at Harvard's Commencement saw conflict. He spoke of Teilhard's globalization as a "thin veneer" forcing interdependence even as it exacerbated tensions in the world's "underside," among cultures, religions, tribes, traditions, and nations. "Every valley cries out for its own interdependence or will even fight for it." And Teilhard's "global energy" includes MTV broadcasting *Beavis and Butthead* from Hong Kong to 200,000 Indian households. The Minister of Culture was dismayed but what could he do?

LEGITIMACY

Prickly problems of legitimacy arise as we think about how to minimize conflict in the face of inevitable convergence, and confront the challenges of governance and systemic change mentioned above. Proceeding down this path, I had better follow the advice of those who kindly invited me to prepare this essay — "make it personal" — and say a brief word about my own legitimacy so that you may know, so to speak, where I am coming from, especially since my qualifications for this task are unorthodox to say the least.

I am not an economist. Indeed, academically speaking, I am nothing. When I was chosen by the Harvard Business School faculty to be a tenured professor in 1971, I had no Ph.D. — not even a master's degree — and still do not. In fact, I think I am the only such creature, at least in recent times. My lack of what in academia is called a "discipline" has in all frankness been no handicap. It has allowed me to seek a holistic way to view the world, which I enthusiastically recommend to others.

As perhaps some of my classmates will remember, I left Harvard with a debilitating stutter, which had resisted numerous therapies ("You must relax," the doctor shouted.) I was convinced — quite happily — that my career lay in writing; not fancy writing, at which I was never very good, but journalism, reporting what was going on in the world around me. At first it was the Massachusetts State House, which in retrospect was a good place to start a quest for understanding how the world worked. A chance interview with the Secretary of Labor in President Eisenhower's Cabinet took me to Washington as a speechwriter. Not long after, by luck and good fortune, at the age of twenty-nine I found myself Assistant Secretary of Labor for International Affairs, a post that entailed leading the United States delegation to the International Labor Organization (ILO) conferences in Geneva and lambasting the Soviet Union for their forced labor camps, knowledge of which was coming to the West through the ILO. When Secretary James P. Mitchell told me of his intention to appoint me assistant secretary, I questioned his judgment: my stutter had persisted, and I doubted that I could lead "the free world" against the forces of evil if I couldn't speak. He disregarded my caution and oddly enough my stutter succumbed to trauma: I had to confront one of the USSR's more formidable debaters, Amazasp Arutiunian, in front of representatives from 120 countries in the awesome Palais des Nations. (He turned out to be an amusing fellow with whom I played chess while consuming his excellent vodka. He later went on to become ambassador to Canada, where he organized the Soviets' North American spy ring.)

My job also included traveling the world, studying the role of trade unions, especially in Asia, Africa, and Latin America, where they were prime targets of Soviet subversion and, therefore, deserving of U.S. protection. The late 1950s saw the emergence from colonialism of scores of new countries in Africa and Asia. Trade unions were virtually the only political organizations the colonial powers had allowed to exist (Lee Kuan Yew was a leader of Singapore's port workers), and so with independence they were in the driver's seat. Through their eyes I began to see the problems of "development."

President Kennedy reappointed me to my job but, now that I could speak, a host of career possibilities beckoned. While I was writing a book on the role of unions in developing countries, Dean Teele of the Harvard Business School invited me to come there to finish the book and give some lectures. It was understood that I would leave soon to run for the U.S. Senate in 1962.

I knew nothing about business, not even what the initials "MBA" stood for, but the surroundings were beautiful and I had never met such a bright collection of people. So, after Ted Kennedy defeated me, I returned, supposing, ridiculously, that if I had been hired once I would be hired again. But the deans had changed. George P. Baker was in charge. He was not particularly glad to see me, but he was a kind person and offered me a one (stress one) year appointment. Half the time I would teach — neither he nor I knew exactly what — and the other half was to be devoted to spreading the light of Harvard in the developing world. Remember, these were the Kennedy years. There was no problem the United States — with Harvard's help — could not solve.

Walt Rostow was the head of policy planning at the State Department. I had come to know him in Washington through discussions of his magnum opus *The Stages of Economic Growth*. So I told him about Harvard's desire to help and he suggested Latin America, where the Alliance for Progress was in full swing. We were going to turn the hemisphere, or at least the southern part of it, into a vast "crucible of revolutionary reform." The prospect was thrilling, and in 1964 I found myself leading a multi-million dollar Harvard project to help establish a graduate school of management to serve the six countries of Central America. (It was called INCAE, the Central American Institute of Business Administration, now well established with two campuses in Managua, Nicaragua, and San Jose, Costa Rica.) My yearly appointments continued and Dean Baker became a dear friend and supporter.

I was administering millions of USAID dollars. Teams of case writers had fanned out around Central America to prepare the teaching material for the new school. My particular interest was the development process, which, I thought, future managers of the region needed to understand. In spite of the good work of Rostow, Sam Huntington, and others, there were, it seemed to me, large gaps in our understanding. Hence I was looking for a way to learn about it.

"DEVELOPMENT" AS CHANGE

"Development" then and, for many, even now, was assumed to be an economic process, supervised — naturally — by economists. This conception led to the dangerously misleading notion that it could be nonpolitical and was, therefore, noncontroversial. (The World Bank's charter indeed stipulates that its mission is economic development, and that it is to be strictly nonpolitical.) Who, after all, could be against economic development? But, as I had observed it, development to the extent it existed was in fact change and in most places radical change: a permanent, irreversible reallocation of power to reduce poverty and increase political participation. This was the glorious promise of the Alliance — reform of land ownership, taxes, credit, markets, and more. But, of course, if this was development, it was intensely controversial, and perhaps its least significant aspect was economic; it was political, social, cultural, and psychological. Who was changing whom? For what purpose? In whose interest? At what speed? Did the status quo welcome change or would they fight it tooth and nail?

Not only did real development — that is, radical change — make it highly controversial, it also made it profoundly destabilizing. In the Cold War days the importance of stability generally eclipsed the desire for change. Thus there was tension between what the United States and its agents such as the World Bank preached and what they practiced. There was the pretense that channeling resources to governments would somehow trickle down to produce systemic change and reduce poverty. It was a massive deception. Any government opposed to the USSR was labeled democratic or at least a friend of democracy. Assistance granted for ostensibly good purposes such as education, health, or better roads rarely changed anything. What it did do was strengthen the status quo, enlarging the obstacles to the very process true development required. (Unfortunately, this pretension persists even today long after the Soviet Union has expired.)

In 1964, I wanted to learn about the introduction of change. It seemed to me that INCAE needed to know how to do it. Since I was in charge of INCAE's research, funds were not a problem, but I needed a place, an environment that was typical of the developing world, the poor world, and where I could study how to change it. The opportunity came from an unlikely source.

One night I was at a dinner party in Panama City given by Fernando Eleta, an affluent businessman and staunch supporter of INCAE. It was hot and we had both quenched our thirsts with large quantities of gin. After the guests left, with great generosity he asked me what he could do to help Harvard's effort. I told him about what I wanted to do. He had just the place, he said, Veraguas Province, Panama. His father had bought it thinking it contained gold. It didn't. His rent collectors were routinely beaten up. Cuban guerrillas landed on its uninhabited Caribbean beaches handing out transistor radios beamed in on Havana. It was mine, he said, and furthermore a friend of his, Marcos McGrath, a brilliant young leader of the reform wing of the Roman Catholic Church, was about to become the new Bishop of Veraguas. He had asked the Vatican for it because he had ideas about how to change it.

ENGINE OF CHANGE

Veraguas was a remote province, about the size of metropolitan Boston with a population of 150,000 and located 150 miles west of Panama City. As in much of the rural world, its people had little sense of belonging to a nation. It was the seat of power of two or three families who owned most of the fertile land and it had languished in unproductivity and poverty since Columbus discovered it. He was, in fact, the first Duke of Veraguas.

There is no space here to go into detail about the three years during which my students and I observed and helped the bishop, his priests, and his band of young laymen. They established forty cooperatives for purposes of increasing production and improving the credit and marketing positions of the *campesinos;* an overall multiservice cooperative organization; vocational training schools; a radio station; and a training center for leaders of the cooperatives.

The bishop's movement was an engine of change. Because of it several thousand families moved from a system in which they had no ability to cause change into a system of their own creation in which they had some control. They owned land. They had their own market and thus the notion of a "free market" meant something. They had access to credit, because they created their own cooperative which gave them some financial power. They were motivated. For the first time they knew the value of education; there was indeed a ladder out there which a young person with schooling could climb and gain power and influence over his or her surroundings. They built their own school and hired a teacher who taught what needed to be taught — how to fix refrigerators. They were organized. They had leaders. When the leaders said boil the water, they boiled it, and dysentery was alleviated. Health, it turned out, was not a medical problem. It was a political and organizational problem. In fact, experts who failed to understand the system within which Veraguas' peasants lived were a menace. They made things worse. A seed specialist had told a subsistence farmer to plant tomatoes. He did and they flourished to such an extent that the landowner on the hill decided to extend his fences to include the land which he had previously thought worthless.

The Veraguas movement introduced change. To those involved it was revolutionary change. Two priests were killed in the revolution. The status quo retaliated. But to an outsider the change seemed modest indeed. It was slow, difficult, and always tenuous. Not only was the government of no help, it was a major obstacle. Panama in those years received more U.S. aid per capita than any other country, but if the aid showed up in Veraguas at all it was in the form of technical experts who had no understanding of the system they were entering — or National Guard troops.

At the end of our project in Veraguas my students and I wondered what had been accomplished. Was it progress? Cash wages had risen, but young women now had radios that informed them of the wonders of urban life. Many left to take up a life of prostitution. Subsistence farming had given way to commercial farms which, while more efficient, made individuals in some ways more dependent. We concluded that perhaps the most promising change was political or psychological in nature. The people involved in the bishop's movement believed that they could shape their lives and their children's lives for the better. Eventually some sort of truly democratic government, based on broad consensus, might come to Panama. That would be the day the country would be able to compete in the world, making full use of its resources.

As we observed what had occurred in Veraguas, a doctrine about the introduction of change there and in other places like it emerged:

> The setting into which the change is to be introduced must be viewed as a whole, a circle of inter-related elements which are social, political, economic, cultural, physical, and psychological.
>
> An engine of change, such as the bishop's movement, must be able to use the solution of one problem on the circle — say access to credit — to open the way

to solutions of other problems — health or education, for example.

A successful engine of change follows a sequence of action beginning with agitation, meaning education about a precise need which is relatively easy to meet; confidence then encourages motivation which leads to organization and finally a commitment to a new way.

It also has certain characteristics: authority — when the leader (the bishop and his agents for instance) speaks, he or she must be listened to and believed; communication — the ability to reach the most remote person you are trying to affect; access to power; the ability to protect the change process from the status quo; and competence — that is, skills that vary as the change process proceeds. At first charisma may be important; later accounting. The bishop's movement eventually gained a radio station, which required highly sophisticated skills.

The injection of resources that fall outside an engine of change (i.e., the tomato seeds) does not promote change; it invariably retards it.

In the province next to Veraguas, the Nestlé company had started a powdered milk operation involving several thousand peasants. Its effect was very much the same as that of the bishop's movement, but it generated profits. There isn't enough church, charity, or tax money to introduce the change the world needs; that is why business is so crucial to the development process, and especially business related to agriculture and the development of the countryside, including not only food and food processing but also transportation, energy, and communications.

In 1971 I helped to create the Inter-American Foundation, a new government agency, designed to find and fuel engines of change in Latin America. With a staff of fewer than 100 it made small, quick grants to peasant cooperatives and other engines of change. It has been essentially trouble-free and has reduced a lot of poverty.

Veraguas is in many ways a microcosm of the poor world, whether in northeastern Brazil, rural India, southern Africa. or the depressed neighborhoods of American cities. Systemic change is required to make these regions competitive with the rest of the world and minimize the negative effects of global convergence. Where such systemic change is required, governments are not usually helpful, since they derive their support from the status quo. But they can be useful in subtle ways.

In the early days of the IAF a request for an organizing grant came from the coffee plantation workers in Colombia. Although not required to do so by the legislation establishing the foundation, we checked with the U.S. Ambassador in Bogota. He thought it unwise to proceed. We paid a visit to the country's president, Carlos Lleras Restrepo, a friend of the foundation's president. In his thoughtful way he said that if we made the grant (which was for about $100,000) he would write a letter to the ambassador complaining about inappropriate intervention. He would send a copy of the letter to the coffee growers. The ambassador would write the IAF expressing outrage and would send a copy of that letter to the president, who would forward it to the growers. "But you will have already made the grant," said Carlos Lleras with a smile, "and I urge you to go ahead and do it. If that union doesn't organize our countryside, others far worse will."

OTHER ASPECTS OF POVERTY REDUCTION

"Let me make a categorical prediction," Harvard's Jeffrey Sachs wrote in the November 5, 1998, *Financial Times*. "Until the poor are brought into the international financial system with real power, the global economy cannot be stable for long. The G-7 countries plus the rest of the European Union represent a mere 14% of the world's population. Yet these countries have 56% of the votes in the IMF executive board."

What he meant by "the poor," I believe, are those nations in which poverty is a part of the social, political, and economic system, in fact caused by that system. He was talking about Russia and ex-Soviet countries like Ukraine and Kazakstan — where an old system collapsed and a new one is unformed — most Latin American countries, much of Africa, and, in Asia, countries like Indonesia. IMF and World Bank loans to such countries may buy time in the short run by giving confidence to investors to follow with more money, but they solve little and the loans increase the country's already heavy burden of debt.

Does that mean that the IMF and the World Bank should be abandoned? No, but they need to be redesigned so as to focus on solving problems rather than merely lending money. The conditions that the IMF imposes on a country, furthermore, often worsen the country's problems. Take the case of Brazil which, in December 1998, was on the edge of financial collapse. The IMF put together a $41.5 billion loan package, hoping to cause foreign investors, who had fled the country fearing a collapse of the currency, to return. Brazil promised to reduce government expenditures, maintain the value of the currency, and take other stringent measures that were likely to produce a prolonged recession. The IMF's prescriptions will not stimulate Brazil's exports. They will not make Brazil more competitive in the world economy, able to earn the foreign exchange it needs to service its debts.

It will require massive improvement in Brazil's education system to produce the skilled workers required to raise productivity and make the country's industry competitive. The abysmal levels of education, however, do not result so much from a lack of schools and teachers as they do from the fact that 50% of the country's people live in poverty, trapped in a system in which change is impossible or seen as so dangerous it is to be avoided. In such a situation education appears to be irrelevant. Brazil's president, Fernando Henrique Cardoso, was right when he said : "Brazil is not an underdeveloped country; it is an unjust one."

The engines of change required to restructure Brazil's system are at work. They are Brazilian and multinational firms, running their own educational programs and drawing young men and women out of poverty into jobs. But they are too few and their efforts are too small.

I believe that the IMF and the World Bank should be augmented by a World Development Corporation (WDC), chartered by the Bank and composed of managers from a spectrum of multinational corporations. It could bring to bear the range of competencies required to develop such places as rural Brazil, especially the poverty-stricken northeast. These competencies, as I have mentioned, include agriculture and related industries, and also access to world product and credit markets and the latest technology. At first the WDC would need to be subsidized, but eventually it should return a profit; and virtually any amount of subsidy would be more worthwhile than current practices that frequently put money down a rat hole. I proposed a WDC to the World Bank's president, James Wolfensohn, without success.

Recently I was sent by the World Bank to Kazakstan. (In spite of my disagreements with the Bank, there are those in it who agree with me.) My job was to assist the brilliant young minister of planning, Erzhan Utembaev, to draft an economic strategy for the country. Kazakstan is huge — five times the size of France — with a dwindling population of seventeen million. In the Soviet days it was prosperous, sustained by a vast network of weapons factories and Soviet space program installations. It has immense resources of minerals; as much oil as Kuwait. Foreign companies were quick to move to exploit the country's resources. But 80% of the people live in the countryside. Since independence in 1991, they have moved into abject poverty. The country's wealth has not reached them.

In the Soviet days the rural people worked gigantic farms, producing wheat and other grains. Sustained by $10 billion a year of subsidies from the USSR, these collectives also provided schools, health facilities, and other social services. When the subsidies stopped, the collectives collapsed. Advice from the West was typical: break up the collectives; introduce property rights; provide farmers with their own farms; let them sell in the free market; and competition among them will insure the best results. The only problem was reality. For three generations the farmers had lived in a system that provided cradle-to-grave security. It was neither efficient nor free, but it was safe. Roads and electric power served the old collectives, not the small holdings. There were no markets to speak of; nor was there credit to allow the farmers to buy seed, fertilizer, and equipment.

When I told Utembaev and his staff that the advice from the West was inconsistent with its practice, he was shocked. United States agriculture, the wonder of the world, I pointed out, had been heavily subsidized, assisted, and protected at every turn by government. The same of course was true for Europe. So here Kazakstan had been told to employ an ideology that the West fervently preached but had not practiced for years. Assistance funds to the Ministry of Agriculture and its technicians were pointless. What was needed was a total integrated systemic change, and that is what a World Development Corporation should be doing. The last I heard, starvation was rampant in the Kazak countryside, even as a handful of entrepreneurs and government officials became super-rich selling the country's minerals.

LOOKING FORWARD: MANAGING VOLATILITY AND CONFLICT

Kazakstan and countries like it cannot withdraw from the world and they cannot make it on their own. As globalization forces converge, it will cause conflict unless ways can be found to integrate such countries into the world economy. It will take time and care and will require realism — not ideological dogma. The IMF and the World Bank advised Kazakstan to practice free trade: lower tariff barriers and let international competition force change. Overnight the local textile industry, a major source of employment, was wiped out. We should learn from China the value of a gradual approach to systemic change, especially when moving out of an authoritarian system.

A troubled world greets the twenty-first century. Japan, which was the miracle economy of the post-war years, saw its gross domestic product shrink 2.5% in 1998. But Western pessimism about Japan is misplaced. It is the world's second largest economy with the highest GDP per capita. Its education system is second to none;

income is relatively equally distributed; the Japanese consensus holds. It will recover. But in the meantime other Asian economies that depend on a bouyant Japan flounder. Indonesia, with close to 200 million people, will be a major trouble spot. And South Korea is in deep recession in 1999.

Russia, Brazil, and India have all suffered severe economic declines and have major weaknesses. Mexico, also, is in trouble. Being next to the United States is a mixed blessing. We prevent the crisis the country may need for its reformation because it would be too dangerous for us, but we tolerate the awesome power of its drug criminals.

Given the interdependence of the world's economies, failure in one tends to spread to others. Some have argued that competition in a "free market" is the best way to solve the problems of instability and conflict that beset the world today; we don't need more government, international or otherwise. Although conceptually they may be right, realistically they are whistling in the dark, for several reasons:

> Markets are never completely free; they are managed by those with the political and economic power to do so. For example, sugar, tobacco, peanuts, and textiles are among the many products that benefit from U.S. tariffs and quotas.

> For the poor there often is no market at all and those that exist are designed to benefit the rich.

> There are mounting environmental demands that cannot be met by the satisfaction of consumer desires in the market place.

The financial contagion revealed in the global effects of the Asian crisis will require governmental control. To design this control we need to understand the contagion's causes. They are:

> Investors made nervous about one country naturally have their suspicions heightened about other

countries regardless of the differences that may exist among them. In 1994 when the Mexican peso fell, Bombay had to close its stock exchange. Irrational as it may be, that's the way the world works.

As long as world economic conditions are good, investors are not so careful, but when country after country becomes unable to pay its debts, they are less willing to take risks.

As the amount of debt increases, credit becomes less available. There is thus a perceived shortage of capital and investors become more careful.

Countries that are heavily dependent on trade may devalue their currency to make exports more competitive with those of other countries that have devalued. This makes for a cycle of devaluation which carries with it the threat that investors will withdraw their money in anticipation of devaluation, thus actually causing it.

Investors worry that the IMF and other official lenders will run out of money and thus there will be no safety net to support them in the time of trouble.

These factors suggest steps that should be taken to reduce the volatility of globalization. These include:

Strengthening and augmenting the IMF so that it can identify and diagnose problems early. Especially it needs accurate and complete information that it lacks today. Balance of payments data in many countries is grossly inaccurate; definitions of "foreign investment" differ widely among countries; and investment companies like Long Term Capital Management, which threaten global stability, keep their secrets locked up in the Cayman Islands; if a U.S. government inspector tried to look at them, he would be arrested.

Greater discernment by the IMF of the differences

among the nations upon which it imposes its conditions for assistance. The one-size-fits-all free market, balanced budget dogma was a disaster in Korea, where budgets were already near balance. Calling for high interest rates in countries with high levels of indebtedness and no inflation, as was the case in several of the Asian nations, was disastrously deflationary.

Increased regulation to control capital flows either by governments — national or international — or by industry groups.

To deal with the more profound and long-term problems that afflict a number of nations, the proposed World Development Corporation should work in close cooperation with leading corporations from different countries, including Japan, China, Germany, Britain, and the United States.

The evolving global information infrastructure (GII) contains many points of friction: cultural questions, access to markets, privacy matters, and issues concerning security, monopolization, and control. The GII is composed of the melding of many national information infrastructures, each of which is rooted in a century or more of tradition and ideology. How the melding will come out, nobody knows. Some say, let the market decide; but if history is any indicator there will be community needs that the market fails to meet. National governments are increasingly powerless to control modern information technology. The World Trade Organization and the International Telecommunications Union are trying, but one could hope that industry groups such as the GII Commission, made up of the heads of leading firms in the communications industry, might devise rules and standards so as to avoid or minimize conflict. In doing so they would be following the good example of the chemical and timber industries which, under the gun of government regulations and environmental pressure groups, have developed cooperative ways to set standards and police their membership.

NATIONAL STRATEGIES FOR GLOBAL COMPETITIVENESS

As global governments become more important, national governments will resent the erosion of their power, and people will want
to reshape their political structures. We have already seen the birth
of many new nations, and more are in the offing. With benefits from
old borders declining, these localities look for ways to preserve what
they cherish. At the same time, regions like Europe are coming
together, not because they want to particularly, but because they
know they cannot compete in the world economy unless they do.
So even as global government becomes more important, nations,
albeit often with new borders, will continue to play a critical role.
Their economic strategies and the structures that support and
implement those strategies will shape the world.

I believe that those strategies and structures will converge, but
toward what design will the convergence be aimed? What shapes
will it take? Around what set of beliefs or values will it coalesce? It
seems to me pretty obvious that those national strategies and structures that are most competitive in the world economy, and thus best
able to produce a rising standard of living for that nation's people,
will drive out those which are less competitive.

We can perceive trends today that will shape the next century.
We can identify some inevitabilities, old ways being replaced by
new ones that work more efficiently. Let me emphasize that there
is nothing particularly good — or bad — about these transitions.
Their impact on morality will depend on how they are managed.
Here is a brief and partial list.

First, let us begin with a bit of theory. Many economists still
adhere to the thought of David Ricardo who, in the early nineteenth century, proposed the idea that the place of a nation in the
world economy was properly determined by free trade among individual firms in an open marketplace. The relative position of each
nation was determined by its "comparative advantage," that with
which nature had endowed it. Portugal, the textbook example
went, would properly grow grapes because God had blessed it with

sunshine; England would raise sheep and make textiles. Government's role was to stay very much on the sidelines, blowing the whistle now and again, but not intervening. This was, of course, a great idea for the British (Ricardo was an Englishmen) since textiles were the high value-added, high profit industry of the day. It was not so good for the Portuguese.

The fact is that successful developing countries — the United States in the nineteenth and early twentieth centuries, Korea, Taiwan, Japan, China, and more — all violated the rule. They were unwilling to allow their standard of living to be determined by their resources or lack of them. They used government policies, including trade policies, to create advantage. High tariff walls permitted the development of large, efficient companies that could compete in the world. Once a nation gets to that stage, it naturally wants other nations to practice free trade. It is, of course, quite true that in many countries such protection nourishes inefficiency and is unwise, but in others it can be an effective component of a global competitive strategy. Other components include high rates of savings and investment in export-oriented industries; topnotch education; relative equality of incomes so that pain and gain are fairly shared; a high degree of consensus about the purposes of the nation; and a conception of business that focuses on the needs of the community. Successful economies also have a close, although preferably not collusive or corrupt, relationship between government and business. Examples are Japan and Korea in the 1960s and 1970s; Singapore, Taiwan, and the United States — the Department of Defense — in computers and other high-tech sectors from the 1960s to the end of the Cold War in 1989.

This is not a prediction of protectionism of the sort that worried Kindleberger, but it suggests in all realism that discreet forms of protection, connected to competitive goals and effective policies, are and will be components of national development strategies.

Government policies that support commercial competitiveness can also raise a nation's standard of living. They may not be necessary for spectacular successes by individual firms like

Microsoft, but they may be helpful in insuring that the nation benefits from commercial activity as much as shareholders.

This raises the second set of issues, having to do with property rights. Property rights, according to traditional American ideology, were semi-sacred in that they were held to be "natural," that
is, coming from God. The principal role of government was to protect them. From this notion came the peculiar importance attached
to shareholders as property owners. The purpose of business was
to satisfy the owners. But in the case of large, publicly held corporations those "owners" turned out often to be a fickle lot
who insisted upon quick returns whatever the effects might be on
the long-run fortunes of the company and its employees, or on the
country.

Then, too, these "owners" invariably were really not owners at
all but rather investors who cared little for **their** company. If it did-
n't satisfy their earnings desires, they did not try to fix the company.
They shifted to another one.

In the rest of the world, particularly in Asia, this conception of
property rights is regarded as strange indeed. In the first place, for
Asians property rights are one of a number of rights of membership in the community. (Others include income, health, safety, and
employment.) And they are shaped and constrained by the needs of
the community. Indeed, even in America today property rights are
not what they used to be. They have been infringed upon by environmental strictures as well as a host of other regulations. Thus, in
the future we can expect property rights to be increasingly uncertain and subject to the needs of different communities.

This has obvious implications for the legitimacy of the corporation in different settings and for the sources of authority of its
managers. The purpose of corporations in most of the world is far
more closely related to the needs of their home communities than
in the United States. Recently this may have been a competitive
advantage for American companies but over the long run even
U.S. companies will need to regard their purposes as inseparable
from the needs of the communities they affect, including their
home base.

A third set of issues concerns relations between managers and those they manage. The old idea was that the right to manage came from the shareholders and that it was a manager's right and duty to hire and fire workers as they were needed. Not only have shareholders become increasingly removed from management, but also successful managers throughout the world have come to realize that their ability to manage comes from the people they manage, and employee involvement in management is increasingly essential for high productivity and efficiency. Old-style managers cannot survive, nor indeed can traditional trade unions, whose existence in many countries assumed a fundamental conflict between labor on the one side and management, representing shareholders, on the other.

Asian competition has forced change in a fourth set of Western premises: those concerning rights and duties of membership in the community. Starting with the Great Depression, rights to income, health, and so on escalated. Rights achieved their peak perhaps during the 1990s in the welfare states of Germany and France, and even in the United States, where rights have been slightly less generous, health costs in 1990 were around 16% of GDP. It is now clear that rights cannot exceed for long the capacity of a country to compete in the world economy. Asian competition is causing unemployment in Europe, and a capping of rights in the United States. Indeed, it is doing much more. It is reminding the West that if a community provides its people with rights, it must, and eventually will, stipulate duties (if you have a right to income, you have a duty to work). Politically the imposition of duties is more difficult than the provision of rights. Asian societies have an advantage since their Confucian ways have tended to stress duty more than rights in the first place. But there is bound to be convergence on this question as well as others.

USING CRISIS

These changes exemplify some directions of global convergence. They are shaping the world in which our descendants will live.

They can enhance democratic ways or just as easily erode them. They can promote greater equality — sharing of rights and duties — or they can foster exploitation. So the management of convergence and its inherent conflicts is important.

Convergence proceeds from very different bases. The old ways die hard. They are rooted in history and tradition. The new century will be a time when inspection of old assumptions is particularly important. Dogma impedes pragmatic solutions and, therefore, worsens problems, inviting crisis. Crisis, of course, is educationally valuable; it is probably a prerequisite for change; we don't want to waste it; it is expensive. So we may hope that our leaders are proficient at making maximum use of minimum crisis for maximum change.

Selected Comparisons between the 1950s and the Present

1. World Trade

(millions U.S. $)	1950	1996	1997
Imports	58,250	5,391,100	5,642,000
Exports	55,450	5,289,800	5,546,000
Total	113,700	10,680,900	11,188,000

Sources: United Nations *Statistical Yearbook,* various years; *IMF Direction of Trade Statistics Yearbook, 1998.*

2. GDP

(current U.S. $ millions)	1950	1996
World	732,100	28,583,721
U.S.	286,700	7,636,000

Sources: World GDP: *Azila Amjadi the World Bank (202) 473–3840;* U.S. GDP: International Monetary Fund, *International Financial Statistics Yearbook, 1998; A Review of World Trends in Gross Domestic Product, 1964.*

3. World Trade as Percent of World GDP

	1950	1996
	15.53%	37.37%

4. International Tourist Travel

(thousand of tourists)	1950	1955	1995
Arrivals–Worldwide	25,681	50,866	566,384
Arrivals–U.S.	2,964	5,671	61,137

Source: United Nations *Statistical Yearbook,* various years.

5. Motor Vehicles in Use (World)

(thousands)	1950	1951	1955	1995
Passenger Cars	n/a	55,820	73,050	n/a
Commercial Vehicles	n/a	16,320	20,070	n/a
Total	n/a	72,140	93,120	n/a

Source: United Nations *Statistical Yearbook,* various years.

6. Motor Vehicles in Use (U.S.)

(thousands)	1950	1951	1955	1995
Passenegr Cars	40,334	42,683	52,136	134,981
Commercial Vehicles	8,828	9,231	10,558	65,465
Total	49,162	51,914	62,694	200,446

Source: U.S. Bureau of the Census *Statistical Abstract of the United States,* various years.

7. Civil Aviation (World)

(millions)	1950	1951	1995
Kilometers flown–Total	1,177	1,557	19,345
Kilometers flown–International	n/a	n/a	8,527
Passenger km–Total	26,503	34,008	2,244,813
Passenger km–International	n/a	n/a	1,252,329

Source: United Nations *Statistical Yearbook,* various years.

8. Civil Aviation (U.S.)

(millions)	1950	1951	1995
Kilometers flown–Total	759	836	8,191
Kilometers flown–International	n/a	n/a	1,501
Passenger km–Total	16,445	21,186	854,223
Passenger km–International	n/a	n/a	240,219

Source: United Nations *Statistical Yearbook,* various years.

9. Appliances Used by Households (U.S.)

(percent of households)	1953	1993
Room air-conditioners	1.3%	26.6%
Dishwashers	3.0%	45.2%
Televisions (b&w)	46.7%	19.6%
Televisions (color)	n/a	97.7%
Refrigerators	89.2%	99.8%
Ranges	24.1%	94.7%
Home Freezers	11.5%	34.5%
Water Heaters	13.8%	91.4%
Clothes Dryers	3.6%	71.2%

Source: U.S. Bureau of the Census *Statistical Abstract of the United States,* various years.

10. Households with Telephone Services (U.S.)

(percent of households)	**1950**	**1955**	**1995**
	61.8%	71.5%	93.9%

Source: U.S. Bureau of the Census *Statistical Abstracts of the United States,* various years.

11. Communications (U.S.)

	1950	**1955**	**1995**
Number of Television Stations	107	437	1,532
Number of Radio Stations	2,143	2,704	9,880
Number of Daily Newspapers	1,772	1,760	1,533
Circulation (millions)	53.8	56.1	58.2
Number of Sunday Newspapers	549	541	888
Circulation (millions)	46.6	46.4	61.5

Source: U.S. Bureau of the Census *Statistical Abstracts of the United States,* various years.

ENVIRONMENT

The Evolution of a Concept

Gordon J. F. MacDonald

Mention the term "environment" today, and it conjures up any number of associations (perhaps emotionally colored, depending upon the political convictions of the hearer): "greenhouse" warming and climate change, air and water pollution, ozone hole, wildlife conservation and biodiversity, natural resources, desertification. The issue has gained such public currency that in 1988 the Republican candidate for presidency (a Yale man) promised to be the "environmental President," and proposed to counter the "greenhouse effect" with the "White House effect." In 1992, the vice presidential candidate of the Democratic Party (a Harvard man) published a book on environmental issues, *Earth in the Balance.* "Green" parties, the fringe elements in Europe in the late 1960s, spearheaded the rebellions that toppled several Communist governments in the late 1980s and early 1990s. Yet in 1950 the term "environment," if used at all, was used in the context of "I have a good/bad work/home environment." Indexes of books on social issues in 1950 do not even contain the term.

In 1950, to the extent that "environment" was a concern at all, Americans honored presidents such as Teddy Roosevelt, who had taken the lead in setting aside some of the more pristine and unique landscapes in the country as the basis of our national park system. But Roosevelt was more a preservationist than an environmentalist. The conservationist in Teddy Roosevelt harmonized with the thinking of the liberal and wealthy Republicans of the time. They favored preserving natural resources so that members of the upper classes could enjoy them through hunting and fishing. Worries about the impacts of industrial pollution on health of workers and nature were far from their thoughts. By 1950, sights and stenches of industrial pollution had become as familiar as those of agriculture.

Production and consumption of goods generate waste; waste, in turn, contaminates the air, water, and land, with adverse effects on both human populations and ecological systems. For the first time, a large number of people recognized that the consumer economy had an unavoidable consequence: pollution. Events of the 1940s through the 1960s began to change attitudes toward the relationship of humanity to nature and the environment. Changes came gradually, although a few dramatic incidents accelerated the pace.

FOG AND SMOG

Many Americans first heard about air pollution through comedian Jack Benny's radio show, in which he made numerous jokes about Los Angeles smog and its impact on people and pigeons. The Native American name for Los Angeles was Yang na, which translates into "the valley of smoke." When there is a temperature inversion — meaning that the temperature of the air increases with altitude — pollutants cannot escape from the valley, and in American Indian times the burning of wood created a persistent brown cloud. By the late 1930s and 1940s, automobiles had replaced wood fires as the cloud-makers. The interaction of abundant sunlight with chemical products from hundreds of thousands of internal combustion engines produced yellowish clouds that stung the eyes and interfered with breathing. In 1947 Los Angeles established the nation's first air pollution control district to study the formation of "smog" and determine how it could be controlled. This move indicated that the public and politicians thought that air pollution might have a significant impact on the quality of life — and therefore on real estate values.

Air pollution incidents were not confined to sunny Southern California. In 1948, in the valleys near Donora, Pennsylvania (birthplace of Stan Musial), temperature inversion trapped a deadly combination of sulfur oxides and particulates, pollutants that come not from automobiles, but from industrial plants that use sulfur-rich coal. The Donora tragedy led to twenty deaths and 600 hospitalizations. Similar incidents in the coal-burning areas of the Northeast prompted President Truman in 1950 to issue a call that would become familiar in later years: he asked government and industry to join forces to deal with the problem. Like those of future presidents, Truman's appeal went largely unnoticed.

Neither was air pollution confined to the U.S. In 1948, a fog laced with particulate matter and sulfuric acid was blamed for 600 deaths in London. Then, in December 1952, London experienced the worst such incident in history, a killer fog that led to 4,000–7,000 excess deaths. During the four-day temperature inversion, day became night. Buses could run only if a guide walked in front of the bus to lead it through the darkened streets. The fog resulted from almost universal use of sulfur coal as a fuel for household heating — a causative chain recognized as early as 1273 and 1306, when historians record prohibitions against burning soft coal within the city.

The events of the 1940s and 1950s prompted the British government to pass the Clean Air Act of 1956 making emission of smoke from homes illegal in controlled areas and placing regulations on the heights of chimneys.

U.S. air pollution events continued through the 1940s and 1950s. In October 1954 an especially intense smog event in Los Angeles shut down industry and closed schools. Research in the 1950s clearly identified automobile emissions as the principal source of smog. High-temperature combustion in car engines leads to the formation of nitrogen oxides, which, when released into the atmosphere, undergo a series of chemical reactions that result in the formation of ozone. Ozone, a molecule consisting of three oxygen atoms, is highly reactive with organic materials. Indeed, one crude measure of ozone concentration, which I used in Los Angeles in the 1950s, involved measuring the size of the holes — dime, penny, quarter, half dollar — observed in stretch nylon panties exposed to the atmosphere. In addition to nylon, ozone affected delicate lung tissue.

The U.S. Congress responded by passing the Air Pollution Research Act of 1955, which authorized the U.S. Public Health Service to undertake research into the effects of air pollution, but did not require any limitations on emissions. This action came at a time when the symbol of the Small Business Administration was a tall chimney belching smoke — a relic of the Depression, when active smokestacks meant jobs.

As research progressed, California contemplated a number of measures to reduce the ozone-forming compounds. The first requirement, issued in 1959, was that automobiles be equipped with a blow-by valve to recycle crankcase emissions. Although this restriction applied only to automobiles sold in the Los Angeles Air Pollution Control District, it was fiercely resisted by industry. The blow-by valve cost $7, and industry leaders feared that sales would be negatively impacted by this additional cost. The industry did not understand that the demand for new vehicles is probably inelastic, and anything that uniformly raises costs is likely, through price mark-up policies, to raise revenues and profits. The real fear, later to be realized, was that the simple device would be only the first of a series of much more stringent requirements, which would force the automobile industry to interact continually with hated Washington regulators.

RACHEL CARSON

Many would agree with Al Gore, who, in his introduction to the 1992 reprinting of *Silent Spring,* noted that Rachel Carson's writings could properly be seen as the beginning of the modern environment movement. While journalists of the 1940s, 1950s, and

1960s called attention to specific pollution events and the resultant dangers, their stories died promptly. In contrast, the impact of Rachel Carson's eloquent prose reached beyond the boundary of her specific concerns, whether pesticides in *Silent Spring,* or ocean pollutants in *The Edge of the Sea.* She emphasized the interconnection of human beings and the natural environment. Her books brought environment issues to the attention of not only industry and government, but also the public, and prompted the first steps in putting our democracy itself on the side of saving the earth.

Rachel Carson's career mirrors the history of her times. Friends and sponsors were dismayed when, in her junior year at college, she changed her major from English to zoology. Science was not thought of as an appropriate avenue for a woman, especially one whose writing held such promise. After graduating in 1928 from Pennsylvania College for Women, she continued her scientific investigations at Johns Hopkins, obtaining in 1932 her M.A. degree in marine zoology. In 1936 the Bureau of Fisheries hired her as their first-ever female biologist. During her sixteen-year stint in government, Carson rose within the bureaucracy, as well as within her literary circle. She published *Under the Sea Wind* in 1941 to critical acclaim from both scientists and writers. Publication in 1951 of *The Sea Around Us* gave her the financial independence to leave the Fish and Wildlife Service and devote herself to writing. *The Sea Around Us* was a Book-of-the-Month Club selection, and remained on the *New York Times's* best seller list an astounding eighty-one weeks.

The Edge of the Sea expressed in lyrical language her own philosophy of ecology and love of nature. "The shore is an ancient world," she explained. "each time I enter it, I gain some new awareness of its beauty and its deeper meanings, sensing the intricate fabric of life by which one creature is linked to another and each with its surroundings." Carson described the fragility of the coast, where disturbances could lead to total destruction of the whole system, and her prescient work anticipated disasters to come.

Silent Spring, published in 1962, remains the best known of Carson's works. It summarizes her many years of investigating the influence of pesticides and other chemicals placed in the environment. In evocative language, Carson describes the slow but certain disappearance of songbirds. But in 1962, only The *New Yorker* was brave enough to resist pressures from the chemical industry and acquire pre-publication rights. Its condensed three-part series prompted more mail than any other article in the magazine's history.

Manufacturers of pesticides, including the major chemical companies in the United States, mounted a vicious personal attack on Rachel Carson, and much of the criticism directed at her played to gender stereotypes. She was called hysterical and extremist — charges still heard today whenever anyone questions those whose financial position depends on maintaining the environmental status quo. Her views that the balance of nature is a major force in the survival of society were contested by claims of industrialists that modern scientists know that it is man's destiny to control nature.

Attacks on Carson by industry contrasted with praise from scientific and academic communities. U.S. Supreme Court Justice William O. Douglas called *Silent Spring* "the most important chronicle of this century in human rights." Not long after the *New Yorker* series appeared, President John F. Kennedy announced the formation of a special governmental group to investigate use and control of pesticides, under the direction of the President's Science Advisory Committee (PSAC). On May 15, 1963, the committee's report, *Pesticide Use and Control,* confirmed every point highlighted in *Silent Spring.*

Carson's writings, together with the PSAC report, led to Congressional legislation that tightened controls over the sales of chemicals. But even today the alliance of chemical and agricultural industries has succeeded in delaying the implementation of protective measures called for in *Silent Spring.* Control mechanisms instituted by Congress over the years have led to a system of laws and regulations with loopholes that permit delays and exceptions. In terms of quantity, twice as many chemicals are applied to the environment today as at the time when *Silent Spring* was published. Some chemicals that were of concern in 1962, such as DDT and PCBs, are virtually banned in the United States, but government regulations do not prohibit export of these chemicals to countries where the dangers are either not known or ignored.

ENVIRONMENT ON THE U.S. AGENDA: THE 1970S

The Birth of an Environmental President

Rachel Carson raised the awareness of the fragile interrelations between people and nature. But even in the early 1960s, "environment" had not entered the lexicon of public policy. In the 1960 party conventions, conservation, precursor of environmentalism, was mentioned, but only in passing and almost entirely in the context of national parks and natural resources. In a last-minute bid to win California and thus the Presidential election, Senator Hubert Humphrey decided in October 1968 to raise the issue of pollution, even though he had not previously considered waste control a viable political theme. As a leader of California Scientists and Engineers for Humphrey, I campaigned with the senator in California. In TV spots and at political rallies we argued that the Democratic Party was better equipped than were the Republicans to deal with air and water pollution problems. The belated introduction of the environment into the campaign resonated with public opinion and reversed the trend for Nixon in California, with Humphrey almost level with Nixon in pre-election polling. The effort came too late to prevent Nixon's election, but events of the afternoon of January 29, 1969, permanently altered the political priority accorded to the environment.

Just two weeks after Richard Nixon's inauguration, an environmental nightmare began in Santa Barbara. Oil workers on a Union Oil Company platform stationed six miles off the coast had drilled a well 3,500 feet below the ocean floor. Operators had begun to retrieve the drilling pipe in order to replace a drill bit when suddenly a natural gas blowout occurred. The initial attempt to cap the hole succeeded, but it led to a tremendous buildup of pressure below the surface. The expanding mass of natural gas and oil created five breaks in an east-west fault, releasing oil and gas from sediments deep beneath the ocean floor. For eleven days, oil workers struggled to control the flow of gas and oil from the ruptures. During that time, some 200,000 gallons of crude oil bubbled to the surface, and oil was spread into an 800–square-mile slick by winds and swells. Incoming tides brought oil and tar to beaches all along the coast south of Santa Barbara.

Animals that depended on the sea were hard hit. Tides carried the corpses of seals and dolphins to the view of horrified spectators crowding the beaches. Oil clogged the blowholes of the dolphins, causing massive lung hemorrhages; it poisoned the animals that ingested it; and it soaked migrating birds that must get nourishment from the waters. Thousands of sea birds died despite the efforts of hundreds of volunteers.

Television media covered the blowout and the impacts on the birds and sea life on an hour-by-hour basis. Unlike the air pollution events, which largely took place before television, the oil spill provided a continuing — and visually powerful — picture of the impact of man on the environment. The media focus on environmental problems intensified in weeks following the blowout, as long-term consequences of the oil spill became clear, and reporters and the public recognized that the spill was only one of man's many insults to nature.

The new administration faced its first real crisis by quickly appointing a small group of scientists and engineers to recommend solutions to the continued gushing of oil. I was a member of that group, which recognized that the only workable solution was to pump the oil and gas as rapidly as possible to lower underground pressure. Citizens of Southern California greeted this solution with great skepticism; it seemed to play into the hands of Union Oil Company, because the platform continued to produce profit-making oil. At the local level, one day after the oil spill began, citizens of Santa Barbara established an organization called "Get Oil Out" (GOO). The organization urged the public to cut down on driving, burn oil company credit cards, and boycott gas stations associated with Union Oil. Volunteers helped the organization gather some 100,000 signatures on the petition banning offshore oil drilling.

As weeks passed, and television coverage continued, the White House became increasingly concerned about the political implications of the spill and subsequent public reaction. Democrats criticized President Nixon and the Republicans for their inaction. Six weeks after the blowout, Nixon decided to visit Santa Barbara and demonstrate his personal concern over the environmental disaster. I learned about his impending visit while in Princeton, giving a set of lectures on the origin of the moon. The White House called me to request that I accompany the President to Santa Barbara. At that time I was Vice Chancellor of the University of California, Santa Barbara, and at the same time a holdover member of President Johnson's Science Advisory Committee. I quickly flew to Los Angeles to meet the President.

By the time I arrived, President Nixon was already in his helicopter, ready to fly north to Santa Barbara. I was asked to sit in the aisle seat next to the President, whom I had not met before. He clearly was anxious about the upcoming trip. The Secret Service noted that the gathering crowd in Santa Barbara was in an angry mood. Anxiety was heightened when the Secret Service asked the President to exchange seats with Mrs. Nixon, so that he would be less exposed with his back to the bulkhead, while Mrs. Nixon now faced forward. As we flew north, President Nixon continued to show his anxiety, with sweaty palms and twisting thumbs. I attempted minor conversation by pointing out the oil slick that appeared as the helicopter traveled over the Pacific. His reply was, "Gordon, I know all about oil slicks; I served in the Navy."

The helicopter landed on the beach in Santa Barbara. The beach was pristine, with not a sign of oil anywhere. Union Oil workers had been active all night, raking and cleaning up all evidence of the oil spill. In the background, we could hear the noise of the chanting crowd, but barbed wire and California state troopers kept them at a safe distance.

In order to demonstrate to the public that all was well, the President was to walk along the beach, with coverage by TV photographers who would be backing up. I was to be on Nixon's right, and on his left, Fred Hartley, president of Union Oil Company. As the choreographed walk proceeded, Hartley continually asserted that there had been no damage. He kept repeating, "I don't like to call it a disaster, because there has been no loss of human life. I am amazed at the publicity for the loss of a few birds." He also emphasized that there really was no oil on the beach. Upset at Hartley's statements, I contradicted him, stating that the tide came in, the tide went out, and each time the tide came in it deposited a layer of oil. Impulsively, I kicked at the sand, sending an oily glob of sand onto a highly strategic area of the President's trousers. Hartley apologized profusely for my action, and began brushing off the President's pants, much to the delight of the TV cameramen.

At a press conference following this episode, Hartley repeated his pronouncement that the spill was a disaster only in press accounts. President Nixon's comments were much more to the point. "It is sad that it was necessary that Santa Barbara should be the example that had to bring to the attention of the American people [sic]. What is involved is the use of our resources of the sea and of the land in a more effective way, and with more concern for preserving the beauty and natural resources that are so important to any kind of society that we want for the future. The Santa Barbara incident has frankly touched the conscience of the American people."

With this incident, "environment" became a central issue of American politics for the next decade. This political shift was strengthened by the 1969 Apollo 8 mission, which broadcast to the world the haunting, lyrically beautiful image of "Earthrise," accompanied by the crew's message to all inhabitants of the "good Earth." The far off Blue Earth contrasting so sharply with the nearby reddish dust of the lifeless moon emphasized the importance of all living things.

National Environmental Policy Act

During 1969 Congress considered legislation proposed by Senator Henry ["Scoop"] Jackson of Washington. Jackson was a most powerful senator, and a potential Democratic opponent to Nixon in the

1972 election. In pushing for a strong environmental agenda for the Democratic Party, Jackson was joined by Senator Ed Muskie of Maine, who had a long-standing interest in control of water pollution. Maine's economy depended heavily on the pulp and paper industry, but the resulting pollution discouraged tourism.

President Nixon believed that environmental political issues would become the focus of attacks on his administration by the Democrats, and he decided to counter by identifying his administration as the true defender of the environment. His thinking was heavily influenced by his domestic chief of staff, John Ehrlichmann, who as a land-use lawyer had become familiar with numerous environmental issues.

Nixon's views about the environment were pragmatic, rather than based on writings of Rachel Carson. As a good politician, he wanted to give the public what they desired, and throughout 1969 signals coming from the public and media indicated that Americans had taken a very strong interest in remedying water and air pollution. He had to be cautious, however, since such an environmental agenda would surely run into opposition from large elements of the business community, historically backers of the Republican Party. A decision point was reached late in 1969, when Congress passed the National Environmental Policy Act (NEPA), and sent it to activist environmental organizations, which were only in their infancy in the 1960s. Congress, in producing the legislation, was responding to its own view of the national interest.

NEPA was not a regulatory measure. Instead, it was designed as a statement of national policy. The act considers a broad range of public interests, including ecological, economic, aesthetic, and ethical concerns. Its clear orientation is to the future; it does not provide a prescription for near-term solutions to pollution problems. These unfamiliar features led many to dismiss NEPA as vague and inconclusive.

Nonetheless, Republican leaders and many in the business community advised Nixon to veto NEPA. Given his decision to use the environment to his political advantage, Nixon instead signed NEPA into law on January 1, 1970, at his vacation White

House in San Clemente, California. A strong statement accompanied the signing, with Nixon declaring that the decade of the 1970s was to be the decade of the environment.

Few people, especially those in Congress who enacted the law, anticipated the impact that this simple, four-page statute would have on environmental management. NEPA became the foundation of modern American environmental protection. In fact, it is NEPA that first used the term "environment" in the comprehensive sense it has today. A quarter of a century before the notion of sustainable development gained popularity, NEPA provided a clear definition of what that often ill-used term means:

> The Congress, recognizing the profound impact of man's activity on the interrelationship of all components of the natural environment . . . declares that it is the continuing policy of the federal government in cooperation with state and local governments, and other concerned public and private organizations, to use all practicable means and measures . . . to create and maintain conditions under which man and nature can exist in productive harmony and fulfill the social, economic, and other requirements of present and future generations of Americans.

NEPA anticipated the concept of sustainable development "that meets the needs of the present without compromising the ability of future generations to meet their own needs," a notion given worldwide currency by the Brundtland Commission Report, titled *Our Common Future,* in 1987, and by the 1992 United Nations Conference on Environment and Development in Rio de Janeiro. In the years since 1970, NEPA has done much to merit Senator Jackson's description of the act and its passage as "the most important and far-reaching environmental and conservation measure ever enacted by Congress."

Almost hidden in the simple language of NEPA is the requirement that government agencies prepare an environmental impact statement (EIS), with input from state and local governments,

Indian tribes, other federal agencies, and the public, when considering a proposal for a major federal action that would have a significant impact on the environment. These action-forcing provisions of NEPA opened up government decision-making to an unprecedented extent. Section 102 of NEPA specifically calls for an interdisciplinary approach to decision making, drawing on the full range of "natural and social sciences and their related arts." This requirement anticipated the trend toward integrated, ecosystem thinking that is now recognized as crucial to sustaining the environment in the twenty-first century.

Council on Environmental Quality

NEPA also created a Council on Environmental Quality (CEQ) in the Executive Office of the President, requiring that the CEQ report yearly on the state of the environment. The council was to be composed of three members, nominated by the president. Early in 1970, President Nixon nominated Russell Train, Bob Cahn, and me to the Council, with Train as chairman. At the time of his appointment Train served as Deputy Secretary of the Interior. He has been a federal judge, and was well known in the conservation community as a liberal Republican with interest in maintaining world wildlife, particularly in Africa. Bob Cahn had been a reporter for the *Christian Science Monitor* and had won a Pulitzer Prize for a series of articles on the national parks. I was to be the council's tame scientist.

President Nixon's mandate to the newly formed council was to initiate those actions that would lead to a betterment of the environment, and to establish his administration as a leader in environmental matters. The formation of a Council with a presidential mandate in a new field opened up unparalleled opportunities for policy innovations. Government bureaucrats knew that it had the president's backing and Train recruited from the federal bureaucracy a stellar staff, with deep insight into the ways bureaucracy could be manipulated. The staff was essential in accomplishing what we did in the first three years of the council's existence.

The very first step was to define the regulations that were to govern the EIS procedure. Because of my background in national security, derived from a decade as a member of JASON, a small group of the nation's leading physicists who devoted their summers to analyzing national security issues, I had oversight of the Atomic Energy Commission (AEC), the Department of Defense, and the intelligence agencies.

CEQ's earliest and most creative work, however, set out a legislative program to deal with the most urgent environmental issues and in this way establish the nation's environmental agenda. An early priority was the Clean Air Act developed by CEQ and passed by Congress in 1970, and later amended in 1977 and 1990. The Clean Air Act's far-reaching proposals sought to protect the health of all people, including those who suffered from respiratory ailments. It limited the emissions of sulfur oxides, oxides of nitrogen, particulates, and volatile organic compounds.

The actual implementation of the legislation was left to the newly formed Environmental Protection Agency (EPA), itself a product of CEQ. Our strategy was to bring together in a single agency all units of government that had environmental responsibilities, but were scattered throughout the bureaucracy. For example, responding to Rachel Carson's comments, we moved responsibilities for pesticides from the Department of Agriculture and the Department of Health, Education and Welfare (HEW) to the new agency; thus, the advocates for the use of pesticides within the Department of Agriculture no longer regulated their use. Similarly, the EPA assumed HEW's responsibilities for air pollution and the Department of the Interior's responsibilities for water pollution. The reorganization was accomplished by executive order, though Congress with its many interests was kept informed.

In 1972 the Clean Water Act became law despite a Nixon veto based on technicalities. The act's goal was to make all waters in the United States swimmable and fishable. Amendments adjusted the requirements in 1977, 1986, and 1995, but, again, the basic structure of the Clean Water Act today is that fashioned during the first two years of CEQ's existence.

CEQ also conducted numerous analyses that formed the basis for later legislation. Work on toxic chemicals in the first three years of the council led to the passage in 1976 of the Resource Conservation and Recovery Act, which regulates the on-site handling of toxic chemicals, within one's facility. Also in 1976, the Toxic Substances Control Act provided for regulation to protect the public against toxic substances in consumer and industrial products. This act was based on a council study published in 1972.

The framework of laws that today give the federal government authority to protect the environment all came out of the work carried out by CEQ between 1970 and 1972, but by late 1972 the shadow of Watergate had crept over the White House, and I resigned, fearing that the freedom that President Nixon had given the council would be lost as he became entrapped in myriad legal difficulties.

Nixon certainly was not an environmentalist in any sense of the word. Rather, he was a good politician who saw his environmental moves as giving people what they wanted; and at a political level, he wished to take the environmental issue away from the Democrats. History will show what Nixon accomplished. He rightly deserves to be known as the Environmental President.

EARTH DAY

The history of Earth Day illustrates the growth of environment as a political issue. In the early 1960s Senator Gaylord Nelson of Wisconsin was frustrated by the lack of interest his Senate colleagues showed in protecting nature. In 1963 he persuaded President Kennedy to give the issue national visibility by going on a nationwide conservation tour, spelling out in dramatic language the seriously deteriorating conditions of air, land, and water and proposing a comprehensive agenda to begin addressing these problems. President Kennedy at first adopted the idea, and began a conservation tour of Pennsylvania, Minnesota, and Wisconsin in the fall of 1963, accompanied by Senators Hubert Humphrey, Eugene McCarthy, Joe Clark, and Gaylord Nelson. When the trip attracted little media attention, further efforts to raise the environment into the political limelight were abandoned. The assassination of President Kennedy leaves open the question as to whether he would have returned to this initiative.

However, Senator Nelson persevered. In 1969 he noted the effectiveness of antiwar teach-ins across college campuses, and in September of that year he announced that a national environment teach-in would take place sometime in the spring of 1970. In the aftermath of the Santa Barbara oil spill, this announcement immediately received nationwide attention.

Harvard Law Public Policy student Dennis Hayes, who was organizing a teach-in in Cambridge, went to Washington to interview Senator Nelson. Hayes impressed the senator, who proceeded to convince the idealistic student to coordinate the nationwide activities that would become the first Earth Day. They chose April 22 as the best date to reach the primary audience, college students. That day was a Wednesday, and it was selected so as not to interfere with student weekend activities. The weather in the northern states would be warming; it was after the annual student southern migration of spring break, and well before final exams.

The result was a spectacular demonstration. Earth Day was a beautiful spring day across the United States. Folk singer Pete Seeger performed at the Washington Monument, and cars were banned from New York City's Fifth Avenue to accommodate rallies and speeches. Speeches, parades, marches, and rallies were held on college campuses across the country. Congress closed its doors as politicians went home to participate in local events.

I took part in Earth Day by debating Najeeb Halaby, then chief executive officer of Pan American Airways, on the value of the proposed United States supersonic transport (SST). The debate was held at Princeton University; it had been organized by Halaby's daughter Lisa, a student there. She was later to become very well known on the world scene as Queen Noor, the wife (now widow) of Jordan's King Hussein. Given the occasion, it was easy to convince a college audience that government should not spend taxpayers' money to build a plane that would carpet the country with

sonic booms, pollute the high atmosphere, and be an economic disaster. I would later argue the same points before the Congressional
Joint Committee on Economics, then chaired by Senator William
Proxmire. In the end, the Senate killed the U.S. SST program,
despite strong efforts by President Nixon's White House to maintain the funding.

During this period, environmental groups grew and multi-
plied. A group of recently graduated lawyers from Harvard and Yale
started the Natural Resources Defense Council (NRDC) in early
1970. Together with the Environmental Defense Fund (EDF),
founded in 1967 by four scientists concerned by the effects of DDT,
NRDC was soon going to court to block environmentally harmful actions. In this, NRDC and EDF were joined by older organizations that had conservation goals, such as the Sierra Club,
National Audubon Society, and National Wildlife Federation. In the
early years the litigation approach achieved many successes, such as
a nationwide ban on DDT. But in the end, using the courts to
attempt to steer government proved clumsy and frustrating to all
parties.

ENVIRONMENTAL IMPACT STATEMENTS, NATIONAL
SECURITY, AND GREENPEACE

Since the passage of NEPA, many thousands of EIS's have been prepared. For example, in 1972 alone, the number of draft, revised, sup-
plemental, and final EIS's numbered 2,000. A significant fraction of
these statements led to court challenges by stakeholders, and in
many cases, the courts sided with the intervenors rather than the
government. In one area, national security, the courts have almost
always supported the government's position.

The experience of the AEC in the case of the Canniken
nuclear test illustrates the judicial limits that the courts have placed
on EIS's dealing with matters of national security. In 1965 and 1969,
the AEC, predecessor to the Department of Energy, set off explo-
sions deep beneath the tundra-covered surface of Amchitka, an
island in the Aleutian chain. In 1971, the AEC planned to detonate

a nuclear device releasing the equivalent of five million tons of dynamite at a depth of 5,800 feet.

The proposed Canniken test prompted protests from environmentalists, scientists, and the Canadian and Japanese governments. Critics said the test was needless and argued that it might kill marine life and possibly trigger destructive earthquakes and tidal waves. After many delays, the test was scheduled for November 6, a Saturday. Objecting groups, which had exhausted petitions to the lower courts, requested a Supreme Court injunction prohibiting the test. In a rare Saturday session, that body ruled for the AEC.

James Schlesinger, then AEC chairman, brought his wife and two of his daughters to Amchitka for the Canniken blast, saying he wanted to underscore the test's safety. The bomb went off on the afternoon of November 6. Nine-year-old Emily Schlesinger said the ground shook "like riding a train." Fortunately, the explosion neither triggered an earthquake nor set off a tsunami, but it did kill otters and sea birds, although the numbers are uncertain.

The two earlier tests had ignited anti-nuclear feelings in nearby British Columbia. On the day of the 1969 test, 10,000 protesters blocked a major U.S.-Canadian border crossing, carrying placards that read, "Don't make a wave." "It's your fault if our fault goes." When the Canniken test was announced, protestors banded themselves together in an organization called Greenpeace. The term symbolized the dynamic combination that joined concern for the planet with opposition to nuclear arms. Greenpeace's proposition was to take a boat to Amchitka to observe the test, but stormy seas forced the vessel to turn back. A second boat tried to make the journey but was some 800 miles away from Amchitka at the time of the test.

The attempt by Greenpeace to stop the nuclear test was a failure, but it acted as a catalyst for changing public opinion. Opposition to Canniken was strong enough that the following year President Nixon canceled the Amchitka portion of the nuclear weapon testing program, and the island was eventually turned into a bird sanctuary. The Amchitka campaign also set the pattern for future Greenpeace actions that continue to this day.

Concern about nuclear matters had actually reached a peak in the 1950s, with extended debates about the safety of testing nuclear weapons in the atmosphere. The consequent international ban on atmospheric tests, signed in 1963, could be considered an arms control measure or, alternatively, an early form of clean air legislation. Unfortunately, nuclear weapon testing strengthened many people's association of nuclear power reactors with bombs — a misunderstanding further heightened in the 1970s and 1980s by the events at Three Mile Island and Chernobyl. The arrogant secrecy of the AEC during the atmospheric test ban debate inspired Tom Lehrer to write the song "We Will All Go Together When We Go," and did much to erode the AEC's credibility, contributing further to public mistrust of nuclear energy. This has unfortunate implications for the environment, since modern nuclear power plants, properly managed, release fewer harmful substances than do plants that burn coal or even natural gas. The incorrect perception fusing weapons with electricity production has also clouded the endless discussions regarding the safety of nuclear waste disposal.

ENVIRONMENT ON THE MULTINATIONAL AGENDA

Environmental issues have come to play a leading role in international policy making. The international dimensions of environmental issues became increasingly evident during Nixon's terms in office. In 1970, the U.S. business community expressed deep concern to the White House that actions taken to remedy environmental harm in the United States could put U.S. industry at a disadvantage compared to industries located in countries where environmental measures were not enforced. I suggested that since both Los Angeles and Tokyo-Yokohama were suffering through severe air pollution episodes in the summer of 1970, the United States should take the initiative to discuss air pollution issues with the Japanese government. In a rare burst of rationality, the Department of State strongly supported such a visit. When Chairman Train and I traveled to Tokyo, our visit received intense media coverage, particularly in Japan. The meetings in Tokyo achieved all our objectives. Japan, like the United States, was beginning to recognize the economic cost associated with environmental pollution. In addition, we discussed the need to adopt agreements so that countries could not use the environment to obtain trade advantages. Japan and the United States decided to urge the Organisation for Economic Cooperation and Development (OECD) to establish an environmental committee to consider these issues. OECD did form such a committee, to which I was the U.S. representative. At a very early stage, the committee reached an agreement on the "polluter should pay" principle; that is, governments would not subsidize pollution control and thereby give subsidized industry a competitive advantage in the international market.

United Nations Conferences

In the late 1960s and early 1970s the Nordic countries became particularly concerned that sulfur oxides released by tall smokestacks in the United Kingdom were acidifying their waterways and killing fish. These countries joined the United States and Canada in pushing the United Nations to hold an international conference on environment. The United Nations Conference on the Human Environment, held in Stockholm in June 1972, proved to be the major international event on the environment in the 1970s.

President Nixon viewed the conference as an opportunity for the United States to establish itself as the world leader in environmental matters. He also recognized the dangers: countries such as Canada and Sweden, which opposed his Vietnam policy, would use the conference as a forum to indict the United States; and developing countries at the conference might take irresponsible actions, blaming past colonial practices for their current plight. But Nixon was willing to take the risks to put the United States in a leading international position. His instructions were clear: use the conference to highlight U.S. environmental accomplishments.

As it happened, China did use its attendance at its first U.N. conference to blast U.S. destruction of the environment in Vietnam. The U.S. delegation to the conference was under instructions not to respond directly but to point to the advances made by the United States in dealing with environmental problems. Developing countries did blame their environmental difficulties on the rapacious appetites of the industrialized nations, but the conference received worldwide media attention highlighting U.S. actions to protect the environment.

Substantively, the conference made little progress. The delegates approved establishment of a new organization, the U.N. Environmental Programme (UNEP), with the mission to coordinate and catalyze environmental activities among the various U.N. agencies. Groundwork for developing a convention on the dumping of waste into the ocean was put forward and approved. The conference also approved a ten-year moratorium on whaling.

The real value of the conference was that it exposed delegates from many countries to environmental issues. Very few countries had developed the infrastructure needed to deal with problems of the environment and, particularly in the developing world, there was no organizational basis to tackle these complex problems. In the end, participants, outside observers, and the media united in hailing the conference as a great success.

The 1980s and 1990s have seen an increased emphasis on environmental problems that have a global reach. Nixon's determination to play a leadership role in the 1972 conference contrasts sharply with the timidity with which President George Bush approached the U.N. Conference on Environment and Development (UNCED), held in Rio de Janeiro twenty years after the Stockholm meeting. In fact, Bush decided to participate at such a late date that hotel space was limited, and some of the supporting staff had to be housed in motels whose usual customers took the hourly rate.

While the United States had taken the lead in the 1972 conference, lack of leadership and diplomatic ineptness led to a U.S. role as a spectator more than participant in Rio de Janeiro. The European Union and Japan took the leadership role, while the United States had no clear agenda, other than attempting to prevent countries from moving too rapidly to control energy use.

UNCED produced a voluminous document titled *Agenda 21,* which set out totally unachievable goals. The grandiose rhetoric satisfied participants but only frustrated governments attempting to implement its provisions. More importantly, countries at Rio adopted a framework convention on climate and another one on biodiversity. The climate convention, much like the Vienna Convention on Ozone-Depleting Substances, to which I will return, pointed out the potential dangers that would result from the uncontrolled emissions of those gases that affect the radiative balance within the atmosphere: carbon dioxide, methane, oxides of nitrogen, *et cetera.*

In the years following Rio de Janeiro, nations around the world feverishly worked to construct an action-forcing instrument. The states of the European Union wanted prompt and decisive action to limit greenhouse gases, while the United States, Canada, Japan, Australia, and New Zealand favored a go-slow process, fearing that rapid action would lead to economic dislocations. The world's nations agreed to convene in Kyoto, Japan, to prepare an action-forcing protocol, and in the early hours of December 11, 1997, negotiators reached an agreement on a number of goals, but no agreement on means by which these goals were to be attained. A group of thirty-nine industrialized countries, including the United States, would limit their annual average greenhouse emissions during the 2008–2012 time period to a specified percentage of their 1990 emissions. The United States agreed to a 7% reduction. The Kyoto protocol stipulates that greenhouse gases should be treated as a basket and does not single out carbon dioxide. In addition to emission of gases, consideration was also given to sinks of greenhouse gases, processes such as growing trees, which remove carbon from the atmosphere.

Environment has also played a decisive role in international political shifts. During the years 1989–1992, which saw the collapse of the Iron Curtain and of the governments of its component countries, "green" parties spearheaded many of the political revolutions. Motivated by the environmental disasters that decades of Communist rule had produced in their countries, such parties grew from purely environmentalist groups to major forces questioning the entire structure of their governments. Green parties continue to exert political influence in a number of countries. In Germany, where the Green Party in 1968 was considered almost as much a part of the lunatic fringe as the Bader-Meinhof gang, the Greens routinely win some 5% of the national vote, and the mainstream parties have adopted many of their initiatives.

ENVIRONMENT IN TRANSITION

Many would agree that the initiatives taken by governments, industries, and others during the 1970s furthered the goal of improving the environment. The domestic achievements had largely been built into the system, but more was required in the international environmental regime. Progress continued through the following years, with a number of ups and downs.

In the 1980s another California Republican, Ronald Reagan, undertook to dismantle some of the advances made by Richard Nixon. During Reagan's administration, especially when James Watt headed the Interior Department and Anne Gorsuch ran the EPA, environmental know-nothings reached the peak of their influence. Watt, Gorsuch, and their followers regarded destruction of the environment as a sign of hard-nosed economic pragmatism. Under Gorsuch, the EPA was specifically instructed to forget the lessons taught by Rachel Carson. An alternative to chemical pesticides, integrated pest management, was declared a subject never to be discussed. EPA banned publications about it, and outlawed certification for use of integrated pest management methods. The political process worked, and despite Reagan's popularity, the resulting outcry led to dismissal of Gorsuch and reappointment of William Ruckelshaus, EPA's first administrator.

Events of the 1980s showed that even with the technical advances of the 1970s, environmental catastrophe lurked near the surface. Shortly after midnight on March 24, 1989, the tanker vessel *Exxon Valdez* ran aground in Alaska, spilling almost 11 million gallons of Alaska's North Slope crude oil. It was by far the largest spill in U.S. history. The oil affected a national forest, four national wildlife refuges, three national parks, five state parks, four state critical habitat areas, and a state game sanctuary. Oil eventually reached shorelines nearly 600 miles southwest from the Bligh Reef, where the spill occurred.

Again, television captured the images of oiled sea life, struggling sea birds, and wiped out coastal communities. But by 1989 environment was no longer a novelty, and an oil spill many times larger than that in Santa Barbara, but thousands of miles away from media centers, did not ignite public opinion to the same extent.

In the United States the 1990s have seen a linkage between environment and national security concerns. Under the leadership of first Senator and then Vice President Gore, the U.S. intelligence community agreed that a group of scientists, known as the Environmental Task Force (ETF), could examine its resources and particularly its technologies for monitoring the Earth. I chaired the group, consisting of some seventy scientists, which reviewed classified technologies of the national security agencies and concluded that many could be fruitfully applied to the study of the environment. The release of some formerly classified information has led to significant advances in the understanding of the environment, and a follow-up group of scientists, MEDEA, applies classified technology to environmental processes. For example, underwater sensors formerly trained on Soviet submarines now listen to the mating sounds of whales in order to gain insight into the life-cycle of a potentially endangered species.

SCIENCE AND PUBLIC POLICY

The sharply focused process leading to the limitations on ozone-depleting substances shows a remarkable contrast to diffuse U.N.-sponsored activities, whose reach far exceeded their grasp. The ozone hole issue and consequent Vienna Convention and Montreal Protocol provide a textbook example of how science is supposed to influence public policy.

At low altitudes in the atmosphere, ozone is a bad actor as a principal component of smog; but in the high atmosphere it provides a protective shield against damaging incoming ultraviolet radiation from the sun. In 1974 two University of Michigan scientists, Richard Stolarski and Ralph Cicerone, reported in a *Canadian Journal of Chemistry* paper that chlorine released into the high atmosphere could unleash a chemical process that would destroy ozone. This discovery received little attention because there was no apparent source for the chlorine. Also in 1974, under a research program established by President Nixon to examine the environmental effects of supersonic transports, F. Sherwood (Sherry) Rowland and Mario Molina discovered that a class of chemicals, chlorofluorocarbons (CFCs), could provide large quantities of chlorine. CFCs are extremely stable hydrocarbons invented in the early 1930s to provide a safe, inexpensive heat-transporting gas for refrigerators. CFCs have atmospheric lifetimes measured in decades and centuries. As they drift upwards in the atmosphere, they enter into a set of complicated chemical reactions that lead to the destruction of life-protecting ozone.

In the following years a variety of laboratory studies and models supported the chlorine–CFC–ozone link, but there was not yet evidence that the posited reactions took place in the atmosphere. This did not occur until 1985, when scientists associated with the British Antarctic Survey published the astonishing finding over Halley Bay of an ozone hole, which they identified using ground-based instruments. This discovery was confirmed by U.S. scientists, who found their ozone-measuring satellite had been programmed to reject ozone levels as low as those seen over Antarctica. These scientific determinations were turned into international environmental agreements through productive interaction among scientists, politicians, diplomats, and environmental activists.

During 1985 industrialized countries of the world, along with many developing countries, entered into the Vienna Convention for Protection of the Ozone Layer — basically a framework convention pointing out dangers of permitting continued production and use of CFCs. Two years later, in Montreal, countries adopted a protocol on Substances that Deplete the Ozone Layer, with a timetable established for phasing out the production of ozone-depleting substances. Measures were strengthened by revisions agreed upon in 1990 (London), 1992 (Copenhagen), and 1995 (Vienna). Between 1987 and 1995, global consumption and production of the main ozone-depleting substances first stopped expanding and then began to decrease. By early 1996, 156 nations had ratified the 1987 protocol. Most developed countries have substantially phased out consumption of CFCs. Helped by the protocol's multilateral fund, many developing countries are implementing programs to phase out consumption of CFCs by the first decade of the twenty-first century.

In other cases the links between science and policy-making are much less clear. Rachel Carson had a deep understanding of ecology, but her principal contribution was communicating her scientifically based beliefs to the public in crystal-clear writing devoid of jargon. The authors of NEPA were obviously influenced by Carson's general philosophy but not by her particular scientific specialties. Pollution-control legislation was based only in part on scientific evidence, and the terms "swimmable" and "fishable" found in the Clean Water Act are hardly exact.

The ozone layer protection regime is widely regarded as one of the success stories of international environmental negotiations, and as a model for tackling other global environmental problems, in particular greenhouse warming. "Science" again played a role in drawing public attention to this issue — in this case, David Keeling's measurements of the carbon dioxide content of the atmosphere — but the issues covered in the ozone negotiations are simple compared to problems relating to reducing greenhouse gas emissions. Production of ozone-depleting substances is limited to a few chemical companies, and the uses are similarly circumscribed. The total economic impact of phasing out these chemicals is minuscule compared with the total economic activity associated with energy use and the consequent production of greenhouse gases. Burning of any hydrocarbon fuel — coal, oil, or natural gas — produces carbon dioxide, the most important man-made cause of global warming. If the principal component of natural gas, methane, leaks into the atmosphere, it also enhances the greenhouse effect.

The basic facts about the greenhouse phenomenon were well known in 1970 and received extensive discussion in the First Annual Report of CEQ. But neither Congress nor the public was ready to take action. In fact, over the next twenty years I testified to Congress some fifteen times on the greenhouse effect and gave countless seminars on the topic to Congressional staffs and government groups. These educational efforts did contribute to the demise of President Carter's ill-advised program for synthetic fuels and to increased support of research, but not to any limitations on greenhouse gas emissions.

FURTHER DEVELOPMENT OF THE CONCEPT OF "ENVIRONMENT" IN THE TWENTY-FIRST CENTURY

Environment is certain to be an important political issue in the twenty-first century, but one that will not have the urgency — born of novelty — voiced in the late 1960s/early 1970s. Many nations have made much progress, but experience has brought recognition of numerous deficiencies in the handling of environmental problems, and the focus may shift from identifying needs to identifying and applying new methods for solutions.

Control Mechanisms

Recent years have heard a steady drumbeat of criticisms of environmental regulation. The primary target is the "command and control" framework that forms the basis for most existing environmental rules. Vehement critics argue that such rules are economically inefficient, and instead propose a variety of "market-based" alternatives. In the early years, environmental groups strongly opposed one such market mechanism, emission fees, since these were viewed as a license to pollute.

Despite the abysmal failure of centralized command and control to manage complex societal problems, as demonstrated by the experience of the former Soviet Union, command and control remains the dominant mechanism for environmental management. In general, command and control rules impose detailed, legally enforceable limits, conditions, and requirements on a variety of societal activities. For example, environmental rules limit air emission of pollutants from each regulated source to specified amounts, with regulated industry further required to install a particular technology and monitor emissions continually. Critics note that government bureaucrats are seldom up to the task of defining the technologies that would be appropriate in individual cases.

The efficacy of command and control was questioned even in 1970. In a minor debate within the CEQ, I held that in the longer term economic instruments would provide far more flexible tools than those available under command and control. My arguments persuaded President Nixon to propose to Congress a control regime whereby a tax or charge would be placed on emissions of sulfur oxides into the atmosphere. I was given the assignment to convince Congress of the virtues of such charges.

Meetings with the chairman of the House Ways and Means Committee, at that time Wilbur Mills, quickly convinced me that Congress, with its overabundance of lawyers and scarcity of economists, would not buy into a system based on market economics. Mills argued that the Constitution required that taxes should only be imposed to raise revenues, not to influence behavior. Counterexamples, such as taxes on alcohol and tobacco, had no impact on his position. In fact, they may have been counterproductive, since not long afterwards Chairman Mills drove his car and his companion — the well-known strip artist Fanne Foxe — into the Reflecting Pool in Washington, D.C.

The 1990 Clean Air Act amendments illustrate the shift in thinking with respect to use of market mechanisms. While these amendments contain numerous new command and control features, they also incorporate the most ambitious free-market approaches yet enacted. The 1990 act permits establishing a national market for allowances to emit sulfur dioxide in a way that limits total national emissions to nine million tons annually. A market for emission permits has developed in the Chicago Board of Trade. The theory is that plants that can reduce emissions relatively cheaply by installing modern pollution-control equipment have an incentive to reduce overall emission below their assigned allowance. They can then sell their unused allowances to other industrial plants that would face higher compliance costs.

Other market-based controls may become increasingly important. In fact, the insurance industry may play a very significant role in improving environmental conditions. After the *Exxon Valdez* disaster, Congress enacted the Oil Pollution Act of 1990, requiring that all tankers, foreign or domestic, over 5,000 tons calling on U.S. ports be equipped with a double hull by the year 2010. The insurance industry then established insurance rates that greatly favored double-hulled vessels, thereby ensuring that the U.S. requirement would be met on a worldwide basis.

The private insurance industry provides other powerful tools. For example, asbestos abatement insurance, developed in 1987, protects contractors involved in the removal of asbestos from third-party claims. Similarly, property transfer insurance protects property owners from costs associated with contamination discovered on their land after they have made settlement. The insurance firm judges the level of risk and sets the premium accordingly. Responding to the catastrophic losses resulting from recent natural disasters, such as hurricanes, the Northbridge earthquake, and the recent floods in Europe, insurers have set homeowners rates at levels that discourage building in environmentally vulnerable areas.

Environment and Development

As the world moves into the twenty-first century, international dimensions of environmental problems will become ever more important. Global economy, worldwide communication and information networks, and rapid development of biotechnology all have important consequences for the world's environment.

Economic and political reforms currently under way in Asia imply that the continent's vast human resources will decisively influence the world's environment. As populations and economies grow, Asia will experience rapid urbanization, together with the enhanced opportunities and vulnerabilities associated with densely populated urban communities. Economic changes and growing prosperity will stimulate demand for energy, food, and natural resources. If these demands are met in traditional ways, they will place intolerable burdens on the environment.

Currently, both China and India expect their very large coal resources to provide energy for the future. Burning of coal will lead to increases in the emission of the principal greenhouse gas, carbon dioxide, and will also foul the air with sulfur oxide and particulates. Neither China nor India has indicated that it will abide by the greenhouse gas limitations placed on industrialized countries by the Kyoto Protocol on Climate Change.

By the middle of the next century about ten billion people will be placing stresses on the natural resource base of the globe. The experience gained in managing transboundary air and water pollution problems in Europe will be of great value in understanding and managing future environmental issues that will come about from economic development in Asia, Latin America, and Africa. While our world has made great progress toward limiting environmental harm, much remains to be done as country after country moves toward a consumer-based economy. Problems will arise not from the exhaustion of natural resources but from how those resources are used. New technologies can and will lessen damaging environmental impacts if they are employed wisely, guided by the market system.

CONCLUDING THOUGHTS

As NEPA makes clear, "environment" embraces not only science, but also aesthetics and ethics. The concept of environment would not have developed without science, but its evolution also required contributions by politicians, journalists, artists, and philosophers. Such a broad concept incorporates many diverse subjects and their interrelationships.

Perhaps this helps to explain why, even though "realists" continue to sneer at "tree-huggers," the issue has — and will continue to have — special resonance. Some people claim they would rather nuke the whales than save them, but most people have an instinctive wish to preserve especially beautiful landscapes or appealing animals. The arguments tend to focus more on the various mechanisms used in the name of "environment" than on the importance of the issue. The owners of scenic areas often believe that it is they, not the government, who should determine how to use their land. People who wish to save tigers from extinction may feel less strongly about preserving a rare type of slug for the sake of "biodiversity" — especially if the alternatives are posed in terms of "slug versus food/water/economic advancement." Poor communities may feel antagonistic toward what they see as elitist campaigns to preserve the wilderness, and meanwhile site waste dumps in low-income areas. New Englanders who experienced the snows of 1996 may question the existence of global warming. Such questions will continue to be asked in the future as environment remains a politically important issue.

Environment has, in fact, become a given on both national and international agendas — a development that we could not have foreseen in June 1950. It is inconceivable that a political campaign for national office in the United States would not deal with some aspects of environmental issues. At the international level, the establishment of the Global Environmental Facility and the "greening" of the World Bank demonstrate the close linkage between environment and economic development in the minds of decision makers worldwide. Military strategists recognize the role that environmental issues such as desertification or access to water play in leading to armed confrontations, and acknowledge the need to consider "environmental security."

Harvard, like other colleges and universities throughout the world, clearly understands the central role environment will play in the years to come. The university has responded to student needs by developing an interdisciplinary curriculum focused on environment — and many of the most talented students have chosen to concentrate on this area. If "the best and the brightest" have identified environment as central to their lives, can we doubt that it will play a central role in the twenty-first century?

A COTTAGE INDUSTRY IS
GETTING ORGANIZED

Miles F. Shore

In the summer of 1952 I had a dramatic response to a course of sulfa antibiotics. I cannot remember who gave me the prescription or exactly what it was for, but I do know that I got well rapidly despite a startling allergic reaction that has kept me from taking sulfas ever since. At that time there were only three effective antibiotics — penicillin, the sulfa drugs, and streptomycin, although broad spectrum antibiotics were on the horizon. Most people had known about antibiotics since just before the World War II, but they had not been routinely available to civilians until after the war. This was my first encounter with them, and as a second year medical student I naturally regarded this event with some interest. Like many others my age, I had been excited by reading Paul deKruif, a pioneer medical journalist whose articles in the *Reader's Digest* predicted a glowing future for medical miracle workers who were certain to produce medical miracles. My rapid recovery thanks to this first experience with an antibiotic solidified my expectations that life as a doctor would involve a lot more exposure to the wonders of scientific medicine as touted in the *Reader's Digest*.

These expectations were actually much too modest, for the reality of biomedical science has far outstripped even the grandest of what I might have imagined. Who in the early 1950s could have foreseen kidney, liver, heart, and lung transplants as relatively commonplace events? Who could have guessed that operating on the heart would become a routine matter with very low mortality rates and highly predictable outcomes? In 1950 poliomyelitis was a cloud that hung every summer over children, adolescents, and young adults, for whom life encased in an iron lung or limping with braces were possible outcomes. Babies who weighed less than five pounds had almost no chance of survival, and if they did survive, little could be done to correct the sad collection of birth defects that were all-too-common lifetime burdens. The 500,000 people in public mental hospitals had almost no hope for treatment or rehabilitation unless they were lucky enough to respond to insulin or electric shock treatments. In 1950 it was only fanciful writers of science fiction who might have speculated that diagnosis and treatment would someday depend on understanding how DNA and genes work.

Now it appears that there is no theoretical limit to the useful application of science to human disease and yet, paradoxically, because of those extravagant possibilities, medicine at the end of the twentieth century is in turmoil, for science-based technology has been an expensive proposition. Employers who, through an accident of history, pay for a good deal of U.S. health care are increasingly resistant to the rising costs of their employees' health benefits. Taxpayers, impatient since Colonial times with public dependency, have been concerned by the costs of Medicaid for indigent persons. Elected officials are worried about the political fallout of Medicare costs that threaten the financial viability of a program with great appeal to senior citizens, who vote more often than any other group. Practicing physicians who matured professionally in an era when resources seemed unlimited are irate that managed care seems to be telling them how to practice and has squeezed the time they can spend with their patients. Meanwhile, members of the public as patients — in contrast to the public as employers and taxpayers — are alarmed at the possibility that market forces may deprive them and their loved ones of high-technology medicine. The paradox of public attitudes is a tacit acknowledgment that in buying health care we get a lot for what we spend. But when the bill arrives there is a curious disengagement of the mind from the pocketbook and we are upset at the amount that we have to pay. This preoccupation with cost has driven a painful process of reorganization of the health-care system for more than ten years.

While the contributions to patient care of science-based medical technology are so great that they threaten to outstrip society's capacity to pay for them, surprisingly little has been done to advance the way in which services are delivered. The decoration on a Greek vase, circa 410 B.C., depicting an Athenian doctor bending solicitously over a sick man, is little different from the 1929 Norman Rockwell *Saturday Evening Post* cover in which a country doctor pretends to listen to the heart of his little patient's doll. The message of both is the same as today's controversial ads for HMOs: "The physician cares for you, the patient, with technical skill and with human concern." That model of the physician who represents both the science and the art of medicine is a solo model — the physician as captain of the ship, assisted by other professional and non-professional helpers, but individually and solely accountable for the nature and quality of medical care.

Much of the present turmoil in health care and the practice of medicine can be understood by tracing the fifty-year history of the growing chasm between the content of medical care and the way in which it is delivered. The content has undergone a scientific revolution; the delivery of care is very little changed from what it was fifty years ago. The future of health care and the practice of medicine will depend to a large extent on whether or not patient care can be brought up to date through innovations that will match the revolution in medical science.

This model of solo practice, featuring almost unlimited professional autonomy, was defended by U.S. physicians for more than a century against a succession of challenges that could have resulted in a much more corporate, organized model of practice, sharply curtailing physicians' professional freedom. These challenges included the rising power of private, voluntary hospitals in the nineteenth century that sought to control medical practice by hiring staff physicians and restricting access to hospital privileges; large nineteenth century corporations in the steel, railroad, mining, timber, and other newly consolidated industries that threatened to compete with private practice by marketing their employee medical services to the general public; a post–World War I move to create compulsory national health insurance; and, following World War II, President Harry Truman's proposal of compulsory national health insurance that was defeated in the anti-Communist era by being labeled "Socialized Medicine."

Although organized medicine resisted Medicare and Medicaid when they were proposed in the early 1960s, a number of factors made them viable politically and they were adopted in the middle of that decade. Medicare, because it was associated with Social Security and was based on contributions by potential beneficiaries, had strong public support. Medicaid evolved gradually from block grants to states to pay vendors to care for indigent patients and was a boon to states burdened by the costs of welfare. Physicians' fear of government domination was neutralized by relying on fiscal intermediaries, usually Blue Cross and Blue Shield plans, rather than government agencies, to pay providers. But most important, both hospitals and physicians were paid according to exceedingly favorable arrangements. Medicare offered hospitals cost reimbursement, rather than negotiated rates; physicians were paid according to "customary" fees just as they were by private health insurance. Thanks to these financial safeguards, both Medicare and Medicaid turned out to be bonanzas for practicing physicians and for hospitals. And although there were sizable limits to the coverage provided to patients, from the point of view of hospitals and physicians these new payment schemes offered vastly better reimbursement than had previously been available, and at first both hospitals and physicians prospered. Between 1945 and 1969, while the consumer price index rose at an annual rate of 2.8%, physicians' annual incomes rose 5.9% a year. The average net profit from medical practice rose from just over $8,000 in 1945 to $32,000 in 1969.[1] This was the period in history when the practice of medicine became, for the first time, a highly lucrative profession.

Young doctors like me knew little more about these maneu-
verings than lay persons, for at that time "health policy" was something you bought from Mutual of Omaha rather than an academic
discipline. For us, the chief point of Medicare and Medicaid was
that it increased access to care for our patients. It meant that we
could treat more patients with dignity, and that was very important.
Of equal interest to us was the cascade of scientific discoveries, also
supported by the federal government through research grants
administered by the National Institutes of Health. These discoveries had intrinsic intellectual interest, and they gave us more things
to do for our patients so we tended not to think about what they
cost. After all, it was the time of the Great Society, which was ener-
gized by the widespread assumption that there was no economic
limit to what could be done if only the establishment, i.e., people
over forty, would loosen up and change their ways. Even though it
was clear to those of us who were a little older that the class of 1969
puffed a good deal of self-important hot air, we took satisfaction
from the fact that the Great Society seemed to be making a commitment to social justice through expanded coverage of health care.
We had only sketchy awareness that the amount of patient care was
actually quite limited, and we had no idea that the golden eggs of
scientific discovery were on their way to disabling the goose, the
economic engine, that had produced them. Instead we appreciated
the funders at the National Institutes of Health who supported
research, and we admired the clever hospital chief financial officers
who found ingenious ways of milking the cost reimbursement system, because the result of both seemed to be that we could do better by our patients. Increasing access to more and better care was
then the issue, not cost.

Of course the oil crisis and stagflation of the early 1970s
brought the social revolution to a standstill and took some of the
wind out of the class of 1969 who had to struggle to find work. By
1970, the incentives for increased spending built into Medicare and
Medicaid had run up the costs of health care and generated a public crisis for which physicians and hospitals were roundly criticized.
For the first time, it became clear that there were stark trade-offs

between access to care and the costs of care. If care were broadly available, the costs might well be unbearable. With that awareness, the battles to contain costs began in earnest, and they continue to this day. Staunchly defending access for patients, the providers of care based their arguments on an ethical assumption that more health care was automatically better; the convenient corollary was that any limitation of care endangered human life. That is a tenacious and *prima facie* attractive assertion, which plays to patients' fears of death and disability and continues to drive the debate despite the fact that in many cases it is not true at all.

Despite the recognition that fee-for-service and cost reimbursement drove up costs, unprecedented amounts of money from Blue Cross and Blue Shield, private insurance, and Medicare and Medicaid poured into hospitals. And the deluge of research findings stimulated hospitals to increase capital investments in expanded and improved facilities and equipment to apply these findings to patient care. This so-called "edifice complex" had begun with the passage of the federal Hill-Burton legislation in 1946 to fund hospital construction. That the cost of capital could be included in Medicare and Medicaid rates, supported the demand for new technology and turned hospitals into much more sophisticated fiscal institutions, springing them loose from their dependence on voluntary donations from local community benefactors to upgrade and expand their facilities.

The new medical technology strained the traditional ways that physicians took care of their patients. New diagnostic tests and therapeutic procedures were adopted enthusiastically because they promised better care for patients and because of the financial incentives created by the way procedures were reimbursed. Payment rates were set when the procedures were new, took a lot of time, and could be done by only a few people. Soon, with familiarity and technical refinements, these procedures took less time, and many people could do them, yet they were rarely repriced to reflect the new, lower cost. As the margins on procedures grew disproportionately, physicians who specialized in such things as cardiac catheterization, endoscopy, x-ray therapy, and new surgical techniques could make very large amounts of money, as could hospitals that provided the space and the hardware.

Non-specialist physicians, too, had to respond to the demand for more sophisticated medical technology. They had to learn when and how to order new diagnostic tests, when to use new medications with dangerous side effects and interactions, and how to refer patients for new therapeutic procedures, even if those procedures were actually performed by others. One penalty of the new technology was an increasingly complex and often frustrating administrative system that physicians had to master in order to get paid. They also were forced to accommodate to a succession of administrative annoyances — many of them cumbersome and demanding — imposed by government and private purchasers of care to restrain cost increases.

Despite the pressures of this technical and administrative complexity, the organization and delivery of care changed very little. The "social architecture" of medical practice — the solo physician, the private office, the trip to attend patients in the hospital, the hospital itself, the odd relationship between the physician and the hospital, vitally connected but officially separate — stayed pretty much the same. Even the early health maintenance organizations and multispecialty group practices were structured to support the individual doctor seeing one patient at a time. Instead of pushing experimentation and innovation to revise fundamentally the structure and the process of care, physicians accommodated as best they could, adding complexity and cost to the traditional system of practice by hiring physician assistants and nurse practitioners to pick up some of the clinical tasks, and clerks to wrangle with Medicare, Medicaid, and private health insurance companies. The technological revolution that so decisively changed the care that was delivered hardly touched the delivery of that care. It was as if a jet engine had been lifted from a Boeing 747 and installed in a World War I biplane.

From the perspective of history, it may not be surprising that the delivery of care lagged so far behind scientific medical technology, for healing has been a feature of every society, and its history is that of the human race, whereas scientific medical technology is relatively new. Of course healers have always relied on some form of technology. Egyptian physicians set fractures in ox-bone splints supported by resin-soaked bandages; Dioscorides, a Greek surgeon to Nero's army in the first century A.D, wrote five books of remedies that included aromatics, oils, salves, roots, juices, herbs, and salts of lead and copper; the physician in Chaucer's *Canterbury Tales* ("loved he gold exceeding all") often "kept a patient from the pall by horoscopes and magic natural" and "ready he was with his apothecaries, to send him drugs and all electuaries."

In contrast to the practice of healing, the science of medicine is little more than 450 years old. It dates roughly from 1543, with the publication of *De humani corporis fabrica* by Andreas Vesalius, which presented his dissections of human bodies that challenged traditional "truths" about anatomy, and 1628 when William Harvey published *De motu cordis,* which documented his experiments on the circulation of the blood and the heart's role as a pump. Thus medical science as we know it, a relative newcomer with all its complexity and ever-evolving series of "truths," has had to be incorporated into the healing role with its much longer tradition of devoted service to patients. It has not been an easy fit.

Each of us as a patient wants a personal physician who is paying attention to us and is an advocate for our needs. And so physicians have been criticized for at least thirty years for being so preoccupied with complicated technical wizardry that they had too little time to listen to their patients. Furthermore, patients are ambivalent about technology. They want it desperately, but they are suspicious that it may possibly hurt them. This has been called the "Andromeda Strain" syndrome after the Michael Crichton novel that traded on the fear of technology run amok. And unfortunately there has been too little development of technology aimed at enhancing personal care. The continued popularity of alternative medicine, based largely on credulity and anecdote, is further evidence that science gets mixed reviews in the public arena, and that it is sometimes upstaged by the wish for healing.

The upshot of this history is that the delivery of medical care has continued to be for the most part a cottage industry of individual craftspersons: physicians, working away in their isolated workshops doing piecework, i.e., the care of one patient after another. Physicians are professionally socialized to value this approach; they expect to enjoy its benefits; and they are mightily upset when it is threatened. The benefits of this traditional approach include great autonomy in choosing how to practice, how much to practice, and the freedom from scrutiny by anyone except other physicians with comparable experience. The price of this freedom has been the heavy weight of individual responsibility for professional decisions and for the outcomes of these decisions that burdens every doctor. For society, the price is even higher — the growing inability of practitioners working essentially alone to deliver scientific medicine that is up to date, safe, and of the highest quality. The problem is that as medical knowledge explodes, and the process of treatment becomes increasingly complex, there is no adequate, organized system to make sure that physicians keep up with the latest developments; that they share in the best practices; and that they practice safely. This is fundamentally because of a lack of real accountability for standards of practice.

In medical specialties that involve procedures, accountability to other professionals is automatic and inescapable. Practice is typically carried out in public and involves members of other professions who can observe and comment on the quality of what is done. But in the so-called cognitive specialties — general and family practice, psychiatry, and general internal medicine — there is no systematic provision for continuous constructive review of practice by others so that, *de facto,* most physicians practice without the peer review that is supposed to be the professional guarantee of quality. Doctors are of course accountable to their patients for those elements of care a patient can judge. These include what used to be called "bedside manner": the way in which the physician connects with the patient by spending time in the examination, being genuinely interested in his or her well-being, and impressing the patient with knowledge, competence, courtesy, and respect. Patients also continuously evaluate the "customer service" aspect of care —

waiting time, civil treatment by ancillary personnel, the atmosphere of the office. In this cybernetic era, patients capture the latest medical news from the internet and from television, and they expect their doctors to know at least as much as they do. Patients also know when there has been a grossly bad outcome, but they generally are unable to judge whether it was due to bad care or bad luck. Without a bad outcome, in what might be called the "middle ground" of care, it is difficult for patients to evaluate the degree to which their medical care meets the highest professional standards. As a result, most patients are satisfied with the care provided by their personal physicians and are unaware of problems that they are in no position to identify or judge.

Doctors are also accountable to the legal system when bad outcomes result in malpractice suits. These occur typically when there is injury and a poor relationship with the patient. But this legal accountability does not improve the quality of care much at all. In fact, it may well decrease quality by encouraging the practice of defensive medicine that results in the overuse of tests and procedures.

Accountability for those aspects of practice that are beyond the scrutiny of patients, usually the province of governmental regulation, is virtually nonexistent. There is no national or uniform legal or regulatory requirement for physicians to upgrade their knowledge and skills through continuing education; that is supposed to be largely a matter of individual professional responsibility. Many, but not all, states require physicians to attend continuing education courses, but these may cover a wide variety of topics, not necessarily those in which the physician is deficient. These courses usually have no examinations, either before or after, so it is possible to attend them without improving the quality of practice.

As a result of the inadequacy of traditional professional accountability, and the lack of effective regulatory accountability, there is growing concern among leaders of the medical profession about the quality of care that is actually being delivered. Two recent studies found that 21% of all antibiotic prescriptions given to children and adults in 1992 were used to treat colds, upper respiratory infections, and other conditions for which antibiotics are ineffective and, in fact, dangerous because of the risk of adverse drug reactions and increasing antibiotic resistance.[2] A study of elderly patients who had suffered heart attacks found that 79% of them had not received Beta-blockers, the standard post-coronary treatment. Over the next two years, this group had a 75% greater death rate than those who had received the medication.[3] Unfortunately, there is no easy way to identify physicians who are deficient in their practice, and it is even difficult for individual physicians to find out if they, themselves, are deficient compared to others. A famous story concerns researchers studying practice variation who found that the rates of tonsillectomy in a small, northern New England town were vastly higher than in any other place in the state. The anomaly was due not to higher rates of diseased tonsils in that town, but rather to the fact that one family doctor was taking out every set of tonsils that he could find. When shown the figures he was quite surprised, for he had never seen data comparing his practice to others. With some relief he readily decided that he should stop taking out so many tonsils — relief because he had been worried for some time about the number of gallstones in town and he wanted to get busy taking them out![4]

The same line of research found geographic variation in patterns of practice that could not be explained by disease severity. In 1989, for example, the residents of Boston used more than 4.3 hospital beds for every thousand residents; in New Haven fewer than 2.3 beds were used per thousand residents. The difference was accounted for by the fact that in Boston, persons with common conditions like pneumonia, heart failure, and gastroenteritis were admitted for treatment, whereas in New Haven similar cases were treated outside the hospital.[5] Were Bostonians hospitalized too often, or were New Havenites hospitalized too little? These data leave such questions open; what they do demonstrate is that the lack of systematic standardization of medical practice has serious and expensive consequences.

Another line of research — studies of patient safety and medical error — raises somewhat different concerns about individual practice. It is estimated from reviews of hospital charts that 180,000 patients each year die partly as a result of medical errors.[6] That is the equivalent of three jumbo jet crashes every two days! These errors include missed diagnoses, failure to treat promptly, drug overdoses, giving the wrong drug, and failure to get a follow-up culture to check for antibiotic resistance when the patient does not respond to treatment. Even though errors occur in as few as 1% of the many events that happen to a patient in the course of an illness, this is a much higher error rate than is tolerated in many other industries that apply technology to human safety and welfare. As Leape points out, commercial aviation, nuclear power generation, and naval aviation have all been successful in vastly improving the safety of their operations.

Experts on medical error cite numerous factors that account for the fact that medical care is relatively unsafe. Most of these factors reflect the reliance on individual physicians and other medical professionals to perfect their practice methods. The assumption is that doctors can practice safely and at the highest standard if they are sufficiently intelligent, well trained, and conscientious. Unfortunately, in medicine, error-reduction all too often relies on punishment of the offending practitioner, which interferes with open investigation of the process failures that are typically responsible. No consideration is given to the finding of human-factors studies that human error is inevitable, but that it can be minimized or prevented by creating systems around individuals that make it much more difficult or even impossible for them to make mistakes. This is very different from other high-hazard professions — piloting airplanes, running nuclear power plants — that rely heavily on standardization of processes and a variety of technological aids to improve the safety of their work. Doctors frequently reject such solutions as "cookbook medicine" that violates their professional autonomy and fails to take into account the fact that each patient is different.

The best example of such a system solution comes from the automobile industry. It was once possible to start a car in gear. Tragedy and deep guilt were the result if the car started in reverse and one's two-year-old child was playing behind the car, unseen.

Now it is impossible to start cars in gear, and that particular accident cannot take place. In a few hospitals with advanced information systems, the requirement that hospital medication orders must be entered into the computer reduces both errors and cost. If a physician orders a medication that interacts dangerously with the patient's other medications, the computer refuses to process the order until the physician justifies it. In some cases, the potential error is automatically referred to higher clinical authority for review. Similarly, abnormal laboratory tests are entered into the hospital computer system, setting off the beeper of the physician who ordered the test, and continuing the warning until there is a response. Both of these measures interfere with physician autonomy, but they represent the kind of system that is demanded by high technology medicine that is too complex to be practiced alone, unaided. In the past, a not uncommon hospital error was for an intern or resident to give the wrong blood to a patient who needed a transfusion. Such mistakes can be fatal unless, with good luck, the blood turns out to be compatible. Now the patient may be spared the danger, and the house officer the anguish, of that mistake, because in a few places innovative systems of barcoding the patient and the blood substantially reduce the likelihood of such a human error.

These deficiencies in the delivery of care are, in themselves, exceptionally costly. It is estimated by knowledgeable observers that as much as 30% of what is spent on health care is wasted. That amounts to $300 billion per year.[7] This significant amount is consumed by duplicated and unnecessary laboratory tests; by the "rework" necessary to correct mistakes of various sorts; by the costs of treating illnesses prolonged by inadequate or mistaken treatment; and by the wide variation in practice patterns that affect the system. These variations range from geographical differences in rates of hospitalization, to the fact that eight surgeons in the same hospital, performing the same procedures, may use at least eight different sets of operating instruments, sutures, and techniques.

A recent report of the Institute of Medicine of the National Academy of Sciences titled *The Urgent Need to Improve Health Care*

Quality reviewed many of these data.[8] The authors found evidence of three categories of quality problems. The first was underuse: failure to immunize 100% of children; prenatal care begun too late to prevent the complications of pregnancy. (Counter to expectations, a number of the studies cited by the report found that underuse was more common in fee-for-service than in managed care plans.) Misuse, the second category, involves injury from preventable complications of treatment and is related to medical error. The report cites research indicating that there are, on average, 2,000 patient injuries per year from the administration of medications in *each* large teaching hospital studied. Some 24% of these injuries were preventable, and each of them added, on average, $5,000 to the cost of the hospital stay during which it occurred.[9] The RAND Health Services Utilization Study, performed seventeen years ago, long before managed care was an issue, found that 17% of coronary angiographies (visualizing the blood supply to the heart), 32% of carotid endarterectomies (clearing out clogged arteries to the brain), and 17% of upper gastrointestinal tract endoscopies were performed for inappropriate reasons.[10] The Institute of Medicine report made the obvious point that poor quality is expensive, and that reducing overuse and misuse would be a constructive approach to reducing cost. Correcting underuse would increase cost in many cases, although cost increases should be assessed over the long haul because in some conditions reducing underuse now could prevent expensive complications later.

The report comes down hard on the inadequacies of the system of care that I have identified in this essay: "The burden of harm conveyed by the collective impact of all of our health care quality problems is staggering." And it sounds the alarm of urgent need for rapid change. "Meeting this challenge demands a readiness to think in radically new ways about how to deliver health care services and how to assess and improve their quality. Our present efforts resemble a team of engineers trying to break the sound barrier by tinkering with a Model T Ford. We need a new vehicle or, perhaps, many new vehicles. The only unacceptable alternative is not to change."

With the failure of the Clinton administration's attempt to reform the health care system, employers have joined public health officials in pushing managed care as a solution to rising costs. Using techniques developed by health maintenance organizations and the peer review activities of the 1960s, managed care seeks to restrain cost increases by undoing the fee-for-service, cost-reimbursement system and making physicians accountable to the market. By discounting fees, requiring physicians to justify treatment plans, carefully managing hospital lengths of stay, and similar mechanisms, managed care companies, responding to the demands of employers, state Medicaid agencies, and now the federal Health Care Finance Administration that manages Medicare, have substantially reduced the sharp increases in health care costs that marked the 1980s. They have also set off a media firestorm of anecdotes fueled by the rage of physicians at interference with their professional autonomy and the anxiety of patients that they or their loved ones may be denied lifesaving but expensive treatments by physicians who have too little time to pay attention to them, and who stand to gain financially by limiting care.

Some managed care companies, responding more to Wall Street than to their patient care responsibilities (the standard term for what they spend for medical care is "the medical loss ratio"), have made their founding entrepreneurs lavishly wealthy by cutting care to the bone. Other companies, placing value ahead of profit, have sought to improve the quality of practice by using best practices from the literature and from clinical guidelines prepared by specialty societies — i.e., by responsible peers. This is particularly the case in staff model health maintenance organizations whose physicians, paid by salary, work in groups under the same roof and under the same administration, where peer relationships and a common set of purposes can guide practice.

Someone once said that great ideas at times appear in offensive guises, and it may be that the cottage industry of medical care has actually begun getting organized through managed care that was created for the quite different aim of cutting costs. The elements of a rational reorganization of medical care are already present in some of the characteristics of the managed care industry, particularly in the incentives inherent in the assumption of care of defined populations by prepaid systems. And some of the technical aids of the future have been adopted, piecemeal, by various health maintenance organizations, hospitals, group practices, and integrated systems of health care in an effort to meet accreditation standards. However, these advances are limited to a few unusually forward-thinking organizations, and the technology of quality assurance found in the accreditation standards is still in a rudimentary stage. A recent news article in the *Economist* reported that the health care industry spends only 1% of its budget on information systems, compared to 7% in banking and finance.[11] A significant development is the national accreditation standards for integrated health systems put out by the National Committee on Quality Assurance, and more recently by the Joint Commission on the Accreditation of Health Care Organizations. Attempts by better managed care systems to market quality of care collide with the fact that at the moment the medical marketplace is dominated by fierce price competition. Street lore has it that employers who purchase health care talk about quality until it comes down to closing the deal, at which point price is the only issue.

Changes in market conditions — particularly a commitment by businesses to purchase for quality rather than price — will be required to realize the potential of managed care for improving the delivery system. Again, the heart of the problem is to expand the limited professional accountability to which physicians have been so intensely committed. Over and over, discussions of these matters among knowledgeable professionals turn on the issue of motivating physicians to accept changes in their way of practicing. The organized systems that have been set up by managed care companies to save money can assist physicians and other providers to do better work if they can motivate clinicians to change, and if these companies can reorient their own business strategy to compete in terms of quality rather than price. For example, in many systems, profiles of physician practice habits keep track of the cost implications of what they do. Such "economic profiling," which shifts medical practice toward cost-cutting, could be replaced or at least supplemented by "quality profiling" to determine the degree to which individual physicians deliver the highest quality care. Using such data, health care systems could insist that physicians keep up with the latest developments and practice accordingly.

Systems of managed care could assist practitioners to deal with the overload of scientific information by linking primary care physicians with specialists for official and "corridor" consultations, and they could make capital investments in accessible information systems so that the world's medical literature is on each physician's desktop. Unlike the physician working in relative isolation in solo practice, managed care companies can assemble population data to identify likely targets for preventive activities, enhancing so-called "disease management" that focuses intensive outpatient care on chronic conditions like diabetes, asthma, and hypertension, to improve health and prevent medical disasters that require expensive hospitalizations. Technical aids, the reallocation of tasks to ancillary personnel, and attention to improving processes of care can free up the physicians to spend more time listening and talking to patients, thus realizing more fully the ideal of personal care.

Much has happened in medical practice since 1950. The cascade of scientific advances, and the implications of those advances for the economics of health care, mean that the practice of medicine of the highest quality probably exceeds the capacity of the human brain to function adequately without assistance. To move into the future, health care needs the medical equivalent of power steering, of fly-by-wire aircraft, or of the combination of global positioning system and automatic pilot that guides ships through the Norwegian fjords. Many of these aids to medical practice are already developed and are being applied, albeit piecemeal; others are in the developmental stage almost ready for implementation; while still others lie in the future. For such aids to be adopted across all of health care will require a change in the health care marketplace so that value is placed ahead of profit, and a change in the medical culture to accept a host of technological innovations as a valuable step toward the results that patients and health professional alike desire — health care that is broadly accessible, affordable, safe, and of the highest quality.

NOTES

1. P. Starr, *The Social Transformation of American Medicine* (New York: Basic Books, 1982), 354.

2. A. C. Nyquist et al., "Antibiotic Prescribing for Children with Colds, Upper Respiratory Tract Infections, and Bronchitis," *Journal of the American Medical Association* 279 (1998): 875; and R. Gonzalez, J. F. Steiner, and M. A. Sande, "Antibiotic Prescribing for Adults . . ." *JAMA* 278 (1997):904

3. S. B. Soumerai et al., "Adverse Outcomes in Elderly Survivors of Acute Myocardial Infarction," *JAMA* 279 (1997):115.

4. P. Caper, private communication, 1998.

5. J. E. Wennberg, *The Dartmouth Atlas of Health Care in the United States* (Chicago: American Hospital Association, 1996), 3.

6. L. L. Leape, "Error in Medicine," *JAMA* 272 (1994):1851.

7. D. Skinner, M.D., and D. Berwick, M.D., private communications, 1998.

8. M. R. Chassin and R. W. Galvin, "The Urgent Need to Improve Health Care Quality," *JAMA* 280 (1998):1000.

9. T. Brennan et al., "Incidence of Adverse Events and Negligence in Hospitalized Patients: Results of the Harvard Medical Practice Study 1," *New England Journal of Medicine* 324 (1991):370.

10. M. Chassin et al., "Does Inappropriate Use Explain Geographic Variations in the Use of Health Services? A Study of Three Procedures," *JAMA* 254 (1987): 2533.

11. "Hardly Wired," *The Economist,* Oct. 24, 1998:68.

THE NEW PRUDENT INVESTOR RULE

John Train

The mission given to this volume's contributors was to write about the past and present of their specialty — in my instance, investment, notably trust investment — and provide intimations as to the future.

Although investment is a form of futurology, I am not sure the assignment is possible. One often goes wrong in life by having confidence in long-range prospects, because they are subject to so many variables. One thinks of Wellington's aide at Waterloo, asking what the army should do if the Duke were rendered *hors de combat.* Wellington was brusque, "Do I know what Napoleon will do?"

"No, my lord."

"Since what I do depends on what Napoleon does, how am I to tell you what to do if I am absent?"

Much futurology is like that. Things happen because they happen — these days often unpredictably, in technology — and we react.

In the investment business we would all give anything to be able to predict the economic future. In fact, though, we can't. The Reagan boom, which carried the stock market from 1,000 to over 10,000, was foreseen by almost nobody; the sudden collapse of Asia and Russia was foreseen by almost nobody; and the next great inflection point will be foreseen by almost nobody. I find that usually one can only understand what has happened a while after the fact. Furthermore, long-distance forecasting gets less and less accurate the further out it goes; thus, if you are projecting ten years or twenty years, huge errors are all but certain. Ever since the machine gun, wars have been regularly pronounced impossible because they were too horrible. If Alexander Graham Bell had foreseen the universality of the telephone, he would have concluded that all the women in America would be needed to staff the switchboards. Forty years were required to build an audience of fifty million radio listeners; who would have imagined then that it would require only months to gain fifty million internet users?

It seems increasingly recognized that linear or classical economics, which calculates clearing prices and assumes that markets will approach that point, doesn't work. Too many variables. I understand that Gosplan, which ran the Soviet economy, had a computerized matrix of ten thousand variables, but didn't work. Instead, the best approach may be through complexity theory. (If you aren't familiar with complexity theory, I strongly recommend a look into it, since it seems to clarify many puzzles. Perhaps that's my big message in this essay.)

Then, here is another problem: All human affairs are cyclical, including such staples as faith in science, democracy, and religion. But once again, how does one catch the inflection point?

Anyway, rather than peering far into the distant fog of the future, one is well advised to examine minutely, like Darwin, what is happening around us at this very minute. By studying the *hic et nunc* under a magnifying glass, as it were, one perceives things that others may not, and if one can purge the mind of preconceptions, one may well develop powerful insights. As an example, there is an aspect of investment that is already here, that few of us are aware of; and that most of us will need to come to grips with very soon indeed. I refer to the drastic change in the principles governing trusteeship.

The next decade will see the greatest transfer of wealth in our history. Over ten trillion dollars — the value of all the companies listed on the stock exchange — will pass from our generation to its families, often in the form of trusts. IRS statistics indicate that over the next five years the number of trusts could increase by 50%.

Few of us are familiar with the rules that trustees must follow. Then a parent or spouse dies, or grandparents create a trust for our children. We are named trustee, and thrust into a new responsibility. We soon discover that trusts have many mysteries, and that the office cannot be learned on the job. Furthermore, the rules governing how trustees must act have just changed profoundly. The Prudent Man Rule that has governed trustees for over a century was replaced beginning in 1992 by a uniform model statute that has already been adopted by most states. The New Prudent Investor Rule should soon apply in all fifty states. It sets forth principles that every trustee must follow.

WHAT IS PRUDENCE?

Trust prudence is a *process,* not a result. Prudence is a flexible and unspecific standard of care. It lacks the "safe harbor" features found in most other regulatory areas, such as federal securities and tax law. For the trust to grow in value is not enough. A trustee must *act prudently* in all he does for a trust and its beneficiaries, and should *record* the logic of his actions.

Care, Skill, and Caution

Prudence is of two types: administrative and investment. As to each, it consists of three elements: care, skill, and caution.
- *Care* means the duty to be diligent, to investigate fully before acting.
- *Skill* means familiarity with business and investment matters.
- *Caution* means being attentive, and avoiding undue risk.

Administrative prudence means exercising care, skill, and caution in safekeeping trust assets, disposing of trust income and principal, maintaining trust records, keeping beneficiaries informed and treating them impartially, particularly as between income beneficiaries and remaindermen.

Investment prudence means exercising care, skill, and caution when dealing with all aspects of a trust's investments. For instance, before investing, a trustee should establish written investment objectives that suit the purposes of the trust and the needs of the beneficiaries; act diligently in selecting investments; determine the risk tolerance of a trust and choose only investments that suit that risk level; diversify the trust's holdings; focus on the portfolio's liquidity; determine whether he should seek advice from experts; if so, choose and monitor them with great care; and *keep down costs.*

THE OLD PRUDENT INVESTOR RULE: HARVARD V. AMORY

The Old Prudent Man Rule arose from a celebrated 1830 Massachusetts court decision, *Harvard College v. Amory.* Amory was a trustee of a $50,000 testamentary trust. The income went to the decedent's widow for life, while at her death the remainder passed in equal shares to Harvard and the Massachusetts General Hospital. The will gave Amory broad power to invest the trust fund, including in stocks according to "his best judgment and discretion." Amory invested the entire $50,000 fund in stocks, which yielded 8% in dividends. Five years later the widow died. Amory filed his account with the local court, showing a trust value of only $38,000: about a quarter less than when he started. When he asked the court for his discharge, Harvard and Mass. General objected, demanding that he restore the $12,000 of lost capital. Judge Putnam ruled in favor of Amory, couching the rationale for his decision in words renowned in trust lore: "Do what you will, the capital is at hazard." He went on to pronounce in powerful language a legal principle that became a universal standard for fiduciary conduct, known as the "Prudent Man Rule":

> All that can be required of a trustee to invest, is, that he shall conduct himself faithfully and exercise a sound

discretion. He is to observe how men of prudence, discretion, and intelligence manage their own affairs, not in regard to speculation, but in regard to the permanent disposition of their funds, considering the probable income, as well as the probable safety of the capital to be invested.

These trenchant sentences helped shape the actions of trustees of hundreds of thousands of trusts for more than a century and a half. Not without battles, though, as the philosophies of state legislatures and courts changed from favoring flexibility in trust investing to a desire for more certainty and conservatism. In the first half of the twentieth century many states enacted specific legal lists of investments for trustees, and courts established a series of subrules on what was prudent and what was off limits. Often these restrictive rules and limitations were in conflict with what trustees in their best judgment considered wise. Many trustees were thus investing for their own families in one way, and for the trusts they managed in quite another.

PRINCIPLES OF PRUDENCE UNDERLYING THE NEW RULE

The New Rule, then, returns to the old idea of broad investment discretion. On the other hand, it has become extremely fussy about procedures. It brings several new principles into trust investment law, and recasts some old ones for clarity and emphasis. It finally gives up on specific investment limitations for trustees, and declares that *no* investments or techniques are imprudent *per se* — a startling development, considering that the Old Rule held that investments that were speculative, non–income-producing or novel were intrinsically imprudent. Here are some other central ideas of the New Rule:

- Diversification is fundamental to risk management, and is therefore ordinarily required of trustees.
- Risk and return are so directly related that trustees have a duty to analyze and make conscious decisions concerning the levels of risk appropriate to the purposes, distribution

requirements and other circumstances of trusts they administer.

- Previously, every security had to be prudent, to stand on its own bottom, as Harvard says. Under the New Rule, this is not so. A trustee can take account of the overall position in making investment decisions.
- Trustees have a duty to avoid fees, transaction costs and other expenses that are not justified by the realistic objectives of the investment program.
- The fiduciary's duty of impartiality to present and future beneficiaries requires a conscious balancing of current income and capital growth.
- Trustees are permitted, and may have a duty, to delegate investment and administrative duties to professionals and other agents.

These principles profoundly change how trustees must approach investment.

THE NEW RULE

The New Prudent Investor Rule reads, in part, as follows:

> The trustee is under a duty to the beneficiaries to invest and manage the funds of the trust as a prudent investor would, in light of the purposes, terms, distribution requirements, and other circumstances of the trust.
>
> (a) This standard requires the exercise of reasonable care, skill, and caution, and is to be applied to investments not in isolation but in the context of the trust portfolio and as a part of an overall investment strategy, which should incorporate risk and return objectives reasonably suitable to the trust.
>
> (b) In making and implementing investment decisions, the trustee has a duty to diversify the investments of the trust unless, under the circumstances, it is prudent not to do so.

(c) In addition, the trustee must:
> (1) conform to fundamental fiduciary duties of loyalty and impartiality;
> (2) act with prudence in deciding whether and how to delegate authority and in the selection and supervision of agents; and
> (3) incur only costs that are reasonable in amount and appropriate to the investment responsibilities of the trusteeship.

CARE AND SKILL

In addition to exercising care — being thorough and diligent in all matters — a trustee must exercise skill. A person of ordinary intelligence can serve as a trustee even if he does not possess the investment skills required, but then he may have to hire specialists in order to meet the fiduciary standard of necessary skill. The Old Rule in general forbids investment delegation, but the New Rule holds that a trustee may have "a duty to delegate investment authority to others, as a prudent investor would in the circumstances." In so delegating, "the trustee must exercise appropriate care and skill in selecting and supervising agents and in determining the degree and terms of the delegation."

CAUTION

The New Rule requires caution when investing trust funds, with a view both to "safety of capital" and securing a "reasonable return." Safety of capital includes preserving its real (as against nominal) value; that is, seeking to limit the erosion of the trust's purchasing power by inflation. That is a big change. In the old days, if over many years a trust showed even a modest profit before inflation, the trustee was safe, unfortunately. No longer!

In a major departure from the Old Rule, the New Rule defines a "reasonable return" as *total* return: capital growth as well as income. Nevertheless, the trustee must provide a suitable current return to the income beneficiary. Furthermore, under the New Rule capital growth does not necessarily mean only preservation of the trust's purchasing power, "but may extend to growth in the real [i.e., after inflation] value of principal in appropriate cases." An interesting development! It is in reality quite enough to preserve buying power in real terms while providing a reasonable income that rises to offset inflation. Seeking much more than this — swinging for the fences — often achieves less. Nevertheless, says the New Rule, the trustee can try, if doing so is consistent with the situation of the trust. In recent years one has achieved remarkable growth even without trying, but bull markets do not go on forever. Let us hope not to repeat the experience of 1973–1974, when inspired by the Ford Foundation report urging educational distributions to be bolder, many of them plunged in near the top and went over Niagara.

COSTS

I find the New Rule's insistence on a trustee's seeking low costs for all services entirely proper and extremely important. Don't buy a mutual fund with a sales charge! Don't buy an index fund with higher fees than the lowest industry standard! Negotiate all custody and brokerage fees!

RISK

The New Rule, along with the Old Rule and indeed common sense, requires that a trustee give due weight to risk factors in choosing investments. A trustee may take risks if the reward is commensurate. (A master investor can, nevertheless, secure exceptional gains with little risk by deploying superior knowledge and judgment, like a chess master.) In everyday life most of us know what risk is. But institutional and academic investment theorists have in recent years frequently equated risk with volatility — in Modern Portfolio Theory, "beta." I consider this a pernicious conception. Do you worry about the market price fluctuations of your house?

For a true investor, who knows the value of what he owns, volatility can be an advantage, permitting him to add to a holding when it is cheap and, if he wants, to cut back when it is high. If risk equals volatility, then several years of steadily higher prices in the face of uninteresting earnings might not be considered risky, even though the valuations toward the end of the period had become grossly excessive. We can see examples in the market as I write. Quite often such steady rises derive from momentum. For instance, shares of a closed-end fund in a popular sector may steadily advance from a discount compared to the value of the underlying securities to twice their value. On the beta theory of risk, the shares of the trust would then be a low-risk investment, whereas common sense would indicate an exceedingly high risk.

(One hears less these days about another academic favorite, the Efficient Market Hypotheses, which as usually recited holds that since all information about securities is available to everybody, the market prices securities correctly or "efficiently." The practical refutation of this notion is simply that some investors consistently outperform the market, and some objective measures, such as closed-end fund premiums and discounts to net asset value, fluctuate wildly over time. The theoretical refutation is that a) *emotion*, along with reason, rules markets; b) nobody can collect and interpret all possible information; c) there are different skill levels in investing, as in chess; and d) when investors do agree on the positive facts about a great company, the stock becomes overpriced: doubts and fears create opportunity. I offer the Efficient Professor Hypothesis: All the profs have access to the same information, so all must agree.)

What, then, other than volatility — "beta" — are the more significant real risk elements to which a trustee must give keen attention? Let us consider four: business risk, country risk, market risk, and inflation.

The most important risk is always the soundness of the business that the trust is investing in. Companies can fail to grow, or indeed can decline, and thus a prudent trustee must be alert to shrinking profit margins, declining sales (unit sales as well as sales measured in dollars), skimpy research and development outlays, intensifying competition, and so on. This is particularly true during a bull market: a company may be losing ground while its stock price remains strong. Bull and bear markets are like love affairs: when the market's rising, all is forgiven; when the next bear market comes along, any fault is pounced on.

When a trust holds foreign securities, another true risk is that a country will get into trouble. Its economic environment may be unsound before its security markets reflect that. The economic collapses in many Asian countries in 1997–1998 were generally not anticipated by the securities markets. (Conversely, of course, things may be better than the market recognizes.)

Market risk is simply paying too much for a stock, so that the price goes down even though the business remains satisfactory. This can occur because a given country's stock market overall, or a particular security, has become overpriced, so that a decline follows.

We all have experienced inflation which, since we were in college, wiped out much of the then value of bonds, insurance policies, and annuities. The New Rule requires that a trustee take inflation into account (as well as deflation).

These, then, are risks that can involve a true impairment of value. Mere quotational fluctuations against a background of improving company conditions need concern the trustee little, as long as the trust in question has a long-term viewpoint.

The New Rule does not rule out any investment category, contrary to Judge Putnam's pregnant admonition, "not in regard to speculation, but in regard to the permanent disposition of their funds." In other words, commodities, derivatives, and art are all theoretically suitable. Nevertheless, I do not consider these categories prudent holdings for private trusts. Almost all commodity speculators lose money. That business is a legalized casino, whose purpose is not to build the suckers' wealth but to relieve them of their savings. Much the same is true of speculation in derivatives. Here I'm not talking about Harvard Management, which doubtless knows what it is doing, but the typical private trustee. Even large banks, and one *central* bank, have been wiped out by derivative speculation. As to art, in general it declines in value in real terms, allowing for a modest opportunity cost, from the time it is first sold until it disappears into the attic or crumbles into dust. The exceptions are few, and then mostly achieved by dealers or collectors with a trained eye. A work of art should be bought because you love it and know all about it, and out of income, not trust capital.

So for me, all these categories, where there is no intrinsic buildup of value from earnings, and where the future is unknowable, are almost always imprudent on a risk-return basis, and were thus rightly unacceptable under *Harvard v. Amory,* even if under the New Rule they are now theoretically permissible. We can look forward to some interesting court cases testing these principles.

DEFENSIVE TRUST ADMINISTRATION

A trustee is not a guarantor of his investment success. However, by imposing a very high standard of care the Rules set a low hurdle for establishing his liability. If a breach of that standard — imprudence — causes a loss, the trustee can be held liable to the trust and to the beneficiaries.

When settlors grant extended powers to trustees, they often seek to relieve them of correspondingly extended liability by adding exculpatory clauses to trust instruments. Courts view such clauses unfavorably, but they are generally enforced and are commonly used in living trust agreements; less so in testamentary trusts.

However, public policy places limitations on such exoneration provisions. Generally a trustee may not be excused from liability for deliberate violations of fiduciary obligations, including the duty to act with care, skill, and caution, nor for gross negligence, bad faith or dishonesty, nor for acts of self-dealing not specifically authorized by the trust or the beneficiaries. In addition, although many trusts grant the trustee the power to act with "absolute discretion," public policy limits that authority. A trustee may not exercise discretionary powers or authority dishonestly or in bad faith, regardless of contrary provisions in a trust document.

A trustee has the right to render an account of his or her

trustee stewardship and to be discharged from any liability or responsibility for all actions fairly and fully disclosed in the accounting. In certain circumstances, beneficiaries also have the right to force a trustee to account for his actions as a trustee, even if the trust instrument dispenses with that duty.

Accountings are to inform beneficiaries, and to provide a method for resolving questions about a trustee's activities and his possible surcharge liability for losses sustained by the trust during the accounting period.

Trustee accountings are conclusive as to the actions of the trustee, assuming proper notice to beneficiaries and adequate disclosure. They may be reopened only by necessary parties who are not notified, if there was fraud or misrepresentation by the trustee. If an issue regarding a trustee's action or inaction is not raised by a notified beneficiary, a completed and properly executed accounting proceeding, whether informally or judicially settled, will resolve any such issues. The trustee will have been discharged as to all matters during the accounting period.

Each time a trustee accounts and proper disclosure and notice have been given, the slate is wiped clean. The trustee's future responsibility for the trust assets is reset to their market value on the date of the accounting.

SPECIFIC MEASURES

What steps can you take, as a trustee, to avoid incurring personal liability for investment losses? Beside requesting exoneration in the trust document, and asking the settlor to state his priorities as between income beneficiaries and remaindermen, the answer is to do things right.

- Master the fundamental duties of a trustee.
- Avoid even a semblance of self-dealing.
- Develop financial and tax profiles for each beneficiary.
- Record analyses of distribution liquidity needs.
- Take out fiduciary malpractice insurance.
- Develop *written* investment objectives.

- Engage any outside professionals under a systematic and detailed screening process, and monitor them carefully.
- *Record* risk/return analysis.
- *Record* your study of the impact of inflation or deflation.
- *Record* considerations of portfolio diversification to reduce the risk of large losses.
- Negotiate all costs at least down to standard levels.
- Minimize taxes.
- Keep the number of investment transactions low.
- Be scrupulously fair as between income beneficiaries and remaindermen, and *record* your reasoning.
- Stay in touch with the beneficiaries, and have them ratify your actions.
- Obtain co-trustee approvals.
- *Record* key actions and their rationale.
- In extreme cases, ask the advice and direction of a court.

To sum up, one way to think of the spirit of the New Rule is to compare the administration of a hospital today with the life of a country doctor earlier in the century. Then, everybody knew old Doc Perkins, who had helped them, and very likely their parents, into this world. He was often the only healer for miles around, and crisscrossed the territory in all weathers. When one called him in one knew what one would get: a conscientious, overworked physician, not rich, who would surely do his best, but would occasionally make a wrong diagnosis or not have the latest remedies. If the patient lived, he would be grateful for that, and not worry much if the doctor's treatment could have been more perfect. If the patient died, the family would know that Doc Perkins had done all he could, had been there at the end, and shared their grief. The last thing they would think of would be suing the poor man. That's still true in Japan, where it's bad form even to ask your doctor for his diagnosis, let alone question the treatment. Here, though, every move a physician makes is influenced by the threat of a malpractice suit, and the cost of malpractice insurance may be his biggest expense in life, until it drives him out of the profession. A similar thing is happening to trustees, particularly under the New Rule. It is no longer enough that the patient should survive — i.e., that the trust should grow in value. Now every trustee act — exercising skill, limiting costs, impartiality, delegation, and the rest — is subject to challenge, and a trustee's prudence, like a hospital's or a doctor's *must be documented*.

The foregoing are only some patchy notes on aspects of the New Rule. They do not constitute a brief general guide. My book on the subject, *Inventing and Managing Trusts Under the New Prudent Investor Rule,* with suggested checklists for various elements of compliance, was recently published by the Harvard Business School Press.

So as I say, don't try to look too far ahead to find the future of trust investing. You can already see it, just up the road.

FROM WORD TO THERAPEUSIS — AND BACK AGAIN?

An Overview of Religion in America Since 1950

John F. Woolverton

FIFTY YEARS AGO: A QUESTION OF WORDS

The names carved into the frontals of libraries reveal cultural and religious attitudes. Convictions change, of course, but from 1890 on, when many of America's largest libraries were built, classical literary figures were the most popular. At the Butler Library at Columbia University, of eighteen names, ten are from the Graeco-Roman world, three from the middle ages, five from the modern period. The names facing the main campus are all ancient authors: Homer, Herodotus, Sophocles, Plato, Aristotle, Demosthenes, Cicero, and Virgil; on the west side are Horace, and Tacitus. Relegated to the building's sides are four Christian writers: Augustine, Aquinas, Dante, and Milton. Shakespeare, Cervantes, Voltaire, and Goethe make up the rest. There are no Hebrew poets: no Psalmist or Isaiah. Moses is ignored.

Not so in Boston. There Moses, at least, fares better. On the frontal of the Boston Public Library he appears just above Confucius, Pythagoras, Mencius, and Muhammad. Together the five represent the new academic study of religion that was gaining prominence just as the library was completed in 1895. Facing Copley Square are similar groups: writers, painters, musicians, and a section for American worthies, mostly legal and local. Emerson, Lincoln, Peirce, and Hegel face busy Boylston Street. There are only twelve women out of a total of 609 names. Along what used to be the less-prominent Huntington Avenue side of the library are the Reformation figures who shaped the Bay Colony: Calvin, Eliot, Mather (Cotton?), Luther, St. Paul, Wesley, Edwards, and Tillotson. Their placement, however, signified that for our society theology was on the margin of modern intellectual culture. It still is. No doubt the frontals of other libraries across the United States tell nearly the same story.

A worse fate awaited those texts with which Christian worshipers themselves once adorned the interior walls of their churches. These names — statements of faith — were not marginalized but erased. There had been a long tradition of placing the communal declarations where, for both comfort and judgment, those entering the building could read and take notice: the Lord's Prayer, the Apostles' Creed, and the Ten Commandments. This last inscription was required by canon law in Colonial Anglican churches.[1] In the late 1940s at St. George's Episcopal Church in New York City, the vestry, after a reconstruction program, debated whether to restore the Lord's Prayer to the apse wall or put a cross in its place. To those responsible the decision was by no means a small matter. The question of whether or not to retain Christianity's most authoritative text gained the attention of such prominent attorneys as vestrymen Charles C. Burlingham and George W. Martin. In the end they chose the cross.

The choice itself was not by any means inappropriate. The cross had been a symbol of Christianity for centuries. But in this case the omission was culturally significant: words either proclaim, teach, or raise questions of truth, whereas symbols do not. While both can be evocative, instruction — Karl Barth's "binding address' — is the most effective means of passing on a tradition of shared public meaning. Commenting on the loss of between a quarter and a third of the Episcopal, Presbyterian, and Methodist churches since the 1960s, Robert Wuthnow declares "the main reason was theological: the church simply didn't teach them [young people] a clear, compelling set of religious beliefs.'[2]

Why was this? What had happened historically? Two things: the privatization of religion and the belief that faith's function was primarily therapeutic. First, religion became a private matter: the Founding Fathers wisely judged that citizens could exercise faiths as freely and devoutly as they desired so long as they did not attempt to curb the rights of others to do likewise. Voluntary organizations of believers then set out on the one hand to enhance the spirituality of their members and on the other to influence civil society for ameliorative ends. Both goals had roots in American Puritanism. Since 1950, however, while there have been significant social gospel initiatives (supremely, Martin Luther King, Jr., and John XXIII's *Mater et magistra* and *Pacem in terris*), the privatization of religion has proved the stronger of the two.

Second, the influence of faith as therapeusis, that is, the "modern imperative of analysis, reflection, and introspection," in order to heal brokenness,[3] was recognized even before the beginning of the twentieth century. In a discussion of the religion of healthy-mindedness, William James declared in 1905 that the mind-cure principles are beginning to so pervade the air that one catches their spirit at second-hand. . . . "[It was] the 'Gospel of Relaxation."[4] In it, duty to God had no place, only to self. James could not bring himself accurately to quote Walt Whitman's "Song of Myself" on the subject: he left out Whitman's line, "They [animals] do not make me sick discussing their duty to God." Richard Rorty, more of an admirer of Whitman than was James, agrees with the poet, that Americans should "spend the energy that past human societies had spent on discovering God's desires on discovering one anothers' desires.'[5]

By the 1940s and 1950s, God had in fact become emeritus while the belief system of the Christian community was preserved for its therapeutic potential. Group Life Laboratories, Encounter Groups, and Transactional Analysis invaded mainline churches. To the puzzlement of the laity, Christian education ceased to transmit the tradition and sought to cure emotional hurts "felt" [a code word] by children, in Sunday Schools and elsewhere. The Gallup Unchurched American Study (1978) found that only half of the children of baby boomers "were exposing their children to formal religious training of any kind, compared with 86% who themselves had received religious training as children.[6]

In 1966 Philip Rieff referred to the death of a culture, which "begins when . . . normative institutions fail to communicate ideals in ways that remain inwardly compelling.'[7] Rieff reported that C. G. Jung had advanced "a religious doctrine in which God is rendered completely interior": no longer the "I am" of Abraham and Moses, he had become the "dark subterranean God of each man's secret life." Such a quietistic faith "denies, in principle," said Rieff, "any significant social responsibility." Was it, as he claimed, "the end of a cultural history dominated by book religions and word-makers?"

In the meantime when there is doubt about the objective reality of God, writes Wuthnow, "Attention shifts inward towards the subjective realm of perceptions and experience.'[8] The rector of a large city parish describes with marked theological tentativeness, the effect of the very architecture of his church:

> Something happens to people inside this space. It's womb-like. The space puts its arms around you. In the Anglican tradition, so unlike the New England meeting-house, the space itself can be sacramental. We become something together in that hour, but its hard to name it. . . . We become a common body of searchers. Something about the music and the building makes people one.[9]

And these searchers in their middle-class affluence clearly have time on their hands. The traditional New England meetinghouse demanded an act of will against adversaries and adversities, either real or imagined. The space that is womb-like and puts its arms around worshipers is quietistic and comforting. It invites introspection, not critical reflection from a special Christian perspective.

In that church I suspect that people do indeed become "one," but primarily in the sense that they all share the given of separate, private destinies.

But while some pursued interior "spiritual journeys" or elected to follow Joseph Campbell's mysticism, others were shocked by the implicit moral relativism of these monistic systems. As a result, in the 1980s many opted for pentecostal religiosity, ethical dualism, and punitive moral absolutism. Ironically Pentecostals also accentuated therapeusis: a subjective feel-good attitude, and human potential (for conversion rather than for escape from pain). Others continued to sing "The Church's One Foundation"; to make their communal confessions of faith; to thank God for what they had received; and to pitch in with Habitat for Humanity and other good works.

TWENTY YEARS AGO: THE GREAT DIVISION

In the mid-1970s in the Episcopal Theological School where I taught, I was challenged one day after class by a visiting evangelical — and pietistic — bishop. The lecture had been on the social gospel in twentieth-century America and the heroic efforts of its champions. I must have entered into the spirit of the subject, for the bishop declared, "You people who were involved in social Christianity and civil rights have no real personal faith." I replied that as an evangelical he might like to sit in tomorrow on my seminar on Jonathan Edwards. I asked him if he had ever read Edwards' *The Nature of Religious Affections,* which the class was studying. No? "Well," I suggested (I was tenured), "it ought to be required reading for all 'charismatics' today." The bishop failed to appear. Our exchange signaled the brief moment when the personal and the social were in converse just prior to the appearance of Jerry Falwell's "Moral Majority" (1979). But then it was too late. The conservative revivalist Billy Graham, who had become increasingly concerned socially, failed to provide a rallying point. With the rise of Falwell, Pat Robertson, and their allies the division between liberals and conservatives deepened.

Robert Wuthnow draws attention to the greater similarity among major denominations and faiths than obtained in the 1950s and notes considerable convergence in social status and educational levels, and, among mainline churches, a similarity in outlook on social issues.[10] Denominations no longer divide as sharply as once they had. Nancy Ammerman remarks on the increasing evidence that Americans are less and less firmly identified with them: "People marry across denominational lines, transfer membership when they move, and drop in and out with impunity."[11] This does not by any means spell the death of denominations; in fact countervailing moves are under way today to rediscover denominational roots in Methodism, Anglicanism, and elsewhere, even to creating separate denominational enclaves. Centers for Anglican communion studies and the like have sprouted in a number of the Episcopal Church's theological schools, while at the General Theological Seminary in New York City a journal is published with the exuberant title *The Anglican: A Journal of Anglican Identity.* The great divide, however, has been and is now between liberals and conservatives, and it cuts directly through the middle of many of the older denominations.[12]

My conservative bishop had a point. Within Protestantism, it seemed to him, those who welcomed pluralism, who sought to sanctify the secular city (to use the title of Harvey Cox's 1965 book), had thrown over "a whole range of beliefs and practices: miracles, prayer, piety, hell, the devil, God as transcendent judge, [and] missionary work (of the 'soul-saving' kind)."[13] Liberal professors in theological schools were often not sure whether their first loyalty was to an analytical, historical method which cut everyone down to size or to the God of the Bible who chose and inspirited his people. For their part students in university divinity schools were often not sure whether they were religious people or those who studied them. When their professors declared that behavior had many motivations, conservative students wondered if there were *any* absolute values. The evangelicals wanted rules, a framework, and "authentic" tradition. They still do. Black theology, liberation theology, and feminist theology seemed to lead away from a "personal relationship" with Jesus Christ and to use scripture for political ends. By the 1992

Republican convention it was clear, however, that Robertson's "Christian Coalition" was doing the same thing. And why not? they said.

What began in 1964 with the nomination for the Presidency of Barry Goldwater culminated in 1994 with control of the House of Representatives falling into the hands of born-again Christians. If in the period 1968 to 1973 religious activists on the left had toppled a government and stopped an unpopular war, by 1998 activists on the right had impeached a president. The score was even, but the price was high: a degraded political culture in which the investigators of the pornographic set out — with curious similarity — from the right as well as from the left.

To return to the liberal academic scene: for their part the divinity schools connected with universities, together with many liberal denominational schools, resisted what they in turn saw as obscurantism. As early as 1957, H. Richard Niebuhr, who was in neither camp, saw tradition as a social process constantly changing but also one which kept memory and value alive. It was with such an attitude that these schools attracted brilliant spokesman such as Reinhold Niebuhr and Paul Tillich. In honoring scholarship, writes Conrad Cherry, the divinity schools "demonstrated that piety and intellect need not occupy hermetically sealed compartments of life.'[14] The integrity of the life of the mind was upheld and not just for white males but for minorities and for women — who by the 1980s counted for nearly 50 per cent of theological students. The divinity schools' legacy of commitment to social justice, succor of the needy, and defiance of unjust laws and institutions was a long one. It eventually came to include concern for those who were the objects of that *timor maximus,* homosexuality. The danger of course was that by immersing ministers in the life of the modern university, professors inadvertently cut them off from the life of the churches. (It was a point well grasped by Harvard's Derek Bok.)

The best (and neglected) religious novel of the post World War II era, was Martin Gardner's multilayered *The Flight of Peter Fromm,* was published in 1973. The novel's central character is a young, conservative Christian who finds himself in a liberal divinity school (Chicago) where he undergoes trials of faith — which sounds trite but is not. Had Gardner written his novel in the late 1970s, however, the story of Peter Fromm would have been very different. By then, through the election of born-again Christian Jimmy Carter (who greatly reduced suspicion about the conversion experience), through the successful adoption of forms of mass televangelism, and by means of the building of new coalitions such as the National Association of Evangelicals, conservative Christian faith stole the limelight. While popularizers like Timothy LaHaye might fail to convince the educated, his Ronald Reagan-like history was read by the masses.[15] On the other hand the work of scholars such as Francis Shaeffer, George Marsden, Mark Noll, Nathan Hatch, and others commanded everyone's serious attention. Thereafter religiously conservative evangelicalism was no longer marginalized but marched triumphantly into the groves of academe.

Among Roman Catholics the great division has been equally acute. However, there is a difference: instead of liberals for the most part in control, as in mainline Protestantism, conservatives dominate. The century began with the rejection of "Modernism" and has ended with the 1998 apostolic letter *Ad Tuendam Fidem* (To Defend the Faith). This apostolic letter raises "definitively held" Catholic teachings to the level of infallibility. Among those matters which Cardinal Joseph Ratzinger's influential commentary on the letter declares are punishable offenses, are opposition to the church's stand on the nonordination of women, on sex before marriage, and on the invalidity of Anglican orders. Vatican II therefore must be seen as a brief moment of liberalization.

But, like the election of the first Roman Catholic president in 1960, the remarkable council of 1962 proved immensely important. Vatican II put the Catholic Church in a commanding religious position. Through its call for collegiality that involved not only the pope and bishops but lower clergy and laity as well; through *Dignitas humanae personae,* the declaration on religious freedom, prompted by the American Jesuit, John Courtney Murray;

through the new openness to dialogue and debate with Protestants, Orthodox, and people of other faiths; and by mandating worship in the vernacular — for all these reasons the church was no longer seen as a "clerically dominated monolith.'[16] Indeed the council inspired within Protestantism itself greater collegiality, a fresh interest in ecumenism, even fascination with liturgical renewal. Increasingly, Protestants were and remain attracted to Catholic "spiritual formation."

Then came the reaction. In 1968, against the advice of his own commission, Pope Paul VI in *Humanae Vitae* condemned "artificial" interference with procreation in the sexual act. While the prohibition of contraception has been largely ignored by Catholic women of childbearing age, it symbolized the end of the liberal period. Increasingly, conservative Catholics sided with evangelicals on such matters as teenage pregnancies, abortion, youth violence, and the secularization of society. But for both Protestant and Catholic conservatives, sexual ethics became the major focus of political concern. No doubt because of his support for abortion funding, the Vatican in 1980 withdrew its ten-year exemption for Jesuit Father Robert Drinan to serve as Congressman from Massachusetts. In the 1984 presidential campaign, abortion prompted New York's John J. O'Connor, Boston's Bernard Law, and others to join Falwell and advise voting against fellow Catholics Geraldine Ferraro and Governor Mario Cuomo.

Nonetheless, following in the footsteps of Dorothy Day, Thomas Merton, Father Drinan, the Catholic Worker movement, and the Women's Ordination Conference, Catholic liberals have maintained their voice in the church in such publications as *The National Catholic Reporter* and *Commonweal*. Conservatives for their part read *The National Catholic Register*. The latter has supported Pope John Paul II, ever conservative — except for his views on social and economic justice, which were echoed eloquently in the National Conference of Catholic Bishops' exemplary pastoral letter, "Economics for All" (1987).

TOMORROW SIGNS OF HOPE

To our plurality of voices — therapeutics, Pentecostals, liberals, conservatives, even those who want creeds restored to church walls (as if assent to propositions was the equivalent of faith!) — to all these must be added other religious groups: Native American and Black religions, Mormons, Adventists, Christian Scientists, Hindus, Buddhists, and newer groups: Branch Davidians, Scientology, the Unification Church, and so forth. Along with the larger faiths of Christianity, Judaism, and Islam, the cults and sects have been studied psychologically, sociologically, economically, and equally important, theologically.

In addition to open scholarly inquiry, free exercise for participants in religious groups has added "a lustre to American democracy," a brightness, declares the distinguished Catholic layman, John T. Noonan, which "has been reflected around the world."[17] Surely ongoing free exercise is a sign of hope in our time, an old one but compelling. It must be held high.

The second sign of hope is that in the midst of our pluralism — really confusion of tongues — eloquent voices concerned for the larger community are now sounding. Whatever their differences, Robert Bellah, Alasdair MacIntyre, and Jeffrey Stout raise the question of a common moral philosophy for our time. They offer diverse remedies such as reclaiming biblical language and civic republican traditions; creating local forms of ethical community in which to sit out a new dark age; or finding agreement on commonly shared rights or freedom. In doing so they have raised the debate to a level of high seriousness. In the important area of church/state relations two critics, Stephen L. Carter and Ronald F. Thiemann, call for greater answerability in the courts on the one hand and among religious opponents on the other. And this leads to the third sign of hope for our time, one that is a significant part of both free exercise and community responsibility: the growing sense of obligation to extend full neighbor-love to the stranger in need. For the Christian, that call begins with Jesus Christ as "the one who embodied this love in word and deed," writes Thiemann.

And there can be no race or gender prejudice. Since 1950 Black Americans have come a long way, and many White churches participated in the outcome of that trek. In church and synagogue women have, with some exceptions, gained positions of authority. While the debate over full participation for homosexual people continues to divide religious communities, the outcome is not in doubt.

Of distinct importance in the last fifty years, anti–Semitism has greatly decreased, so that Jews no longer seek assimilation but expressions of Jewishness. Judaism is embarking on a new phase of development, writes Alan Dershowitz; it is "no longer a civilization characterized by persecution, ghettoization, and anti–Semitism."[18] Jewish intellectuals like Will Herberg, the European Martin Buber, and the powerfully prophetic Abraham Heschel achieved wide national influence. In the meantime the lessons of Judaism remain both important and ambiguous. On the one hand, with the exception of Orthodoxy, Jewish groups such as Modern Orthodox, Conservative, Reform, Reconstructionist, and moralistic and cultural Jews anticipated the lessening of Protestant denominational competition. But Jewish divisions cannot be as readily compartmentalized. In Judaism in America all have been both traditionalists and innovators. No federation has exercised more than an advisory role, and individual synagogues have as often as not gone their own ways. Despite the looseness of Jewish oversight, community support and concern in individual synagogues is extremely high. The lesson here is obvious: strength of commitment does not depend on hierarchical control.

But while communal life, including Jewish charities, flourishes to a degree worthy of emulation, the ancient faith has been eroded; standards of religious literacy have fallen; being Jewish has replaced Torah, and the "holy people," "the American Jewish community." Only the most orthodox Jews in America build their programs and institutions around Jewish religious law and Torah rather than around Zionism. While Jews number four million in America, only half that number attend synagogue or temple worship.

Unlike the inclusion of Jews today in America, the task of

incorporating American Muslims into the republic may not be an easy one. Terrorist activities and American ignorance of and insensitivity toward Islam ill serve free exercise. Christian responsibility to welcome and protect Muslim fellow citizens is mandated. The terrorists themselves have a twisted view of Muhammad's legacy. The Qur'an states both freedom to accept or reject Islam and the Muslim's responsibility to forgive, to show mercy, and even to help an enemy who requests protection. Force is to be used only in self-defense. The concept of *jihad* — the struggle for the truth in the way of Allah — has been misunderstood. The word has many meanings from warfare against unbelievers (Christians and Jews, as people of the book, excepted) to inner struggle with the ego. At no point do the basic texts of Islam enjoin terrorism and murder. During the Middle Ages, under the great Saladin, Christians and Jews were protected in Islamic lands, while Muslims were thrown out of Christian Europe and Jews regularly persecuted. Similarly in our time, Louis Farrakhan's Nation of Islam is not a hate group; neither are its leaders ministers of rage. For the purpose of Black pride and separatism, they preach a missionary "jihad of words" only.

Other Americans tend to think of all Muslims as Arabs, whereas in fact the 3.3 million Muslims in this country include such non-Arabs as Iranians, Turks, Sudanese, Albanians, and Pakistanis as well as African-Americans. These appear, not without difficulty, to be moving toward simple, basic constituents of Islam and a degree of unity. In the meantime a full complement of cultural and professional organizations grace Islamic life in America: scholarly, medical, journalistic, educational, and charitable. All are under the umbrella of the Islamic Society of North America.

The fourth sign of hope is the persistent affirmation of the prevenient, initiatory action of God; the stubborn belief that we are *responding* persons; that we do not govern the course of events, God does. It is the deeply held conviction that we are *observed* as well as being observers. This is perhaps the most difficult sign to affirm when, after our bitter century of wartime displacement, poverty, and murder, all the roads to Zion mourn. Nonetheless this "spirituality" continues to be a force, however circumscribed, in our society. George Steiner argues persuasively that in confronting great art directly (without the "aid" of commentaries), whether it be the poetry of Paul Celan, the slow movement of Schubert's C-Major Quintet, or the welding of myth to religion in Faulkner's *Light in August,* the Other enters into us. We are put in touch with that which transcends our materiality.[19] Steiner's conclusion is that where God's presence — or his absence — is no longer felt, thought and creativity are attenuated.

Similarly in the last fifty years at Yale University, H. Richard Niebuhr, Hans W. Frei, George Lindbeck, Ronald Thiemann (now at Harvard), and others have insisted on the unsubstitutable language of the church's tradition and on discovering the intention of the biblical narratives themselves, especially with reference to Jesus's identity. What, Frei asks, is the "plain sense" of scripture? In addition, these theologians hold that the New Testament texts about Jesus are "our means of access to incorporating ourselves . . . in the world of discourse he shared with us.'[20] The criteria of interpretation are to be derived from and accountable to the Christian community as a whole. Christian language has its own thrust, its own intention and integrity.

The Bible for the Yale theologians has been neither a book of laws (conservatives) nor a source of spiritual archetypes (liberals and Jungians), but a historical almanac in which the reader discovers his or her identity. And that identity is understood collectively in terms of the nation and not of the denomination. Not that the nation is to be defended with flamboyant rhetoric, but rather for good or ill — and surely for repentance — "the nation was *the* crucial collective historical agent of the day.'[21]

Is it too late? "Never before," writes Todd Gitlin, "have hope, greed, and fear had so many channels through which to rush so fast.'[22] What should be clear from the Bible — but is not — is that Jesus was the optimistic agent, not the pessimistic spectator. Will the churches that bear his name themselves become agents or remain spectators? Will they describe their church buildings as "womb-like' — and possibly tomb-like — spaces for "searchers" only? Or, to steal an image from the Venerable Bede, will they liken the church to a great banqueting hall where boisterous thanes converse and dine with their king; where, against the raging storms of winter snow and rain, all are warmed together by the brilliant fire of God's love?

Finally I will return to those names on the libraries' frontals. If we were to choose significant figures, people who contributed to the humanity and the positive achievements of life in the last hundred years, we could come up with a large number. But if we were to name significant *religious* leaders, the list would be in our time shorter than it was in 1895. Probably Albert Schweitzer, Mahatma Gandhi, Billy Graham, Mother Theresa, Desmond Tutu, Pope John XXIII, and Martin Luther King, Jr., would be named. But John R. Mott, Walter Rauschenbusch, Karl Barth, Reinhold Niebuhr, Malcolm X, Dorothy Day, John Courtney Murray, Abraham J. Heschel, Will Herberg, Pope John Paul II? And if we were to place statements of faith on our church walls, what would they be today? We do not seem as eager to carve names into postmodern libraries' glass walls as our grandparents were prone to do with granite and limestone. More's the pity. We need to remember.

NOTES

1. See John F. Woolverton, "Anglicanism," in *Encyclopedia of the North American Colonies,* ed. J. E. Cooke (New York: Scribner, 1993), 3:573; also Roger Kennedy, *American Churches* (New York: Stewart, Tabori & Chang, 1982), 166, for a visual example.

2. Robert Wuthnow, *Christianity and Civil Society* (Valley Forge: Trinity Press International, 1996), 23.

3. James D. Hunter, *Evangelicalism: The Coming Generation* (Chicago: Univ. of Chicago Press, 1987), 210.

4. William James, *The Varities of Religious Experience* (New York: Longmans, Green, 1905), 95.

5. Richard Rorty, *Achieving Our Country* (Cambridge: Harvard Univ. Press, 1998), 16. The assumption, of course, is that the two are antithetical.

6. Quoted in Wuthnow, *Christianity and Civil Society,* 24.

7. See Philip Rieff, *The Triumph of the Therapeutic: Uses of Faith after Freud* (Chicago: Univ. of Chicago Press, 1966).

8. Robert Wuthnow, *After Heaven: Spirituality in America Since the 1950s* (Berkeley: Univ. of California Press, 1998), 149.

9. Richard Todd, "The Stranger in the Back of the Church," *Civilization,* Dec. 1998/Jan. 1999:30.

10. Robert Wuthnow, *The Restructuring of American Religion* (Princeton: Princeton Univ. Press, 1988), 87.

11. Nancy T. Ammerman, "Denominations: Who and What Are We Studying?" in *Reimagining Denominationalism,* ed. R. B. Mullin and R. E. Richey (New York: Oxford Univ. Press, 1994), 112.

12. See Wuthnow, *Restructuring of American Religion,* 138.

13. Richard Wightman Fox, "Experience and Explanation in Twentieth-Century American Religious History," *New Directions* (New York: Oxford Univ. Press, 1997), 403.

14. Conrad Cherry, *Hurrying to Zion: Divinity Schools and American Protestantism* (Bloomington: Indiana Univ. Press, 1995), 298.

15. Timothy LaHaye, *Faith of Our Founding Fathers* (Green Forest, Arkansas: Master Books, 1990).

16. See Peter W. Williams, "Catholicism Since World War I," *Encyclopedia of the American Religious Experience* I: 383–384. It should be noted that the idea of collegiality was begun by Pius XII in *Mysteria corpus.*

17. John T. Noonan, Jr., *The Lustre of Our Country* (Berkeley: Univ. of California Press, 1998), 8.

18. Alan M. Dershowitz, *The Vanishing American Jew* (New York: Simon & Schuster, 1997), 336.

19. George Steiner, *Real Presences* (Chicago: Univ. of Chicago Press, 1989), 227.

20. Hans W. Frei, *Types of Christian Theology* (New Haven: Yale Univ. Press, 1992).

21. Hans W. Frei, "H. Richard Niebuhr on History, Church, and Nation," in *Theology and Narrative* (New York: Oxford Univ. Press, 1993), 216.

22. Todd Gitlin, *The Twilight of Common Dreams: Why America is Wracked by Culture Wars* (New York: Henry Holt, 1995), 224.

Many other works have been consulted as I prepared this essay; and some are particularly recommended for further reading:

Jeffrey Stout, *Ethics after Babel: The Languages of Morals and Their Discontents,* 1988.

John Woolverton, *The Skeptical Vestryman: George W. Martin,* 1997.

Richard Rabinowitz, *The Spiritual Self in Everyday Life: The Transformation of Personal Religious Experience in Nineteenth-Century New England,* 1989.

Ronald C. White, Jr., and C. Howard Hopins. *The Social Gospel: Religion and Reform in Changing America,* 1976.

Joanna B. Gillespie, "What We Taught: Christian Education in the American Episcopal Church, 1920–1980," *Anglican and Episcopal History,* 1987.

H. Richard Niebuhr, *The Purpose of the Church and Its Ministry: Reflections on the Aims of Theological Education,* 1957.

Philip Goll, "Revivals and Revolution: Historiographical Turns Since Alan Heimert's Religion and the American Mind," *Church History,* 1998.

Eric O. Hanson, *The Catholic Church and World Politics,* 1987.

Diana L. Eck et al., *On Common Ground: World Religions in America* (CD-ROM).

Will Herberg, *Catholic, Protestant, and Jew,* 1995.

Martin Buber, *I and Thou,* [1923. tr. 1937],1970.

Yvonne Y. Haddard and Adair T. Lummis, *Islamic Values in the United States,* 1987.

Richard B. Turner, *Islam in the African-American Experience,* 1997.

ABOUT OUR AUTHORS

Arden Albee is currently Dean of Graduate Studies and Professor of Geology and Planetary Science at the California Institute of Technology. He prepared for Harvard at Mount Clemens (Michigan) High School and received his baccalaureate *magna cum laude.* A resident of Leverett House he went on to earn both a master's degree and a doctorate (1957) in geology from Harvard while working with the U.S. Geological Survey. Since 1959, his entire career has been spent at Caltech, where he was a member of the Lunatic Asylum, a group who analyzed the lunar rock samples as they were returned from the moon. In 1976 he received the NASA Medal for Exceptional Scientific Achievement for his research and advisory service. He has served as Chief Scientist at the Jet Propulsion Laboratory and as the Project Scientist for the Mars Observer Mission and he is the Project Scientist for the Mars Global Surveyor Mission, currently in orbit about Mars. Active in a number of professional organizations related to geology, planetary science, and graduate education, he has been an associate editor of *Annual Reviews of Earth and Planetary Sciences* since 1979. Currently he serves on both the GRE and TOEFL boards of the Educational Testing Service. He and his wife have an extended family of eight children and eleven grandchildren. His community activities include various charitable organizations, local churches, the board of a small college, and service on the Citizens Oversight Committee for Measure Y School Bonds.

Among his recent publications, both with F. D. Palluconi and R. E. Arvidson, are:

"The Mars Global Observer Mission," *Journal of Geophysical Research* 97 (1996):7665.

"Mars Global Surveyor Mission: Overview and Status," *Science* 279 (1998):1671.

Address: Office of the Dean of Graduate Studies, M/C 02–31, California Institute of Technology, Pasadena, CA 91125.
Tel: 626 395–6367 ✦ FAX: 626 577–9246
e-mail: aalbee@cco.caltech.edu

Robert Ashenhurst is Professor of Applied Mathematics in the Graduate School of Business at the University of Chicago, and is a specialist in computer and information systems. He prepared for Harvard at Chicago's Francis W. Parker School. A resident of Lowell House, he received his bachelor's degree *summa cum laude*. After graduation he worked at the Harvard Computation Laboratory for seven years while earning a master's and a doctorate (1956) in applied mathematics. Having started his career in Cambridge, he soon followed in his grandfather's footsteps to the University of Chicago, where, besides his appointment to the Graduate School of Business, he has also served as Director of the Institute for Computer Research and Chairman of the Committee on Information Sciences.

Throughout his career, Bob has been deeply involved with the Association for Computing Machinery (ACM), a leading professional organization in the field. Recently he was honored by that society's Fellows Award which cited his thirty-one years of ACM leadership that included fourteen years as editor of the Monograph Series, and seventeen years as editor of its journal, *Communications of the ACM*. He continues active, serving as Parliamentarian of the governing ACM Council and Chairman of the Constitution & Bylaws Committee.

On the nonprofessional side of things, he remains involved with the local Gilbert & Sullivan opera company and other community organizations. He has four children and, as of our 45th Reunion, four grandchildren.

Among some of his recent publications are:

"The Homeless Computer," *Encyclopedia Britannica 1986 Book of the Year* (Encyclopedia Britannica, Inc., 1986), 286.

ACM Turing Award Lectures: The First Twenty Years 1966–1985 (Addison Wesley, 1987)

(co-editor with Susan Graham).

"Ontological Aspects of Information Modeling," *Minds and Machines* 6, no. 3 (1996):287.

"The Nature of Information Modeling," in *Essays on the Future: In Honor of Nick Metropolis* (Boston: Birkhauser, in press).

Address: The University of Chicago, Graduate School of
Business, 1101 East 58th Street, Chicago, IL 60637
Tel: 773 702–7454 ✦ Fax: 773 702–0458
e-mail: robert.ashenhurst@gsb.uchicago.edu

Charles W. Bailey is a free-lance writer and editor living in Washington, D.C. A graduate of Philips Exeter Academy, Exeter, NH, and an Eliot House resident, he received his baccalaureate degree *magna cum laude*. A major part of his career was spent with the *Minneapolis Tribune* where he started as a reporter, and then became Washington correspondent; subsequently he was Chief of the Washington Bureau and then served ten years as Editor. Following this, he became Washington Editor for National Public Radio.

He has served on several boards of trustees, including the Carnegie Endowment for International Peace.

He writes, "Along the way I had the good luck to have several foreign assignments, including trips to the USSR, China, Vietnam (1966–1967), the Middle East, Japan, and other places of interest.

"I am still married to the lady I wed in September 1950. We have two children and two grandchildren."

He was co-author of *Seven Days in May* (1962) a best-selling story about an attempted military coup to overthrow a president.

Among his other, more recent, publications:

The Land Was Ours (1991), a historical novel set in the Great Plains, and various reviews and articles in *The Washington Monthly* and other magazines.

Address: 3001 Albermarle St. NW, Washington, DC 20008
Tel: 202 966−4366

Robert Coles is Professor of Psychiatry and Medical Humanities at the Harvard Medical School as well as James Agee Professor of Social Ethics at the College and at the Graduate School of Education, and a research psychiatrist for the University Health Services. A graduate of Boston Latin School, he was a resident of Adams House and received his bachelor's degree *magna cum laude*. He went on to earn an M.D. (1954) at Columbia University. In addition to his work in Cambridge, Bob has been a visiting professor in the History Department of Duke University for many years, and is a founding member of the Center for Documentary Studies there. He is the editor of *DoubleTake* magazine, published at the Center.

In 1973 he was awarded the Pulitzer Prize; he received a John D. and Catherine T. MacArthur Foundation Fellowship in 1981, and the Presidential Medal of Freedom in 1998.

Since 1961 he has published over 1,300 articles, reviews, and essays in newspapers, magazines, journals, and anthologies. He has written some sixty books. Some of his most recent are listed below.

Bob lives outside of Boston. Two of his sons are physicians and the third is in medical school. His wife, Jane Hallowell Coles, died in 1993.

Recent publications include:

The Story of Ruby Bridges (Scholastic Press, 1995).
The Mind's Fate (Little, Brown, 1995).

Harvard Diary II: Essays on the Sacred and the Secular (Crossroads, 1997).

The Moral Intelligence of Children (Random House, 1997).

The Youngest Parents (DoubleTake/W. W. Norton Books, 1997)(with J. Moses and J. Lee)

Doing Documentary Work (Oxford University Press, 1997).

Old and On Their Own (W. W. Norton, 1998).

Address: Harvard University Health Services, 75 Mt. Auburn
St., Cambridge, MA 02138
Tel: 617 495–3736   ✦   FAX: 617 496–9911
e-mail: robert_coles@harvard.edu

Nicholas Cunningham is Professor of Clinical Pediatrics and Clinical Public Health at the College of Physicians and Surgeons of Columbia University. In addition he serves as Attending Pediatrician and Director of Outpatient Pediatrics at the Babies Hospital Division of the Presbyterian Hospital in New York City. He graduated from the Thacher School, Ojai, California, and was a resident of Leverett House. Following graduation he went on to receive his M.D. (1955) at Johns Hopkins University, his Doctor in Tropical Health (1965) from the University of London, and his Doctor of Public Health (1977) from Johns Hopkins.

The Peace Corps took him to Togo, West Africa, early in his career. Subsequently he has had extensive experience in Lagos, Nigeria, and serves as an honorary consultant in pediatrics to Lagos University.

In 1980 he was co-founder and later director of the Presbyterian Hospital Therapeutic Nursery. For this, in 1993, he was given a United Nations Environmental Programme Award.

More recently, Nick has been associated with an interdisciplinary team working with the Open Society Institute to help new countries of Eastern Europe to develop services to protect children. In November, 1998, he returned from a mission to Baghdad to assess the effect that various sanctions were having on women and children in Iraq.

Nick and his second wife have five children and a grandson, live in Manhattan but drive to Otsego Lake for as many weekends as possible the year around. His wife and daughter are both doctors.

Among his recent publications:

The Columbia University College of Physicians and Surgeons Guide to Early Child Care (New York: Crown Publishers,1990) (with D. F. Tapley, ed.).

"Does Infant Carrying Promote Attachment? An Experimental Study of the Effects of Increased Physical Contact on the Development of Attachment," *Child Development*, 61 (1990):1617 (with E. Anisfeld, V. Caspar, and M. Nozye).

"From U.F.C. to P.H.C.: Five Ways to Integrate Primary Maternal and Child Health Care So It Works." *Tropical Doctor* 25 (1995):1.

"A Children's Lifetime Homebased Health Record: Its Use and Non-use," *Ambulatory Health Care* 25 (1995):1 (with L. Fumanski, L. Bahamonde, et al.).

"The Child's Personal Health Record in New York City: Which Components are Used?" *Ambulatory Child Health* 4, no. 1 (1995):3–11 (with Y. Ghossein, C. Gibbs, et al.)

Address: Columbia Presbyterian Medical Center, 622 West 168th Street, VC 402, New York, NY 10032–3784
Tel: 212 305–6227 ✦ FAX: 212 305–8819
e-mail: nc18@columbia.edu

William Harrop is a retired career diplomat who was ambassador at various times to Guinea, Kenya, Seychelles, Zaire, and Israel. He was also Inspector General of the State Department and Foreign Service. A graduate of Deerfield Academy, Deerfield, MA, he was a resident of Eliot House. After graduation he pursued further studies at the Missouri School of Journalism and later the Woodrow Wilson School of Public and International Affairs. During the Korean War he served in the Marine Corps. He was Deputy Assistant Secretary of State for Africa and Deputy Chief of Mission to Australia. He is a former Chairman of the American Foreign Service Association, and holds the State Department Distinguished Service Award and the Presidential Distinguished Service Award. Currently he is a Director of The American Academy of Diplomacy, The Association for Diplomatic Training and Studies, and the American Foreign Service Association. He is now in private business — specialty coffee bars. He has been married for forty-five years to Ann Delavan, and they have four sons and four grandchildren. Bill plays tennis three times a week and is an enthusiastic skier.

Among his recent publications:

"The Future of the Foreign Service," *Foreign Service Journal*, May 1997.

"The American Chief of Mission in the Late 1990s," *American Academy of Diplomacy*, March, 1996.

Address: 3615 49th St. NW. Washington, DC 20016–3214
Tel: 202 966–1071 ✦ FAX: 202 966–6271
e-mail: HARROPBILL@EROLS.COM

John Dwight Ingram is a Professor of Law at the John Marshall Law School. He prepared at the Middlesex School, Concord, MA, and was a resident of Adams House. He went on to earn a C.L.U. (1957) from the American College of Life Underwriters and, subsequently, his J.D. (1966) at the John Marshall Law School. After a two-year stint with the U. S. Army, he worked in the insurance industry and was an attorney for seven years with the firm Simon and Ingram. Besides his teaching duties, Jack is an expert witness, consultant, and arbitrator in cases involving questions of insurance law.

His family includes his wife, a son, two daughters, and two grandchildren. He spends his leisure in travel and writing law review articles. For twenty-five years he coached junior football teams in Winnetka and Highland Park. His teams won the league championship five times and played in the championship game on five other occasions.

Among his recent publications:

"Date Rape: It's Time for 'No' to Really Mean 'No,' " *American Journal of Criminal Law*, 1993.

"In Vitro Fertilization: Problems and Solutions," *Dickinson Law Review*, 1993.

"Surrogate Gestator, A New and Honorable Profession," *Marquette Law Review*, 76 (1993):67.

"Liability of Medical Institutions For the Negligence of Independent Contractors Practicing on Their Premises," *Jour. of Contemporary Health Law and Policy*, 1994.

"The Right (?) to Keep and Bear Arms," *New Mexico Law Review*, 1997.

"The American First Lady," *Capital University Law Review*, 1999.

"The First 'First Gentleman': The Role of President Jane Doe's Husband," *American University Journal of Gender, Social Policy and the Law*, 1999.

Address: 315 South Plymouth Court, Chicago, IL 60604
Tel: 312 987–1428 ✦ FAX: 312 427–9974

Frank Jones has retired from the Massachusetts Institute of Technology, where he was the Ford Professor of Urban Affairs. Following graduation he received an MBA (1957) from the Business School. Frank's father was for thirty years the president of Bennett College in Greensboro, North Carolina, one of two colleges oriented primarily to the higher education of Afro-American women. Thus, with this heritage, it is not surprising that from 1943 to 1992 Frank dealt with the education and development of himself and others in, successively, Phillips Academy, Andover, MA; Harvard College; Harvard Business School; and MIT. He was awarded an honorary Doctor of Laws degree by Trinity College, Hartford CT, in 1976.

He currently serves on the board of directors of Polaroid Corporation; CIGNA Corporation; Capital Cities/ABC, Inc.; and Scientific Games Holdings Corp.

In 1993 he retired to Atlanta, where he is seeking to become an urban entrepreneur. He is separated from his wife and has two sons.

Address: 2460 Peachtree Rd. NW, #108, Atlanta, GA 30305
Tel: 404 526−7827

George Lodge is the Jaime and Josefina Professor of Business Administration, Emeritus, at the Harvard Business School. He prepared at Groton School, Groton, MA; lived in Lowell House; and received his bachelor's degree *cum laude*. After four years as a political writer for the *Boston Herald,* he went to Washington as a speech writer for then Secretary of Labor James P. Mitchell. In 1958, President Eisenhower appointed him Assistant Secretary of Labor for International Affairs; he was reappointed by President Kennedy. While in that post he was elected chairman of the Governing Body of the International Labor Organization.

In 1961 he returned to Massachusetts to become a lecturer at the Harvard Business School, a post he left in 1962 to run against Edward Kennedy for a seat in the U.S. Senate. Following his defeat he returned to Harvard, where he was elected a tenured professor in 1971. During the 1960s he helped create the Central American Institute of Business Administration and a new governmental agency, the Inter-American Foundation. He retired in 1997 but continues to teach in the Business School's executive program in Boston and around the world.

Nancy, his wife of 48 years, died in 1997. He then married Susan Powers, whose husband had died four years earlier. George has six children and 13 grandchildren. He and Susan spend all the time they can aboard their 39−foot sloop, cruising the coasts of Maine and Nova Scotia.

George plays third clarinet in the fifty-piece Dane Street Community Band in his hometown of Beverly. He finds this a challenge: "The position does not carry tenure and there is no fourth clarinet."

Among his recent publications:

Managing Globalization in the Age of Interdependence (Pfeiffer & Co., 1995).

Perestroika for America: Restructuring Business-Government Relations (Harvard Business School Press, 1990).

Comparative Business-Government Relations (Prentice-Hall, 1990).

And a number of articles in the *Harvard Business Review*.

Address: 275 Hale St., Beverly, MA 01915
Tel 978 922–4534
e-mail: glodge@hbs.edu

Gordon J. F. MacDonald is Director of IIASA (originally the International Institute for Applied Systems Analysis), an international organization that conducts policy-oriented, multidisciplinary research in areas of energy and technologies, population and society, environment and natural resources. A resident of Eliot House, he received his bachelor's degree *summa cum laude* and earned a master's and a doctorate (1954) in geophysics at Harvard. He was Henry Luce Third Century Professor and Director of Environmental Studies at Dartmouth College from 1972 to 1979, when he joined the Mitre Corporation as chief scientist, later also becoming vice president, a position he held until 1990. He then joined the faculty of the University of California at San Diego as Professor of International Relations and Director of Environmental Studies, Institute of Global Conflict and Cooperation. During this time, he founded the *Journal of Environment and Development,* currently published by Sage Publications. In 1992, he served as the first chairman of the Environmental Task Force, sponsored by the Office of the Vice President, and then chaired its successor organization, MEDEA, until 1996. He is a member of several learned societies, including the American Academy of Arts and Sciences, American Philosophical Society, Council on Foreign Relations and the National Academy of Sciences. In 1994 he received the Central Intelligence Agency Seal Medallion, the agency's highest civilian award.

He is currently married to the former Margaret Stone (Radcliffe 1969), and has four children.

Among some recent publications:

"Atmospheric Turbulence Compensation by Resonant Optical Backscattering from the Sodium Layer in the Upper Atmosphere," *Journal of the Optical Society of America A*, 11 (1994):263 (with W. Happer, C. E. Max, and F. Dyson).

Latin American Environmental Policy in International Perspective (Westview Press, 1996) (with D. L. Nielson and M. Stern, ed.).

"Simultaneous Presence of Orbital Inclination and Eccentricity in Proxy Climate Records from Ocean Drilling Program Site 806," *Geology* 25 (1997):3.

"Glacial Cycles and Astronomical Forcing," *Science* 277 (1997):215; "Spectrum of 100–kyr Glacial Cycle: Orbital Inclination, not Eccentricity," *Proc. National Acad. of Sciences* 94 (1997):8329 (with R. A. Muller).

"Regulating Global Warming: Success in Kyoto," *Linkages,* 2 (Oct. 1997); "How to Make Kyoto a Success," *Nature* 389(1997):777 (with D. G. Victor).

Address: International Institute for Applied Systems Analysis, Schloss Laxenburg, A-2361 Laxenburg, Austria
Tel: +43 2236 807n 402 ✦ FAX: +43 2236 72659
e-mail: macdon@iiasa.ac.at

Miles Shore is Bullard Professor of Psychiatry at Harvard Medical School and Visiting Scholar at the Kennedy School of Government. He prepared at Chicago's Lindbloom High School and spent two years at the University of Chicago before transferring to Harvard in his junior year, where he resided in Adams House. He received his baccalaureate *cum laude* and earned an M.D. (1954) at Harvard Medical School. He trained in psychiatry at the Massachusetts Mental Health Center and Boston's Beth Israel Hospital, and in psychoanalysis at the Boston Psychoanalytic Institute. He was on the faculty of Tufts Medical School from 1964 to 1975, when he was appointed Bullard Professor of Psychiatry at Harvard and Superintendent of the Massachusetts Mental Health Center. In 1993 he moved to the Kennedy School, where he is studying the dramatic changes affecting the health care system in this and other countries. He is co-principal investigator of a project studying medical error to improve patient safety, and is co-director of an executive program, "Understanding the New World of Health Care," which offers physicians and other health care leaders an intensive introduction to health policy. He teaches in graduate courses on leadership, health policy, and mental health policy.

He is married to Eleanor G. Shore, Radcliffe '51, HMS '55, HSPH '70, who is Dean for Faculty Affairs at Harvard Medical School. Their three children, Paul '81, Rebecca Lewin '83, HMS '90, and Susanna LeBoutillier '86, are married. They have one grandchild, Monica Lewin. Leisure activities include travel (Iceland, Spain, England, Canada this year), gardening, cooking, and playing four-hand piano.

Among his recent publications:

"A Lesson in History, circa 2047," *Amer. Journal of Psychiatry* 154, no. 3 (1997):307.

"On Spending Other Peoples' Money," *Harvard Review of Psychiatry* 6, no. 2 (July–August 1998):110.

"Medical Leadership and the Future of Health Care," The Ralph Alley Memorial Lecture, *Annals of Thoracic Surgery* (in press).

"Leadership," in *Textbook of Administrative Psychiatry,* John A. Talbot, ed. (American Psychiatric Press, 1999) (with Mark Vanelli).

Address: Kennedy School of Government, 79 John F.
Kennedy St., Cambridge MA 02138
Tel: 617 496–1392 ✦ FAX: 617 496–0250
e-mail: miles_shore@harvard.edu

John Train is an investment counsel and writer, also a Presidential appointee (Reagan, Bush, and Clinton) as a part-time governor or director of independent agencies working overseas. He graduated from the Groton School, Groton, MA; resided in Lowell House; and received his bachelor's degree *magna cum laude* and a master's degree the following year. He was president of the Signet and the *Lampoon* and long a trustee of the latter. He is a founder of the *Paris Review* and of Train, Smith, Investment Counsel in New York, among other endeavors.

He has written eighteen books and about 400 columns in the *Financial Times* (London), *Forbes, The Wall Street Journal, Harvard Magazine,* etc. He has twice been made a Commendatore in different Italian orders in consideration of humanitarian work, and was named to the order of St. John of Jerusalem in the Queen's Birthday Honours, 1997.

Address: 667 Madison Avenue, New York, NY 10021
Tel: 212 451–3457 ✦ FAX: 212 436–1769
e-mail: jtrain@trainsmith.com

John Woolverton, an Episcopal minister and practicing American church historian, resides in Center Sandwich, NH, where he serves as editor for the *Anglican and Episcopal History,* an international, historical journal published by the Historical Society of the Episcopal Church. He prepared at Groton School, Groton, MA, was a resident of Lowell House, and following graduation earned a M. Div. (1952) at the Episcopal Theological Seminary, which also awarded him in 1984 an honorary D.D., and a Ph. D. (1963) at Columbia University. From 1958 to 1983 he was a professor and chairman of the Department of Church History at the Virginia Theological Seminary. This was followed by a six-year stint as Rector of Trinity Episcopal Church in Portland, ME. He was a founder and a trustee of the General Theological Center of Maine and later its president. He has also served as a visiting scholar of the Episcopal Divinity School, Cambridge, MA, and as a visiting professor at the Episcopal Theological Seminary of the Southwest, Austin, TX. Married, with two sons and two daughters, he currently reports seven grandchildren.

Among his recent publications:
Colonial Anglicanism in North America, 1607–1776 (Detroit: Wayne State University Press, 1986).

The Education of Phillips Brooks (Urbana and Chicago: University of Illinois Press, 1995).

The Skeptical Vestryman and Plato's Heavenly Way of Justice: George Whitney Martin (Plymouth, N. H.: Colophon Press 1997).

"Hans W. Frei in Context: A Theological and Historical Memoir," *Anglican Theological Review* LXXIX, no. 3 (1997): 369.

Work in progress: *Robert Hallowell Gardiner III: A Biography, Anglican Millennialism: The Case of Henry Dana Ward.*

Address: P.O. Box 261 / 40 Skinner St.,
Center Sandwich, NH 03227
Office: 603 284–6584   ✦   Home: 603 284–6595